4th Workshop on Technologies for MT of Low Resource Languages (LoResMT 2021)

Held at MT Summit 2021

Online
16 – 20 August 2021

ISBN: 978-1-7138-3922-4

Printed from e-media with permission by:

Curran Associates, Inc.
57 Morehouse Lane
Red Hook, NY 12571

Some format issues inherent in the e-media version may also appear in this print version.

Printed with permission by Curran Associates, Inc. (2022)

For permission requests, please contact the Association for Computational Linguistics at the address below.

Association for Computational Linguistics
209 N. Eighth Street
Stroudsburg, Pennsylvania 18360

Phone: 1-570-476-8006
Fax: 1-570-476-0860

acl@aclweb.org

Additional copies of this publication are available from:

Curran Associates, Inc.
57 Morehouse Lane
Red Hook, NY 12571 USA
Phone: 845-758-0400
Fax: 845-758-2633
Email: curran@proceedings.com
Web: www.proceedings.com

MT SUMMIT VIRTUAL 2021

Proceedings of Machine Translation Summit XVIII

https://mtsummit2021.amtaweb.org

4th Workshop on Technologies for MT of Low Resource Languages

Organizers:
John Ortega, Atul Kr. Ojha, Katharina Kann and Chao-Hong Liu

Proceedings of the 4th Workshop on Technologies for Machine Translation of Low-resource Languages

Organizers
John Ortega[1] jortega@cs.nyu.edu
Atul Kr. Ojha[2,3] atulkumar.ojha@insight-centre.org
Katharina Kann[4] katharina.kann@colorado.edu
Chao-Hong Liu[5] ch.liu@acm.org
[1]New York University
[2]Data Science Institute, NUIG, Galway
[3]Panlingua Language Processing LLP, New Delhi
[4]University of Colorado Boulder
[5]Potamu Research Ltd

1 Aim of the Workshop

Based on the success of past low-resource machine translation (LoResMT) workshops at AACL-IJCNLP 2020[1], MT Summit 2019[2] and AMTA 2018[3], we introduce the 4th LoResMT workshop co-located at the MT Summit 2021[4] conference. Like its predecessors, this workshop will bring together researchers and translators of low-resource languages to compare and contrast how each use digital technology for translation. Specifically, the workshop focuses on novel advances on the coverage of even more languages than past workshops with different geographical presence, degree of diffusion and digitization.

The proceedings of LoResMT 2021 contain original work on low-resource translation which includes, but is not limited to, machine translation (MT) systems that include word tokenizers/de-tokenizers, word segmenters, and morphological analyzers. Additionally, we explicitly solicited novel work covering translations of COVID-related text and their practical use for low-resource communities.

The goal of this workshop was to begin to close the gap between low-resource translation systems and their practical use in the real world. Online systems and original research that used by native speakers of low-resource languages was of particular interest. Therefore, we encouraged the authors of research papers to include a statement about the impact of their proposed approaches on the quality of MT output and how they can be used in the real world.

The need for receiving relevant, fast and up-to-date information in one's language is today more important than ever, especially under the current crisis conditions. MT is a vital tool for facilitating communication and access to information. For most of the world's languages, the lack of training data has long posed a major obstacle to developing high quality MT systems,

[1]http://aacl2020.org
[2]https://www.mtsummit2019.com
[3]https://amtaweb.org
[4]https://amtaweb.org/mt-summit2021

excluding the speakers of these low-resource languages from the benefits of MT. In the past few years, MT performance has improved significantly, mainly due to the new possibilities opened up by neural machine translation (NMT). With the development of novel techniques, such as multilingual translation and transfer learning, the use of MT is no longer a privilege restricted to users of a dozen popular languages. Consequently, there has been an increasing interest in the MT community to expand the coverage to more languages with different geographical presence, degree of diffusion and digitization. Today, research groups on all continents are working on MT. The number of languages offered by publicly available MT engines is increasing, reaching almost 200 languages at the moment of writing. We are witnessing an interesting phenomenon of collaborative projects to promote MT for under-represented languages, involving partners from all over the globe, participating on a voluntary basis. These developments have created a colourful, promising future for low-resource languages on the MT map.

Despite all these encouraging developments in MT technologies, creating an MT system for a new language from scratch or even improving an existing system still requires a considerable amount of work in collecting the pieces necessary for building such systems. Due to the data-hungry nature of NMT approaches, the need for parallel and monolingual corpora in different domains is never saturated. The development of MT systems requires reliable test sets and evaluation benchmarks. In addition, MT systems still rely on several natural language processing (NLP) tools to pre-process human-generated texts in the forms that are required as input for MT systems and post-process the MT output in proper textual forms in the target language. These NLP tools include, but are not limited to, word tokenizers/de-tokenizers, word segmenters, and morphological analysers. The performance of these tools has a great impact on the quality of the resulting translation. There is only limited discussion on these NLP tools, their methods, their role in training different MT systems, and their coverage of support in the many languages of the world.

LoResMT provides a discussion panel for researchers working on MT systems/methods for low-resource languages in general. This year we received research papers covering a wide range of languages spoken in Asia, Latin America, Africa and Europe. These languages are: Arabic, Albanian, Ashaninka, Bengali, Dutch, Eastern Pokomchi, English, French, German, Gujarati, Hindi, Inuktitut, Indonesian, Irish, Japanese, Kannada, Khasi, Konkani, Korean, Mayan, Malayalam, Marathi, Odia, Punjabi, Quechua, Sanskrit, Spanish, Tamil, Telugu, Turkish and Urdu. We received both resource papers (monolingual, parallel corpora, social media, sentiment and formalisms) and methods papers, ranging from unsupervised, zero-shot to multilingual NMT, MT evaluation. The acceptance rate of LoResMT this year is 43.4%.

In addition to soliciting research papers, we organized a shared task to be presented at the workshop, where we asked participants to build novel MT systems for COVID-related texts in low-resource languages, including one sign language. The shared task aimed to encourage research on MT systems for three language pairs: English↔Irish, English↔Marathi and Taiwanese Sign Language↔Traditional Chinese. The corpora along with additional information on downloading videos for sign language for machine translation tasks are freely available on Github[5]. Six shared task papers are published as part of the proceedings, along with the findings of the shared task.

2 Invited Speakers (listed alphabetically)

We are happy our dear colleagues Barry Haddow, Catherine Muthoni Gitau, Mathias Müller and Mona Diab have prepared talks on four important topics for LoResMT 2021.

[5]https://github.com/loresmt/loresmt-2021

2.1 Barry Haddow, Aveni and University of Edinburgh

MT for Low-resource Languages: Progress and Open Problems

Current machine translation (MT) systems have reached the stage where researchers are now debating whether or not they can rival human translators in performance. However these MT systems are typically trained on data sets consisting of tens or even hundreds of millions of parallel sentences. There is an increasing body of research which considers the problem of training MT systems on much smaller data sets. The aim of this talk is to provide a broad survey of the techniques that have been applied to low-resource MT, presenting a data-centric taxonomy, and indicating gaps. The talk is based on a survey paper which is currently being finalised, and that we aim to release during August 2021.

About the Speaker

Barry Haddow is a senior researcher in the School of Informatics at the University of Edinburgh. He has worked in machine translation for more than 10 years, and his current interests include low-resource MT, spoken language translation and evaluation of MT. Barry coordinates the annual WMT conference on machine translation and associated shared tasks.

2.2 Catherine Muthoni Gitau, African Institute for Mathematical Sciences

Challenges and Advances in MT Systems for African Languages

Africa is known to be the highest linguistically diverse continent with over 2,000 languages across the continent representing about 30% of the languages spoken around the world and despite this, African languages account only a small fraction of available language resources making them low-resourced. There's minimal attention that's being given to machine translation for African languages and therefore, there is not much work or research regarding the problems that arise when using machine translation techniques. However, there's been an increase in work around machine translation for African languages in the last couple of years with the aim of addressing some of these challenges. In this talk, I will present on the challenges currently being faced in the development of machine translation systems for African languages as well as work that's being done to alleviate some of these challenges. I will go into detail about the work of the Masakhane community whose mission is to strengthen and spur NLP research in African languages, for Africans, by Africans with a focus on work that's being done on machine translation.

About the Speaker

Catherine Gitau is a natural language processing researcher and engineer at Proto, a company that builds multilingual AI chatbots for contact centers. She recently completed her Masters' in Machine Intelligence at the African Institute of Mathematical Sciences (AIMS) under the African Masters' in Machine Intelligence (AMMI) program and is an active member of the Masakhane Community whose mission is to strengthen NLP research in African Languages. Her research interests include natural language processing and low-resource machine translation.

2.3 Mathias Müller, Institut für Computerlinguistik, Universität Zürich

On Meaningful Evaluation of Machine Translation Systems

In this talk Mathias will discuss best practices for evaluating machine translation systems. The goal of defining such best practices is to ensure that conclusions drawn from experiments are valid, and that perceived scientific progress is in fact real. Areas we will touch on during the talk include selecting data for experiments, significance testing and the special role of low-resource experiments. Mathias is looking forward to a lively discussion, leading to a set of practices that we can all advocate in the future and implement in our own research.

About the Speaker

Mathias is a post-doc and lecturer at the University of Zurich. His current main interests are 1) the meta-sciences of scientific integrity, methodology and reproducibility applied to machine translation and 2) sign language translation. In his personal life, as a father of two, he advocates the best practice of not working on weekends.

2.4 Mona Diab, Facebook, George Washington University

Trustworthy Human Evaluation Frameworks for MT

How do we establish trust in our machine translation systems performance? Typical evaluations rely on reference translations that are curated from humans, serving as gold data annotations. In this talk I will examine this assumption and propose ways to ensure we have trustworthy reference data with closer to real translation perception (higher meaningfulness gauging). I will propose a holistic view of translation evaluation as an ecosystem and a framework especially for low resource scenarios.

About the Speaker

Mona is a Research Scientist with Facebook AI and she is also a full Professor of CS at the George Washington University where she heads the CARE4Lang NLP Lab. Before joining FB, she led the Lex Conversational AI project within Amazon AWS AI. Her interests span building robust technologies for low resource scenarios with a special interest in Arabic technologies, (mis)information propagation, computational socio-pragmatics, NLG evaluation metrics, and resource creation. She has served the community in several capacities: Elected President of SIGLEX and SIGSemitic. She currently serves as the elected VP-Elect for ACL SIGDAT, the board supporting EMNLP conferences. She has delivered tutorials and organized numerous workshops and panels around Arabic processing. She is a cofounder of CADIM (Consortium on Arabic Dialect Modeling, previously known as Columbia University Arabic Dialects Modeling Group), in 2005, which served as a world renowned reference point on Arabic Language Technologies. Moreover she helped establish two research trends in NLP, namely computational approaches to Code Switching and Semantic Textual Similarity. She is also a founding member of the *SEM conference, one of the top tier conferences in NLP. She currently serves as the senior area chair for multiple top tier conferences. She has published more than 230 peer reviewed articles.

3 Co-organizing Committee

- Jade Abbott, Retro Rabbit
- Jonathan Washington, Swarthmore College
- Nathaniel Oco, National University (Philippines)
- Surafel Melaku Lakew, Amazon AI
- Tommi A Pirinen, University of Hamburg
- Valentin Malykh, Huawei Noah's Ark lab and Kazan Federal University
- Varvara Logacheva Skolkovo, Institute of Science and Technology
- Xiaobing Zhao, Minzu University of China

4 Program Committee

- Alberto Poncelas, Rakuten
- Alina Karakanta, Fondazione Bruno Kessler
- Amirhossein Tebbifakhr, Fondazione Bruno Kessler
- Anna Currey, Amazon AI
- Atul Kr. Ojha, National Univerity of Ireland Galway
- Beatrice Savoldi, beatrice savoldi
- Bharathi Raja Chakravarthi, National University of Ireland Galway
- Bogdan Babych, Heidelberg University
- Chao-Hong Liu, Potamu Research Ltd
- Duygu Ataman, UZH
- Eleni Metheniti, CLLE - CNRS, IRIT
- Félix Arturo Oncevay Marcos, University of Edinburgh
- Flammie A Pirinen, UiT–Norgga árktalaš universitehta
- Jasper Kyle Catapang, University of Birmingham
- John McCrae, National University of Ireland Galway
- John E Ortega, New York University
- Jonathan N Washington, Swarthmore College
- Katharina Kann, University of Colorado Boulder
- Koel Dutta Chowdhury, Saarland University
- Liangyou Li, Huawei Noah's Ark Lab
- Majid Latifi, National College of Ireland (NCI)
- Maria Art Antonette, Clariño University of the Philippines Los Baños
- Mathias Müller, University of Zurich
- Mehdi Rezagholizadeh, Huawei Noah's Ark Lab
- Nathaniel Oco, Philippines
- Priya Rani, National University of Ireland Galway
- Rico Sennrich, University of Zurich
- Sangjie Duanzhu, Qinghai Normal University
- Santanu Pal, Wipro

- Sardana Ivanova, University of Helsinki
- Shabnam Tafreshi, University of Maryland
- Shantipriya Parida, Idiap Research Institute, Martigny, Switzerland
- Sina Ahmadi, Insight Centre for Data Analytics
- Sunit Bhattacharya, Charles University
- Surafel M Lakew, Amazon AI
- Thepchai Supnithi, NECTEC, National Science and Technology Development Agency
- Tsz Kin Lam, Heidelberg University
- Valentin Malykh, Huawei Noah's Ark lab and Kazan Federal University
- Vlad Tyshkevich, Brooklyn College, City University of New York

Contents

Dealing with the Paradox of Quality Estimation

Sugyeong Eo* djtnrud@korea.ac.kr
Chanjun Park* bcj1210@korea.ac.kr
Hyeonseok Moon glee889@korea.ac.kr
Jaehyung Seo seojae777@korea.ac.kr
Heuiseok Lim† limhseok@korea.ac.kr
Department of Computer Science and Engineering, Korea University, Korea

Abstract

In quality estimation (QE), the quality of translation can be predicted by referencing the source sentence and the machine translation (MT) output without access to the reference sentence. However, there exists a paradox in that constructing a dataset for creating a QE model requires non-trivial human labor and time, and it may even requires additional effort compared to the cost of constructing a parallel corpus. In this study, to address this paradox and utilize the various applications of QE, even in low-resource languages (LRLs), we propose a method for automatically constructing a pseudo-QE dataset without using human labor. We perform a comparative analysis on the pseudo-QE dataset using multilingual pre-trained language models. As we generate the pseudo dataset, we conduct experiments using various external machine translators as test sets to verify the accuracy of the results objectively. Also, the experimental results show that multilingual BART demonstrates the best performance, and we confirm the applicability of QE in LRLs using pseudo-QE dataset construction methods.

1 Introduction

In the field of machine translation (MT), most of the representative metrics such as BLEU (Papineni et al., 2002) and METEOR (Banerjee and Lavie, 2005) are used to measure the quality of MT output by comparing it with the reference sentence. However, these evaluation metrics limit the amount of datasets owing to the need for a reference sentence (Specia et al., 2010). In cases where end users use MT, they do not have sufficient knowledge of the source or target languages. Specifically, In the case of low-resource languages (LRLs), people are often unfamiliar with such languages. In such cases, it is difficult to determine whether the translation results derived using MT have been translated well.

Recently, studies on quality estimation (QE) have been actively conducted to address this problem (Kim et al., 2019; Wang et al., 2020; Fomicheva et al., 2020). In QE, the source sentence and the MT output are referenced to predict the quality of translation result. QE can be used to express the quality of MT output numerically, rank the results of several MT systems (Specia et al., 2010), and inform end users on MT system's level of trust. Quality annotations resulting from the QE system also allows individuals who are unfamiliar with the translation languages to verify the quality of MT outputs (Specia et al., 2013). Additionally, post-editing efforts can be reduced by filtering out poor-quality MT outputs (Specia et al., 2009; Specia, 2011). As a result, the importance of QE research has been emphasized in the field of MT.

*These authors contributed equally.
†Corresponding author.

We found one paradox pertaining to this useful QE task. QE has an advantage in that it can make predictions about MT results without using a reference sentence. However, efforts to build datasets that require more expertise than building a parallel corpus must be made to ensure the progress of QE. These requirements also limit the construction of large QE datasets. We refer to this paradox as the *paradox of QE*, and we use methods for generating a pseudo-QE dataset to address this paradox.

Because it is difficult to obtain a parallel corpus for LRLs and hinders to build a QE dataset for such languages, there are few QE studies on LRLs, except for those provided by the Conference on Machine Translation (WMT). Based on these limitations, we conduct a study on sentence-level QE with a main focus on LRLs. We construct a pseudo-QE dataset by automatically expanding Korean-based monolingual or parallel corpora without using extra human labor.

We conduct a comparative analysis between QE models based on various multilingual pre-trained language models (mPLMs), and we confirm the possibility of creating a QE model for LRLs through the experimental results. The contributions of this study are as follows:

- We point out the *paradox of QE* and to address this problem, we propose a method for automatically constructing a pseudo dataset using monolingual or parallel corpora and external machine translators without additional human labor.

- We conduct a QE study on LRLs, where previous studies on the same are rare, and we induce the various applications of QE in LRLs.

- We conduct a quantitative analysis based on various mPLMs, and conduct an empirical study using the results obtained through external machine translators, such as Google[1], Amazon[2], Microsoft[3], and Systran[4], to verify the objectivity of the translation results as we construct the pseudo dataset.

2 Proposed Method

2.1 Why Paradox?

In this section, we describe why the paradox of QE occurs at various granularity (sentence/word/document) levels of QE based on WMT20. We also describe methods for generating a pseudo-QE dataset that can address the limitations for the paradox of QE.

Paradox of QE - Sentence Level In the sentence-level direct assessment task, the MT output is evaluated based on perceived quality, which is referred to as direct assessment (DA) (Specia et al., 2020). At least three translation experts rate the quality of the MT output from zero to 100, and the system predicts the mean z-standardized DA. The dataset construction for this task requires DA annotations from at least three human experts.

The sentence-level post-editing task is configured to predict the quality score for the MT output based on the human translation error rate (HTER) (Snover et al., 2006). HTER scores are obtained through the comparison between the MT outputs and human post-edited sentences. Thus, to generate post-edited sentences for measuring HTER scores, humans must consider how minimal changes make the MT output a correct sentence, which tokens in the MT output have been mistranslated, and how to change them. Building a parallel corpus for LRLs is not easy, and hiring language experts is more difficult. These limitations make LRL-based QE studies

[1]https://translate.google.co.kr/
[2]https://aws.amazon.com/translate/
[3]https://www.microsoft.com/ko-kr/translator/
[4]https://translate.systran.net/

more challenging. The tagging process also requires post-edited sentences to be corrected by translation experts, who are quite limited in terms of human labor.

Paradox of QE - Word Level In the word-level post-editing task, the quality of the MT output is predicted using the OK label or the BAD label for each token, and the GAP tag is used in cases where there is a missing word between tokens. The tagging process also requires post-edited sentences to be modified by a translation expert. However, similar to sentence-level, the construction of a large dataset is quite limited in terms of human labor. The number of datasets released annually by the WMT is only 9K, including those on the train, validation, and test for one pair of languages.

Paradox of QE - Document Level The document-level task is configured to find translation errors in documents and estimate quality scores based on minor, major, and critical errors. In the dataset used in this task, the error part is annotated using span and span length (Specia et al., 2020). Error annotations, such as severity, word span, and specific error type are annotated through crowd-sourcing. Human labor is essential for this process because constructing a new dataset requires humans to annotate the errors. In LRL settings, the language itself is sometimes unfamiliar, making it more difficult to hire an expert that can tag translation errors in documents.

2.2 Constructing Pseudo-QE Dataset

We point out that in QE, building a dataset requires additional effort compared to the translation process. To address this issue, we propose two strategies for generating a pseudo-QE dataset for Korean, which is an LRL, and we conduct sentence-level post-editing, a sub-task of WMT.

2.2.1 Monolingual Corpus-based (M-based) Pseudo-QE Dataset Generation

The monolingual corpus-based (M-based) pseudo-QE dataset is a method for constructing a QE dataset based on round-trip translation (RTT). We generate a dataset with a three-step process based on the fact that RTT can be used to generate paraphrased sentences (Mallinson et al., 2017).

The first process involves a backward translation of the source language. In this process, we adopt Google as an external machine translator because it can easily translate large documents and is frequently used by most people. The source text generated through the backward translation process is similar to the source-side text of the parallel corpus, but there are some errors or paraphrased parts. The output of the first process is converted back into the text of the target language via the second process, which is known as forward translation. In the process of combining and traversing monolingual text using external machine translators in the target language, errors easily committed by translators are additionally attached to the plane text, and the skewed output with translation errors is generated.

In the final process, the translation error rate (TER) between the monolingual corpus and the skewed output is extracted. In other words, we consider the monolingual text as a post-edited sentence, and we measure the HTER using the generated pseudo dataset to eliminate human labor.

In this case, the pseudo dataset created through this approach may only be distorted depending on the error tendency of Google translator. Considering this situation, we use the translation results from additional representative external translators, such as Amazon, Microsoft, and Systran, as test sets to ensure that QE models trained using pseudo datasets predict the quality of translation in a general way.

2.2.2 Parallel Corpus-based (P-based) Pseudo-QE Dataset Generation

Utilizing parallel corpora and external machine translators is a method for constructing parallel corpus-based (P-based) pseudo-QE datasets.

Similar to the first step, the source-side text is entered into the external machine translator, after which it is translated to the target language. In the process of translating the source-side text to the target language, the source-side text is translated to the MT output with errors attached. In the second step, the TER is measured for each sentence using the target-side text from the parallel corpus, considering the LRL settings similar to the M-based dataset generation method.

We organize the dataset to enable the measurement of translation quality without additional human labor by solely using the parallel corpus. However, even in a P-based dataset, error types may appear to be biased to only one external machine translator throughout the dataset construction process. Therefore, the objectivity of how well the translation quality was measured, as in the monolingual case, was verified using test sets containing multiple translation results from external machine translators. The overall process of our proposed method is shown in Figure 1.

2.3 TransQuest-based Korean QE Model

We conduct training on the pseudo-QE dataset using TransQuest[5] (Ranasinghe et al., 2020), which is an open-source framework. Ranasinghe et al. (2020) proposes two structures: MonoTransQuest and SiameseTransQuest. We focus on the consistent high performance of MonoTransQuest, and we only utilize the former structure for learning. Three pooling strategies were experimented in MonoTransQuest, of which the output corresponding to the location of the [CLS] token was inserted into the softmax layer and the score was predicted. In addition to XLM-RoBERTa (XLM-R) used by MonoTransQuest, we use the multilingual BART (mBART) and the cross-lingual language model (XLM), which support Korean, for model performance comparison. For mBART model that is not associated with any previous studies on QE, we find it worth fully exploiting this because they are state-of-the-art models in MT, and we utilize additional noising schemes compared to those used in XLM and XLM-R models.

3 Experiments and Results

3.1 Dataset Details

In this study, we conduct experiments on the sentence-level task corresponding to sub-task 2 of the WMT20 based on various mPLMs for Korean, which is one of the LRLs. As the dataset for our experiments, we leverage two methods to build our proposed pseudo-QE training dataset. We use data from AI-HUB[6] (Park and Lim, 2020) and only the sentences of the target-side for the M-based pseudo-QE dataset.

The statistics of the dataset obtained through the two dataset generation methods are listed in Table 1. In Korean, the sum of the total token lengths of the M-based dataset is more than that of the P-based dataset, but the opposite occurs in English. In other words, when translated from the target language to Korean, the average length of the translated sentence becomes longer than that of the original source. However, when it is translated based on RTT into Korean, the number of tokens in the translated sentence tends to be smaller, even if the length of the source sentence is longer. Overall, the TER scores were distributed slightly lower on the M-based datasets.

Based on the datasets constructed using both methods, we segment the TER scores at 0.1 intervals, and count the scores that are part of each range, as shown on the left side of Figure 2. The distribution over the dataset shows that the M-based dataset is lower overall than the P-based dataset, as illustrated in Table 1. Based on these results, we explore the length distribution of the MT token over the range of the TER scores to analyze why the TER scores are low in the M-based dataset. As shown on the right side of Figure 2, both datasets are distributed with lower error rates as the token length becomes shorter in the TER score range from zero to five.

[5]https://github.com/TharinduDR/TransQuest
[6]https://aihub.or.kr/

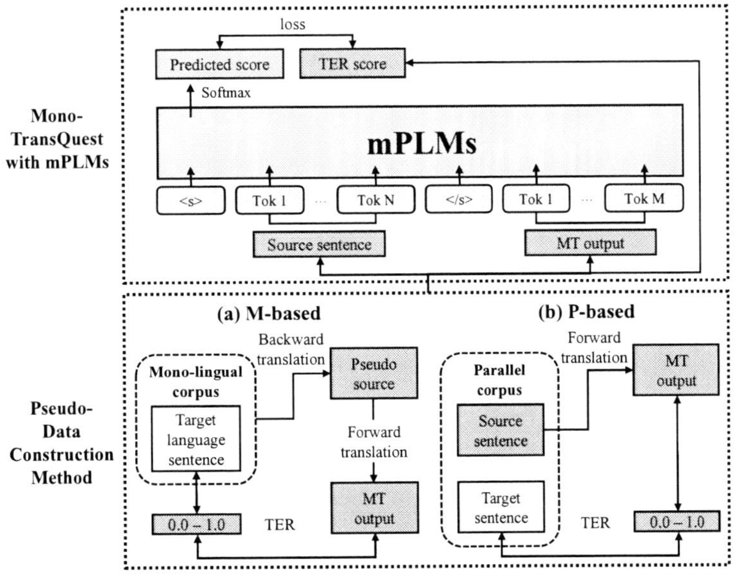

Figure 1: Overall architecture of pseudo QE dataset construction method and model training. (a) corresponds to a monolingual corpus based pseudo-QE dataset generation method, and (b) corresponds to a parallel corpus based method.

However, in the case where the TER score is higher than 0.5, the average token length of the P-based dataset is six to seven times higher overall compared to the M-based dataset. The graph shows that the error rate is also high when MT sentences are generally long and that longer sentences in the P-based dataset result in a negative effect on the TER scores.

	M-based Pseudo Dataset				P-based Pseudo Dataset			
	Train		Valid		Train		Valid	
	SRC	MT	SRC	MT	SRC	MT	SRC	MT
# of sentences	96,000	96,000	12,000	12,000	96,000	96,000	12,000	12,000
# of tokens	1,457,832	2,215,902	183,258	278,451	1,345,381	2,370,791	168,507	297,126
# of min tokens per S	1	1	1	1	3	2	3	2
# of max tokens per S	84	123	60	87	71	143	45	122
Average tokens per S	15	23	15	23	14	24.6	14	24.7
Average TER score	0.419		0.415		0.527		0.525	
Median TER score	0.417		0.417		0.524		0.523	

Table 1: Statistics of the pseudo-QE train and valid dataset. We denote the sentence as S.

	Google	Amazon	Microsoft	Systran
# of sentences	12,000	12,000	12,000	12,000
# of tokens	297,011	264,401	283,450	302,239
# of min tokens in a S	3	3	1	3
# of max tokens in a S	158	120	142	162
Average tokens per S	24.7	22	23.6	25
Average TER score	0.526	0.591	0.591	0.418
Median TER score	0.524	0.6	0.6	0.4

Table 2: Statistics of the pseudo-QE test sets constructed using various external machine translators

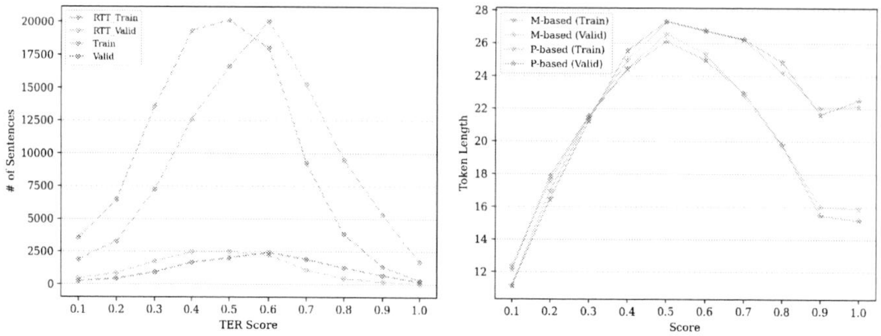

Figure 2: Number of sentences (left-side) and sentence length (right-side) according to TER score range

We build a pseudo dataset without any human labor. In addition, we leverage external machine translators by Google, Amazon, Microsoft, and Systran, to ensure objective evaluation considering the possibility of learning distortion based on the MT results. The statistics for each external machine translator are listed in Table 2. Compared to the train and validation set of the M-based dataset, the TER scores are generally higher, except for Systran. The average token length per sentence is distributed similarly, with 22 to 25 overall.

3.2 Model details

In this study, we conduct a comparative analysis by fine-tuning three representative mPLMs: XLM-R-large, XLM-MLM-100, and mBART. We compare the performance of these models to discover the performance differences that occur depending on the number of language pairs and the noising schemes in the pre-training stage. The description for each model is as follows:

- **Cross-lingual language model (XLM)**: XLM (Lample and Conneau, 2019) is a structure that extends the existing learning method of a language model for the purpose of learning multi-lingual representations. The XLM proposes a causal language model (CLM) that performs unsupervised learning on monolingual corpora, the translation language model (TLM) that implements supervised learning on parallel corpora, and the masked language model (MLM). We used XLM-MLM-100, which is a model pre-trained using a total of 100 languages, including Korean, among various XLM models.
- **XLM-RoBERTa (XLM-R)**: XLM-R (Conneau et al., 2019) significantly increases the number of datasets and conducts pre-training by applying only MLM among the learning methods of XLM. XLM-R faces the curse of multilinguality because it increases the number of training datasets and extends the number of languages. The curse of multilinguality refers to a situation in which the addition of languages improves the performance of LRLs, which have similar linguistic features with high-resource languages, initially by high-resource languages. However, at some point, the performance of both the high-resource languages and the low-resource languages is reduced when the model capacity is fixed. This is because the number of languages increases and the capacity of high-resource languages within the model decreases. By greatly expanding the model capacity, it is possible to improve the performance of low-resource languages and maintain the performance of high-resource languages.
- **multilingual BART (mBART)**: mBART (Liu et al., 2020) is a multilingual extension of BART (Lewis et al., 2019). BART adds noise from sentence permutations, token masking,

token deletion, and text infilling, and document rotations to restore them to a completely original sentence based on the structure of transformer. mBART does not utilize all the noise schemes used in BART. However, it learns by employing text infilling that replaces the span length with one [MASK] token according to the Poisson distribution in sentences and the sentence permutation that shuffles the order of sentences. mBART supports the efficient learning of LRLs by matching the dataset rates between low-resource and high-resource languages. In other words, mBART applies up-down sampling method that increases the number of datasets by copying the same in LRLs and by removing parts of the datasets in high-resource languages.

We fine-tune the pre-trained models by leveraging the framework of the Huggingface model (Wolf et al., 2019). Based on the framework provided by this model, we implement sub-word tokenization, and include the position and language embeddings for XLM. As a loss function for model learning, we use the mean square error (MSE) loss.

3.3 Main Results

As shown in Table 3 and Table 4, according to the tests conducted using datasets built using various external translators, the performance differences based on the Pearson correlation coefficient between the external translators differ by 0.193 on the M-based datasets and 0.052 on the P-based datasets. Specifically, there is no significant difference in performance (0.048), except for the results of the experiments conducted using the Systran translator on the M-based datasets. Therefore, we can conclude that that the performance difference between the external translators is not significant.

	Google			Amazon			Microsoft			Systran		
Model	**Pearson**	**MAE**	**RMSE**	**Pearson**	**MAE**	**RMSE**	**Pearson**	**MAE**	**RMSE**	**Pearson**	**MAE**	**RMSE**
XLM-R	0.236	0.175	0.223	0.307	0.194	0.237	0.278	0.198	0.245	0.076	0.189	0.232
mBART	**0.334**	0.174	0.221	**0.382**	0.199	0.240	**0.360**	0.202	0.247	**0.189**	0.183	0.226
XLM-MLM-100	0.156	0.185	0.234	0.212	0.215	0.257	0.150	0.218	0.265	-0.042	0.188	0.232

Table 3: Results of the M-based pseudo-QE dataset

	Google			Amazon			Microsoft			Systran		
Model	**Pearson**	**MAE**	**RMSE**	**Pearson**	**MAE**	**RMSE**	**Pearson**	**MAE**	**RMSE**	**Pearson**	**MAE**	**RMSE**
XLM-R	0.346	0.157	0.197	0.366	0.158	0.197	0.358	0.164	0.204	0.261	0.194	0.234
mBART	**0.450**	0.146	0.186	**0.445**	0.146	0.184	**0.450**	0.151	0.189	**0.398**	0.185	0.226
XLM-MLM-100	0.285	0.160	0.201	0.269	0.168	0.207	0.259	0.172	0.213	0.272	0.191	0.231

Table 4: Results of the P-based pseudo-QE dataset

3.3.1 Experimental results of M-based Pseudo-QE Model

We conduct a comparative analysis on the models trained using the M-based dataset. The experimental results are similar to those listed in Table 3, and they show the differences in performance in the order of the mBART, XLM-R, and XLM-MLM100 models.

Interpreting Results on Language Capacity The results show that the number of language pairs used in pre-training is not proportional to performance. Although mBART is trained using 25 language pairs, it performs better than XLM-MLM 100 and XLM-R, which are used to conduct pre-training in 100 language pairs. This shows that abundant language pairs do not necessarily benefit the QE of LRLs.

Interpreting Results for the Noising Scheme In XLM-R and XLM-MLM100, only MLM is utilized in the pre-training stage. mBART adds sentence permutation and text infilling during the pre-training process, thereby demonstrating the highest performance. Therefore, we can infer that the additional noising schemes for mBART are the critical factors that result in better results. Liu et al. (2020) also demonstrate that additional strategies for noising schemes are beneficial, and that model capability depends heavily on pre-training methods rather than the number of language pairs.

Interpreting Results for the Tokenization Method Korean is classified as an agglutinative language based on morphological characteristics. Depending on the characteristics of agglutinative languages, a single word may consist of just one word. However, there are some cases in which a substantive (noun, pronoun, numeral) and a post-positional particle appear together or a stem and an ending co-occur. Recent studies have shown that the tokenization method is an important approach that considers morphemes because they have a variety of meanings determined by the post-positional particle (Park et al., 2020, 2021).

mBART and XLM-R employ SentencePiece (Kudo and Richardson, 2018), and XLM-MLM uses byte pair encoding (BPE) (Sennrich et al., 2015). Among them, mBART applies morphological segmentation by considering the agglutinative characteristics of Korean, which can be interpreted as one of the reasons for enhancing the understanding of source text. In the case of the BPE used by XLM, the criteria for pre-tokenization are ambiguous in Korean, and they construct vocabularies in a greedy way. Therefore, there is a high probability of proceeding with incorrect sub-word segmentation. By using the XLM tokenizer, '⟨/w⟩' tokens are attached to the end of every syllable as well as the complete separation of syllables into consonants and vowels. Accordingly, it can be interpreted that the words are completely separated through the use of syllable units, thereby resulting in the poor understanding of the entire sentence and demonstrating the low performance of XLM.

3.3.2 Experimental results of P-based Pseudo-QE Model

Furthermore, we conduct a comparative analysis on models trained using the P-based dataset. As shown in Table 4, mBART and XLM-MLM-100 demonstrate the highest performance and the lowest performance, respectively, for all test sets. This difference in performance can be considered similar to that obtained in the previous analysis. Considering the construction of the dataset, we establish that the overall capability improves when the model is trained using a P-based dataset rather than an M-based dataset. Moreover, it is certain to obtain more desirable results, as they pertain to the measurement of the TER, by comparing the translation of the source sentences in parallel corpora with target sentences, rather than building datasets based on RTT. This result is attributed to the higher intimacy of the test set as a result of translating source sentences into multiple external machine translators and P-based datasets. In contrast, despite the same number of training sentences used in P-based datasets and M-based datasets, the Pearson correlation coefficients differed by a range of 0.063 to 0.209. Because the M-based dataset allows for much more datasets to be added compared to parallel corpora, learning using M-based datasets can also be expected to achieve sufficient performance gains.

4 Conclusion and Future Work

This study points out a paradox in terms of the construction of data for QE tasks. To address this limitation, we propose two methods for generating a pseudo dataset. First, considering the limitations of data construction in low-resource language settings, we generate an RTT-based pseudo-QE dataset using monolingual corpora, and second, we construct pseudo data using parallel data. The experiments are conducted using mPLMs that support Korean, and mBART demonstrated the highest performance. By conducting tests using various external machine translators, we further confirm that the model trained using a pseudo dataset is not significantly skewed on a specific external translator. Therefore, by leveraging pseudo-QE generation methods, we confirm that QE is also available in LRLs, and induce the use of various applicability of QE in LRLs. In our future studies, as we have seen the possibility of sufficient performance improvement for the result of experimenting with monolingual corpora, we plan to conduct further experiments to expand the amount of data to large-scale. We also plan to expand the proposed methodology to various language pairs and conduct detailed verification of the proposed methodology.

Acknowledgments

This research was supported by the MSIT(Ministry of Science and ICT), Korea, under the ITRC(Information Technology Research Center) support program(IITP-2018-0-01405) supervised by the IITP(Institute for Information Communications Technology Planning Evaluation) and the MSIT, Korea, under the ICT Creative Consilience program(IITP-2021-2020-0-01819) supervised by the IITP. Additionally, this work was supported by Institute for Information communications Technology Planning Evaluation(IITP) grant funded by the Korea government(MSIT) (No. 2020-0-00368, A Neural-Symbolic Model for Knowledge Acquisition and Inference Techniques).

References

Banerjee, S. and Lavie, A. (2005). Meteor: An automatic metric for mt evaluation with improved correlation with human judgments. In *Proceedings of the acl workshop on intrinsic and extrinsic evaluation measures for machine translation and/or summarization*, pages 65–72.

Conneau, A., Khandelwal, K., Goyal, N., Chaudhary, V., Wenzek, G., Guzmán, F., Grave, E., Ott, M., Zettlemoyer, L., and Stoyanov, V. (2019). Unsupervised cross-lingual representation learning at scale. *arXiv preprint arXiv:1911.02116*.

Fomicheva, M., Sun, S., Yankovskaya, L., Blain, F., Guzmán, F., Fishel, M., Aletras, N., Chaudhary, V., and Specia, L. (2020). Unsupervised quality estimation for neural machine translation. *Transactions of the Association for Computational Linguistics*, 8:539–555.

Kim, H., Lim, J.-H., Kim, H.-K., and Na, S.-H. (2019). Qe bert: bilingual bert using multi-task learning for neural quality estimation. In *Proceedings of the Fourth Conference on Machine Translation (Volume 3: Shared Task Papers, Day 2)*, pages 85–89.

Kudo, T. and Richardson, J. (2018). Sentencepiece: A simple and language independent subword tokenizer and detokenizer for neural text processing. *arXiv preprint arXiv:1808.06226*.

Lample, G. and Conneau, A. (2019). Cross-lingual language model pretraining. *arXiv preprint arXiv:1901.07291*.

Lewis, M., Liu, Y., Goyal, N., Ghazvininejad, M., Mohamed, A., Levy, O., Stoyanov, V., and Zettlemoyer, L. (2019). Bart: Denoising sequence-to-sequence pre-training for natural language generation, translation, and comprehension. *arXiv preprint arXiv:1910.13461*.

Liu, Y., Gu, J., Goyal, N., Li, X., Edunov, S., Ghazvininejad, M., Lewis, M., and Zettlemoyer, L. (2020). Multilingual denoising pre-training for neural machine translation. *Transactions of the Association for Computational Linguistics*, 8:726–742.

Mallinson, J., Sennrich, R., and Lapata, M. (2017). Paraphrasing revisited with neural machine translation. In *Proceedings of the 15th Conference of the European Chapter of the Association for Computational Linguistics: Volume 1, Long Papers*, pages 881–893.

Papineni, K., Roukos, S., Ward, T., and Zhu, W.-J. (2002). Bleu: a method for automatic evaluation of machine translation. In *Proceedings of the 40th annual meeting of the Association for Computational Linguistics*, pages 311–318.

Park, C., Eo, S., Moon, H., and Lim, H.-S. (2021). Should we find another model?: Improving neural machine translation performance with one-piece tokenization method without model modification. In *Proceedings of the 2021 Conference of the North American Chapter of the Association for Computational Linguistics: Human Language Technologies: Industry Papers*, pages 97–104.

Park, C. and Lim, H. (2020). A study on the performance improvement of machine translation using public korean-english parallel corpus. *Journal of Digital Convergence*, 18(6):271–277.

Park, C., Yang, Y., Park, K., and Lim, H. (2020). Decoding strategies for improving low-resource machine translation. *Electronics*, 9(10):1562.

Ranasinghe, T., Orasan, C., and Mitkov, R. (2020). TransQuest: Translation quality estimation with cross-lingual transformers. In *Proceedings of the 28th International Conference on Computational Linguistics*, pages 5070–5081, Barcelona, Spain (Online). International Committee on Computational Linguistics.

Sennrich, R., Haddow, B., and Birch, A. (2015). Neural machine translation of rare words with subword units. *arXiv preprint arXiv:1508.07909*.

Snover, M., Dorr, B., Schwartz, R., Micciulla, L., and Makhoul, J. (2006). A study of translation edit rate with targeted human annotation. In *Proceedings of association for machine translation in the Americas*, volume 200. Citeseer.

Specia, L. (2011). Exploiting objective annotations for minimising translation post-editing effort. In *Proceedings of the 15th Annual conference of the European Association for Machine Translation*.

Specia, L., Blain, F., Fomicheva, M., Fonseca, E., Chaudhary, V., Guzmán, F., and Martins, A. F. T. (2020). Findings of the WMT 2020 shared task on quality estimation. In *Proceedings of the Fifth Conference on Machine Translation*, pages 743–764, Online. Association for Computational Linguistics.

Specia, L., Raj, D., and Turchi, M. (2010). Machine translation evaluation versus quality estimation. *Machine translation*, 24(1):39–50.

Specia, L., Shah, K., de Souza, J. G., and Cohn, T. (2013). QuEst - a translation quality estimation framework. In *Proceedings of the 51st Annual Meeting of the Association for Computational Linguistics: System Demonstrations*, pages 79–84, Sofia, Bulgaria. Association for Computational Linguistics.

Specia, L., Turchi, M., Cancedda, N., Dymetman, M., and Cristianini, N. (2009). Estimating the sentence-level quality of machine translation systems. In *13th Conference of the European Association for Machine Translation*, pages 28–37.

Wang, M., Yang, H., Shang, H., Wei, D., Guo, J., Lei, L., Qin, Y., Tao, S., Sun, S., Chen, Y., et al. (2020). Hw-tsc's participation at wmt 2020 quality estimation shared task. In *Proceedings of the Fifth Conference on Machine Translation*, pages 1056–1061.

Wolf, T., Debut, L., Sanh, V., Chaumond, J., Delangue, C., Moi, A., Cistac, P., Rault, T., Louf, R., Funtowicz, M., et al. (2019). Huggingface's transformers: State-of-the-art natural language processing. *arXiv preprint arXiv:1910.03771*.

Small-Scale Cross-Language Authorship Attribution on Social Media Comments

Benjamin Murauer b.murauer@posteo.de
Günther Specht guenther.specht@uibk.ac.at

Abstract

Cross-language authorship attribution is the challenging task of classifying documents by bilingual authors where the training documents are written in a different language than the evaluation documents. Traditional solutions rely on either translation to enable the use of single-language features, or language-independent feature extraction methods. More recently, transformer-based language models like BERT can also be pre-trained on multiple languages, making them intuitive candidates for cross-language classifiers which have not been used for this task yet. We perform extensive experiments to benchmark the performance of three different approaches to a small-scale cross-language authorship attribution experiment: (1) using language-independent features with traditional classification models, (2) using multilingual pre-trained language models, and (3) using machine translation to allow single-language classification. For the language-independent features, we utilize universal syntactic features like part-of-speech tags and dependency graphs, and multilingual BERT as a pre-trained language model. We use a small-scale social media comments dataset, closely reflecting practical scenarios. We show that applying machine translation drastically increases the performance of almost all approaches, and that the syntactic features in combination with the translation step achieve the best overall classification performance. In particular, we demonstrate that pre-trained language models are outperformed by traditional models in small scale authorship attribution problems for every language combination analyzed in this paper.

1 Introduction

In cross-language authorship attribution, the true author of a previously unseen document must be determined from a set of candidate authors after training a machine learning model with documents from those candidates in a different language. Applications for this research include plagiarism detection or other forensic analyses, where the authorship of an incriminating document must be determined, but ground truth texts for comparison of selected suspects are only available in different languages.

The language gap imposes difficulties on the machine learning setup, as the training and testing documents have fewer common features. For example, while some languages may share common words, others use completely different alphabets or writing systems. Therefore, this problem requires one of three general strategies to solve: (1) use machine learning features that don't depend on language, (2) use a model that is inherently capable of solving multilingual problems, or (3) transform one feature space into the other to enable the use of language-dependent features (e.g., by using machine translation).

In this paper, we explore these three approaches for the case of cross-language authorship attribution, depicted in Figure 1.

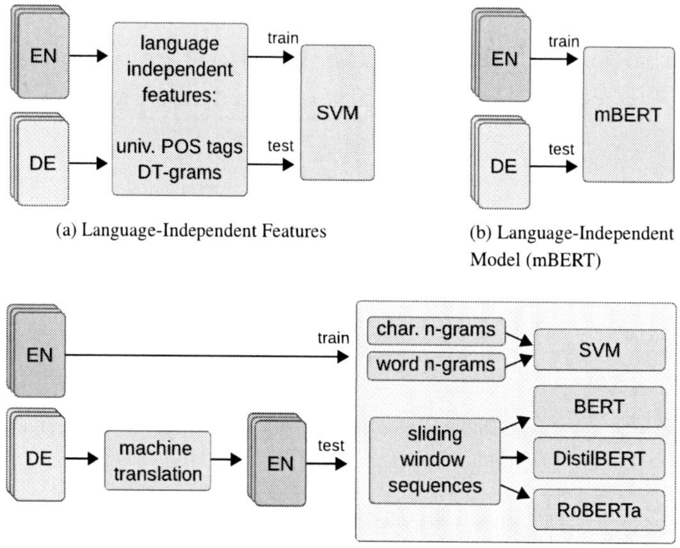

(a) Language-Independent Features

(b) Language-Independent Model (mBERT)

(c) Translation

Figure 1: The three approaches for cross-language classification models tested in this paper. DE represents any of the other languages from the datasets listed in Table 1. Note that in the experiments, both directions of training and testing are executed (i.e., each approach is also evaluated by training on DE and testing on EN for the depicted dataset).

For the first approach, we use universal part-of-speech (POS) tag n-grams (Nivre et al., 2016) as well as DT-grams (Murauer and Specht, 2021) as language-independent features, paired with a support vector machine as a classifier. For the second approach, we utilize a pre-trained multilingual BERT model, which doesn't require a separate translation pre-processing step, and fine-tune it using training part of the attribution problem. To the best of our knowledge, our study is the first to analyze the performance of this type of model to cross-language authorship attribution problems, representing our first contribution. Finally, we utilize the publicly available Marian NMT machine translation system (Junczys-Dowmunt et al., 2018), and perform several experiments with well-established single-language authorship attribution models, including character n-grams in combination with support vector machines, and also more recent approaches including BERT or RoBERTa.

For these experiments, we make use of datasets consisting of Reddit social media comments compiled by Murauer and Specht (2021). We select bilingual[1] authors that write documents in English as well as one of German, Spanish, French, Dutch and Arabic. By using these small-scale datasets, we provide valid and realistic scenarios for forensic application, are able to skip additional human translation steps required in previously used translation-based datasets, and generalize approaches from previous studies by applying them on a different type of texts and authors. This represents our second contribution.

To ensure the reproducibility of our results and promote future research, all of our code is published online [2].

[1] In the context of this paper, we denote an author writing documents in two languages as bilingual, irrespective of whether both languages are spoken natively by that author, or whether that author was raised bilingually.

[2] `https://git.uibk.ac.at/csak8736/small-scale-authorship-attribution`

2 Related Work

Cross-language text classification problems require different strategies to solve. Some problems allow the usage of parallel corpora for training the model, which enables straightforward transformations of output classes from one language to another (Rasooli et al., 2018). However, parallel corpora are not available for many language combinations, and not suitable for many tasks where the output classes can't be mapped between languages directly. Similarly, other approaches include creating a shared low-dimensional embedding space across languages in an unsupervised pre-processing step (Vulić and Moens, 2015; Mogadala and Rettinger, 2016), but it has been shown that these approaches usually can be outperformed by adding a small amount of supervised cross-language training data (Vulić et al., 2019; Karamanolakis et al., 2020).

Transformer-based pre-trained language models have provided many state-of-the-art results in natural language processing (NLP) in general, and models pre-trained on multiple languages show promising performances in a wide variety of NLP tasks (Devlin et al., 2018; Wu and Dredze, 2019), specifically also in document classification (Wu and Dredze, 2019; Keung et al., 2019). However, to the best of our knowledge, these models have not yet been tested on cross-language authorship attribution problems.

When focussing on authorship attribution, few cross-language studies remain. Llorens and Delany (2016) use differently sized windows in which vocabulary richness measurements are aggregated, requiring very large documents. Bogdanova and Lazaridou (2014) use a variety of different features including the frequency of universal POS tags on attribution, and also utilize machine-translation followed by traditional attribution techniques, providing their best results. However, the dataset that they use consists of translated documents in a single language pair (Spanish - English). More recently, Murauer and Specht (2021) have shown that classifying bilingual authors of social media comments by using universal (language-independent) POS tags can be improved by including dependency grammar information.

In this study, we take inspiration from the latter two studies and compare the performance of grammar-based features to translation-based approaches as well as multilingual language models, which have not been applied to this task. In contrast to similar efforts by Bogdanova and Lazaridou (2014), who classify novels by professional authors, we use small-scale datasets consisting of social media comments, which provide untranslated data and focus on a different text and author type.

3 Datasets

Authorship attribution is the task of determining the authorship of an unknown document given a set of candidate authors. An important difference to other text classification problems is that obtaining more data from a specific target (author) is often not possible. A cross-language setup requires multiple documents from multiple bilingual authors who write in the same two languages, further increasing the difficulty of obtaining large quantities of data.

For this reason, some previous studies have used translated corpora as an alternative means (Llorens and Delany, 2016; Bogdanova and Lazaridou, 2014) to solve the availability issue. There, the author wrote all novels in one language, and translated versions of some of them are used as a source of a different language. While this translation does not fully obfuscate the original authorship (Venuti, 2008), it represents a different scenario as the original authors of those novels did not write them in more than one language. Instead, we want to focus on cross-language features originating from the same author and hence use the corpus presented by Murauer and Specht (2021), which consists of comments form the Reddit social media platform, written by bilingual authors. Here, no additional translation step lies between the originally written documents and the classification model. We further add Arabic as a language from a different group of languages to increase the linguistic diversity.

Languages	Authors	Documents	Avg. Doc. Length	Min. Docs/Auth	Avg. Docs/Auth
EN, DE	10	3,479	3,027	22_{EN}, 20_{DE}	139_{EN}, 69_{DE}
EN, ES	20	4,450	3,125	20_{EN}, 21_{ES}	117_{EN}, 52_{ES}
EN, NL	11	2,410	3,232	20_{EN}, 20_{NL}	154_{EN}, 32_{NL}
EN, FR	45	10,131	3,089	21_{EN}, 20_{FR}	102_{EN}, 61_{FR}
EN, AR	10	2,838	2,117	10_{EN}, 11_{AR}	247_{EN}, 18_{Ar}

Table 1: Datasets used in this paper. The document length is measured in characters.

Table 1 shows the datasets used in this study. In the table, each row represents a dataset consisting of bilingual authors that have written documents in the languages displayed in the first column.

The size of any classification dataset can be divided into two parts; the number of target classes (authors) and the number of training samples (documents) per target class. As both of these numbers differ significantly across the datasets in Table 1, we apply two selection steps before each experiment.

To address the first imbalance and make the results across different language combination directly comparable, we select 10 random authors from each dataset. This number is difficult to increase as it is hard to find bilingual authors in general (e.g., the languages in Table 1 can hardly be considered low-resource by themselves, but the additional restraint on authors writing in multiple languages make even those languages difficult to obtain). On the other hand, it does not influence the evaluation results directly: a dataset with more authors does not automatically imply higher quality of the results, but rather is able to model different scenarios.

Regarding the second imbalance, we select 10 random documents from each author for training, and repeat all experiments five times (each time, choosing 10 random documents) to accommodate for this imbalance. This way, each author receives the same number of training documents. We choose 10 as this is the lower bound of how many documents an author has written (in the Arabic dataset). Note that we do not restrict the number of documents used for testing, as it does not influence the training process of the machine learning models, but rather helps to increase the confidence of the evaluation results.

We want to emphasize that having few authors and few documents per author is a valid and realistic scenario for many applications, and therefore, the small size of the datasets is a challenging and central corner stone of our work, rather than a limitation.

4 Methodology

We test three different approaches for cross-language attribution, which are depicted in Figure 1. We follow the same evaluation strategy with each approach: For each dataset, we perform all experiments in two directions, (1) train with the English part of the dataset and test with the respective other language, and (2) the other way around.

Each subsection will discuss any (hyper)parameters of the respective model, the full list of these parameters is shown in Table 2 as a reference.

4.1 Language-Independent Features

In this work, we make use of two language-independent features based on syntactic information, as this type of features has been successfully been used in previous studies (Bogdanova and Lazaridou, 2014; Tschuggnall and Specht, 2014).

Hyperparameters (used in grid search)	
character, word, universal POS tag n-gram size	$n \in [1-3]$
DT-gram shape[1]	$\mathrm{DT_{anc}}, \mathrm{DT_{sib}}, \mathrm{DT_{pq}}, \mathrm{DT_{inv}}$
DT-gram parameter sizes[1]	$\mathrm{sib}, \mathrm{anc} \in [1-4]$
support vector machine regularization factor C	$C \in [0.1, 1, 10]$
Language model parameters (static)	
Fine-tuning epochs	3
Max. sequence length	256
Learning rate	4×10^{-5}
Batch size	8

Table 2: Parameters used in the models. [1]Parameters of the DT-grams features by Murauer and Specht (2021).

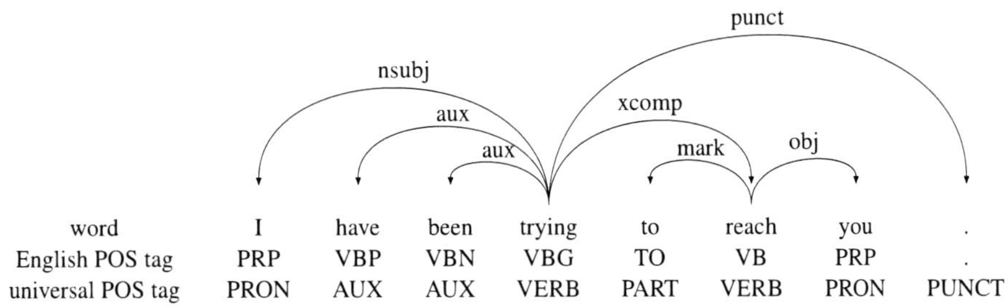

Figure 2: Differences between English-specific and universal POS tags of the sentence 'I have been trying to reach you.'.

1. universal POS tags are the result of a universal mapping of (normally language-dependent) POS tags to a language-independent space, called *universal* POS tags (Nivre et al., 2016). Figure 2 shows both the English-specific POS tags as well as their universal mappings for each word of the sentence "I have been trying to reach you". It can be seen that the mapping produces coarser relationships (e.g., the information that "trying" is a present participle is lost) but enables direct comparisons of POS tags across different languages. From the resulting POS tags, we construct n-grams by using each tag as a token.

2. DT-grams are dependency graph substructures introduced by Murauer and Specht (2021). In addition to using POS tags, the relationship between words is captured. Similar to the POS tags themselves, these dependencies can also be mapped to a language-independent space using universal dependencies (Nivre et al., 2017). We choose the same substructure layout candidates that the original authors suggest, and perform a grid search to determine the optimal candidate as well as the optimal values for the two parameters that each substructure has, from a range of $[1-4]$ (cf. Table 2).

We use a linear support vector machine as a classifier for both approaches, which has been shown to be an effective model for authorship attribution (Stamatatos, 2013; Tschuggnall et al., 2019). We utilize the *stanza* library (Qi et al., 2020) to obtain both the universal POS tags as well as the universal dependency graphs for each sentence in each dataset.

4.2 Pre-Trained Multi-Language Models

We use the multilingual version of BERT called mBERT (Devlin et al., 2018), which is pre-trained using 100 languages and has been successfully applied in many different cross-language text classification tasks (Wu and Dredze, 2019; Keung et al., 2019). While other pre-trained models in multiple languages exist, none of them cover all languages presented in this paper. We use the parameters suggested by the original authors, which are listed in Table 2. As all transformer-based models, mBERT operates on sequences of words, and the maximal length of these sequences is determined by the pre-training step of the model (which is 768 tokens for mBERT). Since the documents used in our classification setup are significantly larger than this limit, we use a sliding window approach to generate multiple samples from each document, so that every part of each document is used for fine-tuning. Thereby, each window overlaps 20% with the previous one.

The results of this model are especially useful to answer the question of whether it is more effective to translate documents in order to be able to use single-language classification models, or if inherently multilingual models are able to render this additional step superfluous.

4.3 Translation

We use the Marian NMT machine translation models (Junczys-Dowmunt et al., 2018) which are available for many language combinations. While the library offers models for both directions, for each dataset, we translate the non-English documents to English rather than the other way around, as there are more pre-trained language models available for English, and the multilingual version of BERT is also pre-trained with more English data. We therefore have more opportunities to compare to other single-language models, and expect mBERT to perform better.

At this point, we test different classification approaches on the now single-language dataset. As suggested in previous (mono-lingual) authorship research (Stamatatos, 2013; Tschuggnall and Specht, 2014), we use a linear support vector machine in combination with frequencies of character 3-grams and word unigrams. The hyperparameters of these models are listed in Table 2. We also analyze the syntactic features from approach 1, but skip the mapping of the POS tags to the universal space. This way, all POS tags are English-specific and therefore finer-grained, increasing the vocabulary size of these features.

Our experiments further include three mono-lingual pre-trained language models: mono-lingual BERT (Devlin et al., 2018), DistilBERT (Sanh et al., 2019), and RoBERTa (Liu et al., 2019). The parameters of these models are set according to recommendations of the original authors, and are listed in Table 2. Following our approach for mBERT, we apply the sliding window scheme to generate samples that fit in the respective maximal sequence lengths.

5 Results

Table 3 shows the results of the three presented approaches for all datasets, where the score is measured in macro-averaged F1.

The results of the language-independent features show that while adding dependency information to the universal POS tag features increases the F1 score for all language pairs consistently, the extent of this increase differs and is most clearly visible for the English/German dataset.

The language-independent model mBERT outperforms the DT-grams+SVM model for some language combinations, but not for the English/German and English/Dutch dataset.

The DT-grams exclusively capture grammatical features while the mBERT model incorporates content-based properties, making the two feature categories largely independent from each other. We therefore suspect them to be suitable candidates for ensemble models, which we aim to pursue in future work.

	ar	de	es	fr	nl
Approach 1: Language-independent models on untranslated documents					
Universal POS tag n-grams	0.110	0.260	0.290	0.239	0.226
DT-grams	0.175	0.400	0.317	0.283	0.262
Approach 2: Multilingual pre-trained language model					
Multilingual BERT	0.228	0.242	0.382	0.368	0.250
Approach 3: Single language models on translated documents					
Character n-grams + SVM	0.375	0.410	0.443	0.443	0.398
Word n-grams + SVM	**0.380**	0.360	0.428	0.413	0.390
BERT	0.291	0.273	0.342	0.425	0.308
DistilBERT	0.160	0.157	0.194	0.186	0.160
RoBERTa	0.298	0.261	0.382	0.432	0.311
English POS tag n-grams	0.281	0.465	0.455	0.503	0.419
English DT-grams	0.347	**0.467**	**0.465**	**0.552**	**0.433**
Combined: Language-independent models on translated documents					
Universal POS tag n-grams	0.256	0.322	0.388	0.362	0.354
DT-grams	0.327	0.435	0.456	0.447	0.416
Multilingual BERT	0.286	0.273	0.322	0.425	0.308

Table 3: Classification score measured in $F1_{macro}$ of the three different approaches, as well as a combination where all language-independent models are applied to the translated documents.

Both the grammar-based features in combination with the support vector machine as well as the multilingual BERT model are outperformed by the translation approach using the character- and word-based n-grams. The former confirms the results of Bogdanova and Lazaridou (2014), while the latter is a novel result showing that a multilingual BERT model is less efficient for such small datasets. In total, the English-specific syntactic features of the machine-translated documents show the best average performance consistently across many different languages. Only for the Arabic dataset, the word n-grams produce the best results.

Machine-translation also improves the performance of the models using language-independent features. The relevant part of our results in this regard is visible in the *Combined* part of Table 3 and shows that translation is able to boost the F1 scores of almost all languages and models, except for the Spanish dataset in combination with mBERT. These results suggest that previous findings by Bogdanova and Lazaridou (2014) are not restricted to professionally written novels, but also apply to small social media datasets. Moreover, the differences between the universal and English-specific grammar-based features demonstrate that the reduced POS tag vocabulary allowing cross-language analyses comes with a notable performance loss.

While the multilingual BERT model is able to compete with the other language-independent features, it's performance is well below all methods using machine-translation. In general, all language models are outperformed by syntactic and lexicographic features in the respective approaches, signaling that the datasets are too small for fine-tuning them sufficiently. We observe an amplification of this effect on DistilBERT, which suggests that models produced by knowledge distillation are more susceptible to smaller datasets than their original teacher model.

Summarized, our findings suggest that for cross-language authorship attribution at a small scale, machine-translation is a highly efficient first step in every case, and syntactic features are a promising candidate for datasets of this size.

6 Limitations

In general, the different datasets show a varying performance, where documents in some languages (e.g., German) are easier to attribute than others (e.g., Arabic). We attribute this effect to the linguistic distance between the language pairs (i.e., German and English are closer related to each other than Arabic and English). More datasets containing additional language pairs are required for more comprehensive comparisons in this regard.

By design, the results using machine translation in the fashion presented in this paper depend on the quality of these translation models. Especially for low-resource languages, this means that differences in translation quality between different language pairs are likely to influence the final attribution results.

7 Conclusion

In this paper, we have demonstrated different approaches to the problem of cross-language authorship attribution for bilingual authors writing in both English and one of Arabic, German, Spanish, French, and Dutch. We have analyzed language-independent syntactic features, using multilingual pre-trained language models as well as performing machine translation followed by several single-language solutions. Eventually, we show that for small-scale problems with very few training documents, using machine translation followed by models using lexicographic and syntactic features yields the best results for all languages analyzed in this work.

In the near future, we want to focus on the influence of the dataset size on the pre-trained language models to see how much data is required for these models to succeed in authorship attribution tasks. Also, we want to investigate recent work suggesting that small translation dictionaries represent a suitable substitution for full translation (Karamanolakis et al., 2020), which is a time and resource-consuming process.

References

Bogdanova, D. and Lazaridou, A. (2014). Cross-language authorship attribution. In *Ninth International Conference on Language Resources and Evaluation (LREC'2014)*, pages 2015–2020.

Devlin, J., Chang, M.-W., Lee, K., and Toutanova, K. (2018). Bert: Pre-training of deep bidirectional transformers for language understanding. `http://arxiv.org/abs/1810.04805`.

Junczys-Dowmunt, M., Grundkiewicz, R., Dwojak, T., Hoang, H., Heafield, K., Neckermann, T., Seide, F., Germann, U., Fikri Aji, A., Bogoychev, N., Martins, A. F. T., and Birch, A. (2018). Marian: Fast neural machine translation in C++. In *Proceedings of ACL 2018, System Demonstrations*, pages 116–121, Melbourne, Australia. Association for Computational Linguistics.

Karamanolakis, G., Hsu, D., and Gravano, L. (2020). Cross-lingual text classification with minimal resources by transferring a sparse teacher. In *Proceedings of the 2020 Conference on Empirical Methods in Natural Language Processing*, pages 3604–3622.

Keung, P., Lu, Y., and Bhardwaj, V. (2019). Adversarial learning with contextual embeddings for zero-resource cross-lingual classification and ner. `http://arxiv.org/pdf/1909.00153v3`.

Liu, Y., Ott, M., Goyal, N., Du, J., Joshi, M., Chen, D., Levy, O., Lewis, M., Zettlemoyer, L., and Stoyanov, V. (2019). Roberta: A robustly optimized bert pretraining approach. `http://arxiv.org/pdf/1907.11692v1`.

Llorens, M. and Delany, S. J. (2016). Deep level lexical features for cross-lingual authorship attribution. In *Proceedings of the first Workshop on Modeling, Learning and Mining for Cross/Multilinguality*, pages 16–25. Dublin Institute of Technology.

Mogadala, A. and Rettinger, A. (2016). Bilingual word embeddings from parallel and non-parallel corpora for cross-language text classification. In *Proceedings of the 2016 Conference of the North American Chapter of the Association for Computational Linguistics: Human Language Technologies*, pages 692–702.

Murauer, B. and Specht, G. (2021). DT-grams: Structured Dependency Grammar Stylometry for Cross-Language Authorship Attribution. `https://arxiv.org/pdf/2106.05677`.

Nivre, J., Agić, Ž., Ahrenberg, L., Antonsen, L., Aranzabe, M. J., Asahara, M., Ateyah, L., Attia, M., Atutxa, A., Augustinus, L., et al. (2017). Universal dependencies 2.1. `https://universaldependencies.org/`.

Nivre, J., De Marneffe, M.-C., Ginter, F., Goldberg, Y., Hajic, J., Manning, C. D., McDonald, R., Petrov, S., Pyysalo, S., Silveira, N., et al. (2016). Universal dependencies v1: A multilingual treebank collection. In *Proceedings of the 10th Int. Conference on Language Resources and Evaluation (LREC'16)*, pages 1659–1666.

Qi, P., Zhang, Y., Zhang, Y., Bolton, J., and Manning, C. D. (2020). Stanza: A Python natural language processing toolkit for many human languages. In *Proceedings of the 58th Annual Meeting of the Association for Computational Linguistics: System Demonstrations*.

Rasooli, M. S., Farra, N., Radeva, A., Yu, T., and McKeown, K. (2018). Cross-lingual sentiment transfer with limited resources. *Machine Translation*, 32(1):143–165.

Sanh, V., Debut, L., Chaumond, J., and Wolf, T. (2019). Distilbert, a distilled version of bert: smaller, faster, cheaper and lighter. `https://arxiv.org/pdf/1910.01108`.

Stamatatos, E. (2013). On the Robustness of Authorship Attribution Based on Character N-Gram Features. *Journal of Law & Policy*, pages 421–439.

Tschuggnall, M., Murauer, B., and Specht, G. (2019). Reduce & attribute: Two-step authorship attribution for large-scale problems. In *Proceedings of the 23rd Conference on Computational Natural Language Learning (CoNLL)*, pages 951–960, Hong Kong, China. Association for Computational Linguistics.

Tschuggnall, M. and Specht, G. (2014). Enhancing Authorship Attribution By Utilizing Syntax Tree Profiles. In *Proceedings of the 14th Conference of the European Chapter of the Association for Computational Linguistics (EACL'2014)*, volume 2, pages 195–199. Association for Computational Linguistics.

Venuti, L. (2008). *The translator's invisibility: A history of translation*. Routledge.

Vulić, I., Glavaš, G., Reichart, R., and Korhonen, A. (2019). Do we really need fully unsupervised cross-lingual embeddings? `https://arxiv.org/pdf/1909.01638`.

Vulić, I. and Moens, M.-F. (2015). Monolingual and cross-lingual information retrieval models based on (bilingual) word embeddings. In *Proceedings of the 38th International Conference on Research and Development in Information Retrieval*. ACM Press.

Wu, S. and Dredze, M. (2019). Beto, bentz, becas: The surprising cross-lingual effectiveness of bert. `https://arxiv.org/pdf/1904.09077v2`.

Morphologically-Guided Segmentation For Translation of Agglutinative Low-Resource Languages

William Chen wchen6255@knights.ucf.edu
Brett Fazio brettfazio@knights.ucf.edu
University of Central Florida

Abstract

Neural Machine Translation (NMT) for Low Resource Languages (LRL) is often limited by the lack of available training data, making it necessary to explore additional techniques to improve translation quality. We propose the use of the Prefix-Root-Postfix-Encoding (PRPE) subword segmentation algorithm to improve translation quality for LRLs, using two agglutinative languages as case studies: Quechua and Indonesian. During the course of our experiments, we reintroduce a parallel corpus for Quechua-Spanish translation that was previously unavailable for NMT. Our experiments show the importance of appropriate subword segmentation, which can go as far as improving translation quality over systems trained on much larger quantities of data. We show this by achieving state-of-the-art results for both languages, obtaining higher BLEU scores than large pre-trained models with much smaller amounts of data.

1 Introduction

Subword segmentation is a common technique used to improve machine translation quality due to its ability to reduce the vocabulary size of input text. Unsupervised techniques such as Byte-Pair Encoding (BPE) (Sennrich et al., 2015) are prevalent in most NLP tasks. On the other side of the spectrum, state-of-the-art morphological segmentation is achieved using dedicated neural seq2seq models (Wang et al., 2016). Neither of these however, are well-suited for Low-Resource Languages (LRLs).

BPE was found to oversplit roots of infrequent words in both English and Japanese (Bostrom and Durrett, 2020). Lower BLEU scores in Quechua-Spanish models segmented by BPE (Ortega et al., 2021) suggest similar side-effects for Quechua. Neural morphological segmentation models require large amounts of morpheme-labeled training data, which often does not exist at all for LRLs. We propose the use of the Prefix-Root-Postfix-Encoding (PRPE) algorithm (Zuters et al., 2018) as an alternative for subword segmentation. PRPE is able to draw upon linguistic knowledge without needing large amounts of labeled training data, making it a middle-ground between BPE and neural seq2seq that is ideal for LRLs.

PRPE is a semi-supervised word segmentation algorithm that uses subword statistics to identify and learn the prefixes, roots, and postfixes of words in a corpus (Zuters et al., 2018), and can be guided using a language-specific heuristic. Using the generated lists of roots and affixes, the algorithm performs subword segmentation that only appears to be morphologically grounded; PRPE does not use any actual linguistic/morphological rules. This makes it well-suited for studying LRLs, as it only requires a surface level of understanding to tune the heuristic for a language instead of dedicated linguistic rules or large amounts of labeled training data.

We experiment with two distinct agglutinative LRLs, Indonesian and Quechua, as we hypothesized that PRPE would naturally work well in the morpheme-heavy environment of these languages. This is because words in agglutinative languages are constructed via a series of affixes, leading to large amounts of information expressed in a single word due to the presence of many morphemes. As such, machine translation for these languages is particularly challenging due to the increased vocabulary size and more frequent appearance of rare words (Koehn and Knowles, 2017). Quechua in particular is highly agglutinative; multiple suffixes are appended to modify a root to denote tense, mood, person, and number (Muysken, 1988).

To investigate the effectiveness of PRPE in improving machine translation quality, we conduct experiments using two distinct language pairs, Quechua to Spanish and Indonesian to English, across multiple domains of corpora. We accomplish this by training LSTM (Hochreiter and Schmidhuber, 1997) and Transformer (Vaswani et al., 2017) models on text segmented by PRPE and compare those with models trained on other segmentation methods. Our experiments show that PRPE subword segmentation can lead to significant improvements in machine translation performance, outperforming prior benchmarks with models pre-trained using masked language modeling (Guntara et al., 2020), transfer learning (Ortega et al., 2021), and models trained on much larger datasets (Guntara et al., 2020).

1.1 Contributions

Our contributions are outlined as followed: (1) we show the ease of extending the semi-supervised PRPE algorithm to new languages by applying it to Quechua and Indonesian; (2) we train several NMT models for those languages to demonstrate the effectiveness of PRPE in improving translation accuracy; (3) we re-introduce a general domain Quechua dataset for NMT by manually cleaning and re-aligning raw data used in early SMT experiments that was previously only available in parallel parse-tree format. Our code and dataset are available at `https://github.com/wanchichen/morphological-nmt`.

2 Related Work

The current segmentation standard for most NMT systems is the unsupervised method of Byte-Pair Encoding (Sennrich et al., 2015). BPE initially represents the corpus at a character level, after which pairs of the most frequently occurring symbols are iteratively merged together to form the vocabulary. However, recent works have shown that a unigram language model for segmentation (Kudo, 2018), another unsupervised method, appears to be the better alternative. Bostrom and Durrett (2020) found unigram models better preserved roots and split affixes compared to BPE in English and Japanese. Richburg et al. (2020) observed similar benefits for two LRLs: Swahili and Turkish.

Zuters et al. (2018) introduced the PRPE algorithm by experimenting with an English-Latvian pairing in both translation directions. PRPE utilizes a proposed 'Root alignment principle' - collecting statistics about prefixes and suffixes before aligning roots with the most frequent prefix and suffix. Aside from the differences in languages used, our work also differs from Zuters et al. (2018) in terms of how the algorithm is incorporated into the overall segmentation pipeline. They also did not consider running PRPE standalone, all text segmented with PRPE in their experiments were post-processed with BPE. In addition to this method, we also explore segmentation results obtained solely with PRPE, as well as those obtained from multiple iterations of PRPE.

There have been several studies on NLP for Quechua. Rios (2016) created a language toolkit for Quechua translation, which included a text normalizer, spell-checking, and morphological analyzer. Ortega et al. (2021) focused primarily on translation from Quechua to Spanish. They proposed BPE-Guided, a method to guide the BPE segmentation algorithm for Quechua by feeding BPE a dictionary of words to ignore during segmentation. They utilized transfer learning from Finnish (a high-resource agglutinative language) to obtain substantial improvements in BLEU. It was also in this study that Ortega et al. (2021) first suggested the use of PRPE for Quechua translation. Oncevay (2021) conducted research on multilingual translation for four Peruvian languages paired with Spanish: Aymara, Ashaninka, Quechua and Shipibo-Konibo. Pre-processing was done using the unigram model (Kudo (2018)) trained across a multilingual corpus. Quechua, the language with the most resources among the four, suffered in performance when trained on the multilingual task rather than solely Quechua and Spanish. Quechua was also recently featured as part of the AmericasNLP Shared Task (Mager et al., 2021), where participants were asked to translate Spanish text to Quechua among other indigenous American languages.

Compared to Quechua, Indonesian has enjoyed much more attention in NLP research. Extensive work has been done on computational approaches in Indonesian morphological analysis, such as MorphInd (Larasati et al., 2011) and later on MALINDO Morph (Nomoto et al., 2018), both of which created morphological dictionaries and supervised morphological analyzers for the language. Guntara et al. (2020) conducted extensive benchmarks of the current state of Indonesian-English NMT, evaluating performance across a multitude of domains such as news, religious text, and conversational text. Ariesandy et al. (2020) extended their work to improve translation for colloquial Indonesian to English by constructing a synthetic training corpus machine-translated from formal Indonesian.

3 PRPE

As suggested by its name, Prefix-Root-Postfix-Encoding (PRPE) separates a word into three main parts, a prefix, a root, and a postfix. Postfixes can be further broken down into a suffix and an ending. Instead of the character pairs of BPE, left and right substrings are used for segmentation. Left substrings are considered as potential prefixes, while right substrings are considered potential postfixes. Similar to BPE, PRPE is also split into a learning phase and application phase, the former of which Zuters et al. (2018) outlines as four main steps:

1. Collect the frequency of left and right substrings for each word.
2. Treat left substrings as potential roots and align them with the middle part of the word to extract potential prefixes.
3. Treat right substrings as potential roots and align them with the middle part of the word to extract potential postfixes.
4. Use obtained prefixes and postfixes to extract roots from left substrings by aligning them with the middle part of the word.

The learning phase of PRPE can also take in a heuristic to help it determine whether a subword unit is a good candidate for a certain affix type. In other words, a set of hyperparameters that determine the threshold for affix candidacy. For example, an English heuristic could help identify *statistically probable prefixes* by using a list of known *linguistic prefixes* (such as pre- or non-) and some maximum character length. A left substring would be considered a potential prefix if it is found in the list or is within the maximum character length. We apply the same principle when creating the Quechua and Indonesian heuristics by using a list of common prefixes and suffixes, obtained from Muysken (1988), Kinti-Moss and Perkins (2012), and Ortega et al. (2021) for Quechua and IndoDic [1] for Indonesian. The exact heuristic implementations

[1] http://indodic.com/affixeng.html

can be found online [2]. This approach is cross-dimensional, and thus makes the algorithm easily extendable to other languages due to the large amount of affix information publicly available.

This learning phase generates 6 files that are used during the application phase: ranked lists of prefixes, roots, postfixes, suffixes, endings, and words that the algorithm has learned. A word is segmented by generating all possible segmentations and choosing the highest ranked candidate. It is important to reiterate that PRPE is not attempting true morphological segmentation of a word into its linguistic morphemes, but rather into subword units that it deems statistically likely to be prefixes, roots, postfixes, suffixes, and endings. This constitutes the "morphologically guided" portion of PRPE, as it allows for sub-word tokenization that resembles morphologically motivated segmentation.

3.1 Additional Segmentation Methods

Different methods to implement PRPE into the larger pipeline were tested. One such method, denoted as PRPE+BPE, originated from Zuters et al. (2018). This technique is derived from the idea that we can obtain more accurate sub-word tokenization if the corpus is already segmented with a morphologically-driven heuristic. The implementation is simple, we first segment the corpus with PRPE. Then, we segment the PRPE-segmented corpus again using BPE.

We also devised Multi-PRPE - a segmentation method where PRPE is iteratively run n times, feeding the segmented text of each run as input to the next iteration. The intuition was that the rigid nature of PRPE (only one of each affix type) may not provide accurate segmentation for highly agglutinative languages. By running multiple times we continually break off affixes allowing new ones, should they exist, to be segmented off the root.

During development, we conducted a brief analysis of segmentation results of randomly sampled words from the training corpora for the sake of testing the different segmentation implementations. Comprehensive morphological analysis of the segmented text remained outside the scope of this paper. The segmentation methods used in the study were BPE (Sennrich et al., 2015) , SentencePiece Unigram (Kudo and Richardson, 2018), PRPE, PRPE+BPE, and Multi-PRPE (for $n = 2$, $n = 5$, and $n = 8$). The segmentation results were evaluated against morphological analyzers as gold standards due to the lack of labeled segmentation data, an analyzer by Rios Gonzales and Castro Mamani (2014) for Quechua and the MALINDO Morph analyzer (Nomoto et al., 2018) for Indonesian. Compared to the other methods, Multi-PRPE ($n = 5$) appeared to best match the gold standard across both languages. For example, in Table 1 PRPE segments the Quechua word *kausashanchej* as *kausashanchej* (no change), while Multi-PRPE segments it as *kausa - sha - nchej*: the exact output of the morphological analyzer.

Method	Quechua Sample 1	Quechua Sample 2	Indonesian Sample 1
Unsegmented	kausakusunman	kausashanchej	kebencian
BPE	kausa - kusunman	kausash - anchej	kebencian
Unigram	kausaku - sunman	kausasha - nchej	kebencian
PRPE	kausakusun - man	kausashanchej	ke - benci - an
PRPE+BPE	kausa - kusun - man	kausa - shanchej	ke - benci - an
Multi-PRPE	kausakusun - man	kausa - sha - nchej	ke - benc - i - an
Analyzer	kausa - ku - sun - man	kausa - sha - nchej	ke - benci - an

Table 1: Sample Segmentation Results

[2] https://github.com/wanchichen/morphological-nmt

4 Datasets

The main dataset used for analyzing performance was the JW300 texts (Agić and Vulić, 2019) from the Opus corpus (Tiedemann, 2012), comprised of Jehovah's Witness scripture across a variety of languages. Despite the dataset's domain specific content, it is also one of the largest parallel texts publicly available for Quechua. For the Quechua-Spanish pair, we used the version of the dataset made publicly available by Ortega et al. (2021), already split into 17,500 training sentences, 2,500 validation sentences, and 5,585 test sentences. For Indonesian-English we use the an altered version of JW300 provided by Guntara et al. (2020), which also includes Bible and Quran texts gathered from Bible-Uedin and Tanzil respectively (Christodouloupoulos and Steedman, 2015). This dataset is split into 579,544 training sentences, 5,000 validation sentences, 4,823 test sentences. We denote both of these as the Religious datasets.

To ascertain the effects of PRPE outside of the religious domain, we also conduct experiments using general language corpora. We include two different general language datasets for Quechua-Spanish. The first is comprised of financial news articles from DW News, originally created by Rios (2016) for statistical machine translation. However, it was only available as parallel parse trees in an XML format, rendering it unusable for NMT models trained on parallel plaintext. We manually align and clean the raw source text data, filtering out uncertain alignments. The entire cleaned 2,018 line corpus is denoted as the Financial dataset. The second corpus used was the 100 sentence Magazine dataset created by Ortega et al. (2021). Both general-language Quechua-Spanish datasets were used solely for testing due to their small size.

For the Indonesian-English pair, despite having access to much larger general language datasets, we chose to use the low-resource News dataset created by Guntara et al. (2020). This is because of the relatively large size of the Religious Indonesian-English dataset compared to many truly low-resource languages (although it is still substantially smaller than most high-resource language datasets); we wanted to examine the benefits of PRPE in a very low-resource setting for both language pairs. The News dataset is split into 38,469 training sentences, 1,953 validation sentences, and 1,954 test sentences.

5 Experimental Setup

We separate our experiments into two stages: development and testing. We use the development stage to experiment with different model architectures and parameter settings, the best performing of which were carried over to the testing stage. In the testing stage, we evaluate the models on both in-domain and out-of-domain corpora after they were trained on a specific dataset.

Our pipeline includes two pre-processing steps: tokenization and subword segmentation. Tokenization is done using Moses tokenizer (Koehn et al., 2007), demonstrated by Domingo et al. (2018) to be effective in translation tasks. Segmentation is done solely on the source language (either Indonesian or Quechua) text, using one of the methods described above: PRPE, Multi-PRPE, and PRPE+BPE. The target language is left unsegmented. To establish a baseline for comparison, we also conduct experiments with unsegmented text and text segmented with BPE and a unigram language model. We use the default SentencePiece vocabulary size of 8000 for all segmentation methods.

We use the sacreBLEU (Post, 2018) implementation of BLEU (Papineni et al., 2002) as our primary metric for evaluation of translation quality to allow for a comparison with other studies. Ortega et al. (2021) used BLEU to evaluate their NMT systems and found it to be correlated with human judgement for the Quechua-Spanish translation direction. Guntara et al. (2020) used BLEU scores from sacreBLEU to benchmark Indonesian-English translation.

5.1 Development Stage

Development was done on the Religious and News datasets for Indonesian-English, and solely on the Religious dataset for Quechua-Spanish. All datasets are used in their original data splits to allow for comparisons with Guntara et al. (2020) and Ortega et al. (2021). Our models were trained and evaluated in OpenNMT (Klein et al., 2017). It provides a variety of encoder and decoder types, however we focus on LSTM (Hochreiter and Schmidhuber, 1997) and Transformer (Vaswani et al., 2017) for better comparisons with previous works.

Most settings from OpenNMT were kept default to allow for comparisons with the results of Ortega et al. (2021), who used default parameters. The Transformer configuration was 6 encoder-decoder layers and 8 attention heads with size 512 word embeddings, a feed-forward network size of 2048, a learning rate of 2, a dropout of 0.1, and the ADAM optimizer (Kingma and Ba, 2014). These were obtained from the recommended OpenNMT Transformer settings also used by Ortega et al. (2021). The default configuration for LSTM is 2 layers with 500 hidden units, a learning rate of 1, a dropout of 0.3, and stochastic gradient descent as the optimizer.

The only parameters changed throughout development were batch size and training step count. The recommended 4096 batch size for the Transformer model resulted in poor performance (regardless of segmentation method used) and was adjusted to the default value of 64. Due to memory constraints, sentences longer than 50 tokens were filtered out when training on the Religious Indonesian-English corpus. We also found the default training step count of 100,000 to be unsuitable for the smaller training sets: the Quechua-Spanish Religious set and the Indonesian-English News set. We instead used values of 20,000 for Transformer and 60,000 for LSTM. Continued training beyond these values led to over-fitting: steady increases in validation perplexity and no increase in validation accuracy.

5.2 Testing Stage

The best performing models during development for each segmentation method on each validation set were carried over for evaluation on the testing set and out-of-domain corpora. During the development stage, translation models trained and tested on text trained with PRPE+BPE or Multi-PRPE performed consistently worse than models developed on text segmented solely with PRPE, although they still produced incremental to moderate gains over the baseline comparisons. Studying the segmented text led us to suspect that this was due to over-segmentation with regards to the task of translating to an unsegmented target language. As such, these segmentation methods were not included in experiments during the testing phase.

Models were tested on both in-domain and out-of-domain text. Quechua-Spanish models were evaluated using the Financial and Magazine corpora, as well as the testing split of the Religious text. Indonesian-English models were tested on both Religious and News text.

6 Results

BLEU scores from the development stage (Table 2) were encouraging, with the standalone PRPE algorithm outperforming the other segmentation algorithms in most instances, gaining as much as 1.9 BLEU compared to the next best method. Notably, the inclusion of PRPE significantly outperformed previous benchmarks on the Indonesian-English Religious validation set (26 BLEU vs 22.5 BLEU), which was established by Guntara et al. (2020) with a model pre-trained with Masked Language Modeling (Devlin et al., 2019) and Translation Language Modeling (Lample and Conneau, 2019) using a training corpus of over 12.9 million non-segmented parallel sentences. A model with language pre-training from Guntara et al. (2020) trained on the exact same Religious training set as ours obtained a BLEU score of 20.2.

Perhaps most interestingly, the models trained on the smaller two training sets (the Quechua-Spanish Religious set and the Indonesian-English News set) consistently yielded better performance when trained on the LSTM architecture compared to the Transformer no matter the segmentation method used, with differences as high as 2.6 BLEU. Ortega et al. (2021) also observed the same pattern in their experiments with Quechua-Spanish translation. These results may suggest that the best performing architectures and techniques in high-resource settings may not be transferable to low-resource translation. We leave further evaluation to future studies. As such, the LSTM models trained on the Quechua-Spanish Religious set and the Indonesian-English News set, instead of their Transformer equivalents, were carried over for testing.

QZ-ES (Religious Validation Set)						
Architecture	Segmentation Method					
	None	BPE	Unigram	PRPE	PRPE+BPE	Multi-PRPE
LSTM	21.7	21.5	22.2	**23.7**	22.9	22.2
Transformer	20.24	19.74	21.1	21.8	20.27	21.03
ID-EN (Religious Validation Set)						
Architecture	Segmentation Method					
	None	BPE	Unigram	PRPE	PRPE+BPE	Multi-PRPE
LSTM	12.2	9.9	22.1	23.8	10.5	22.25
Transformer	19.8	18.7	23.4	**26**	22.4	24.1
ID-EN (News Validation Set)						
Architecture	Segmentation Method					
	None	BPE	Unigram	PRPE	PRPE+BPE	Multi-PRPE
LSTM	9.4	10.1	10.4	**12.2**	10.4	11.9
Transformer	9.8	9.3	9.9	10.1	9.4	9.8

Table 2: BLEU scores in the development stage. Multi-PRPE was run using $n = 5$ iterations. Models generally performed better when text is segmented with some implementation of PRPE.

QZ-ES						
Test Set	Segmentation Method					
	None	BPE	Unigram	PRPE	BPE-Guided*	BPE-Guided (qz-fi)-es*
Religious	20.14	16.5	20.48	**23.4**	17	22.5
Financial	**1.72**	1.06	0.76	1.4	N/A	N/A
Magazine	0.5	0.2	0.56	0.6	0.5	**0.7**

Table 3: In-domain and out-of-domain BLEU scores in the test stage for Quechua-Spanish. All models were LSTMs trained on the Religious training set. *Additional results were included from Ortega et al. (2021) for comparison.

In-domain testing results for Quechua-Spanish were consistent with the development stage with PRPE outperforming other segmentation methods (Table 3). Especially exciting was the PRPE model out-performing models enhanced with transfer learning from Finnish. Quechua-Finnish-Spanish models from Ortega et al. (2021) obtained BLEU scores of 22.9 and 22.5 with BPE and BPE-Guided respectively, whereas the PRPE model obtained a score of 23.4. However, out-of-domain performance for Quechua-Spanish models remained poor, similar to results obtained by Ortega et al. (2021). Segmentation with a unigram language model, the best performing baseline during development, performed especially poorly in out-of-domain evaluation. PRPE had better results than the other segmentation methods in Table 3, but was unable to outperform unsegmented data on the Financial set and transfer learning on the Magazine set.

ID-EN (Religious)				
Test Set	Segmentation Method			
	None	BPE	Unigram	PRPE
Religious	18.5	19.1	20.11	**24.6**
News	10.48	9.8	10.77	**11.47**

Table 4: In-domain and out-of-domain BLEU scores in the test stage for Indonesian-English for Transformer models trained on the Religious dataset.

ID-EN (News)				
Test Set	Segmentation Method			
	None	BPE	Unigram	PRPE
Religious	6.7	6.11	6.44	**7**
News	9.2	9.1	9.5	**10.8**

Table 5: In-domain and out-of-domain BLEU scores in the test stage for Indonesian-English for LSTM models trained on the News dataset.

PRPE performed well during both in-domain and out-of-domain testing for the Indonesian-English pair . In-domain results for the Religious dataset (Table 4) were especially strong, again out-performing a model with language pre-training and a much larger training corpus (24.6 BLEU for PRPE vs 22.1 BLEU from Guntara et al. (2020)). Results for in-domain News (Table 5) and out-of-domain evaluation (Tables 4 and 5) showed much more moderate improvements. A notable result was the poor performance of BPE: it performed worse than no segmentation by producing the lowest scores for 6/7 test sets. This result was surprising given its frequent use in NMT, although still somewhat expected given similar results obtained by Ortega et al. (2021).

Encouraged by the results on the Indonesian-English Religious set, we set up additional experiments using PRPE in an effort to match the Google Translate benchmarks obtained by Guntara et al. (2020) on the validation set (test set scores were not available), which obtained a BLEU score of 29.1 (Table 6). We added the high-resource 1.8 million sentence General dataset from Guntara et al. (2020) as additional training data. Fine-tuning parameters on the validation set, such as increasing word embedding size to 800 from 512 and increasing training steps to 200,000, led to our maximum score of 27.2 BLEU on the validation set and 25.6 BLEU on the testing set (Table 6). With these scores, our PRPE system outperformed the best results of 22.5 validation BLEU and 22.1 test BLEU obtained by Guntara et al. (2020), which was a masked language modelling pre-trained Transformer trained on much more data (10.1 million more sentences in addition to the General and Religious datasets), while performing almost comparably with Google Translate.

ID-EN			
Religious Dataset	Model		
	Our System	Guntara et al. (2020)*	Google Translate*
Validation	27.2	22.5	29.1
Test	25.6	22.1	N/A

Table 6: BLEU scores on the validation and test splits of the Religious set, after adding in additional training data to our system. Our system was a Transformer trained on PRPE-segmented-text from the Religious and General datasets. *Additional results were included from Guntara et al. (2020) for comparison.

Across all datasets, subword segmentation via PRPE consistently improved translation quality over other systems, whether it be unsegmented text or other segmentation methods. Our results demonstrated the importance of selecting suitable subword segmentation methods for low-resource translation. While out-of-domain evaluation remains a challenge for NMT systems, our experiments show that appropriate segmentation techniques can still lead to moderate gains in terms of BLEU. Results are more exciting for in-domain translation, as we show with PRPE that the same segmentation techniques can significantly improve translation quality in place of additional training data, making them especially useful in these low-resource settings.

7 Limitations

While we show that PRPE was able to bring substantial gains in translation quality, there are still constraints that limit its applicability. The most immediate is the pre-requisite for some amount of linguistic knowledge (a list of affixes) during the construction of its heuristics due to its semi-supervised nature. An extension of this limitation is that heuristics are thus language specific, making it less applicable in cross-lingual scenarios (although a multilingual heuristic could be developed to alleviate this problem). Finally, the effectiveness of the algorithm on non-agglutinative languages is unclear. While Zuters et al. (2018) showed that PRPE brought incremental improvements in BLEU score for the non-agglutinative English-Latvian pairing, their experiments also had text further segmented with BPE (which was shown in our results to decrease the benefits of PRPE for agglutinative languages).

8 Conclusion

We introduced the use of the PRPE algorithm for morphologically-guided subword segmentation and evaluate it on two distinct low-resource, agglutinative languages: Quechua and Indonesian. During the development of our experiments, we reintroduced datasets previously unavailable in parallel plaintext for NMT by manually re-aligning raw source data. We found that subword segmentation can have an especially large impact on low-resource translation; unsuitable segmentation methods can actually lower BLEU score when compared to unsegmented text, while effective segmentation can produce moderate to large gains. Our results show that segmentation using PRPE can lead to significant improvements in translation quality when evaluated via BLEU score, out-performing pre-trained, higher-resource models, making the algorithm ideal for low-resource languages that lack the large amounts of training data often necessary for neural machine translation.

References

Agić, Ž. and Vulić, I. (2019). JW300: A wide-coverage parallel corpus for low-resource languages. In *Proceedings of the 57th Annual Meeting of the Association for Computational Linguistics*, pages 3204–3210, Florence, Italy. Association for Computational Linguistics.

Ariesandy, A. S., Amien, M., Aji, A. F., and Prasojo, R. E. (2020). Synthetic source language augmentation for colloquial neural machine translation.

Bostrom, K. and Durrett, G. (2020). Byte pair encoding is suboptimal for language model pretraining. In *Findings of the Association for Computational Linguistics: EMNLP 2020*, pages 4617–4624, Online. Association for Computational Linguistics.

Christodouloupoulos, C. and Steedman, M. (2015). A massively parallel corpus: the bible in 100 languages. *Language resources and evaluation*, 49(2):375–395.

Devlin, J., Chang, M.-W., Lee, K., and Toutanova, K. (2019). Bert: Pre-training of deep bidirectional transformers for language understanding.

Domingo, M., Garcıa-Martınez, M., Helle, A., Casacuberta, F., and Herranz, M. (2018). How much does tokenization affect neural machine translation? *arXiv:1812.08621. Version 4.*

Guntara, T. W., Aji, A. F., and Prasojo, R. E. (2020). Benchmarking multidomain English-Indonesian machine translation. In *Proceedings of the 13th Workshop on Building and Using Comparable Corpora*, pages 35–43, Marseille, France. European Language Resources Association.

Hochreiter, S. and Schmidhuber, J. (1997). Long short-term memory. *Neural Computation*, 9(8):1735–1780.

Kingma, D. and Ba, J. (2014). Adam: A method for stochastic optimization. *International Conference on Learning Representations, arXiv:1412.6980. Version 4.*

Kinti-Moss, N. and Perkins, J. (2012). *Imanhalla An Introduction to Quechua.* University of Kansas.

Klein, G., Kim, Y., Deng, Y., Senellart, J., and Rush, A. (2017). OpenNMT: Open-source toolkit for neural machine translation. In *Proceedings of ACL 2017, System Demonstrations*, pages 67–72, Vancouver, Canada. Association for Computational Linguistics.

Koehn, P., Hoang, H., Birch, A., Callison-Burch, C., Federico, M., Bertoldi, N., Cowan, B., Shen, W., Moran, C., Zens, R., Dyer, C., Bojar, O., Constantin, A., and Herbst, E. (2007). Moses: Open source toolkit for statistical machine translation. In *Proceedings of the 45th Annual Meeting of the Association for Computational Linguistics Companion Volume Proceedings of the Demo and Poster Sessions*, pages 177–180, Prague, Czech Republic. Association for Computational Linguistics.

Koehn, P. and Knowles, R. (2017). Six challenges for neural machine translation.

Kudo, T. (2018). Subword regularization: Improving neural network translation models with multiple subword candidates. In *Proceedings of the 56th Annual Meeting of the Association for Computational Linguistics (Volume 1: Long Papers)*, pages 66–75, Melbourne, Australia. Association for Computational Linguistics.

Kudo, T. and Richardson, J. (2018). SentencePiece: A simple and language independent subword tokenizer and detokenizer for neural text processing. In *Proceedings of the 2018 Conference on Empirical Methods in Natural Language Processing: System Demonstrations*, pages 66–71, Brussels, Belgium. Association for Computational Linguistics.

Lample, G. and Conneau, A. (2019). Cross-lingual language model pretraining.

Larasati, S. D., Kuboň, V., and Zeman, D. (2011). Indonesian morphology tool (morphind): Towards an indonesian corpus. In *International Workshop on Systems and Frameworks for Computational Morphology*, pages 119–129. Springer.

Mager, M., Oncevay, A., Ebrahimi, A., Ortega, J., Rios, A., Fan, A., Gutierrez-Vasques, X., Chiruzzo, L., Giménez-Lugo, G., Ramos, R., Meza Ruiz, I. V., Coto-Solano, R., Palmer, A., Mager-Hois, E., Chaudhary, V., Neubig, G., Vu, N. T., and Kann, K. (2021). Findings of the AmericasNLP 2021 shared task on open machine translation for indigenous languages of the Americas. In *Proceedings of the First Workshop on Natural Language Processing for Indigenous Languages of the Americas*, pages 202–217, Online. Association for Computational Linguistics.

Muysken, P. (1988). Affix order and interpretation: Quechua.

Nomoto, H., Choi, H., Moeljadi, D., and Bond, F. (2018). Malindo morph: Morphological dictionary and analyser for malay/indonesian. In *Proceedings of the LREC 2018 Workshop "The 13th Workshop on Asian Language Resources*, pages 36–43.

Oncevay, A. (2021). Peru is multilingual, its machine translation should be too? In *Proceedings of the First Workshop on Natural Language Processing for Indigenous Languages of the Americas*, pages 194–201, Online. Association for Computational Linguistics.

Ortega, J., Castro Mamani, R., and Cho, K. (2021). Neural machine translation with a polysynthetic low resource language. *Machine Translation*.

Papineni, K., Roukos, S., Ward, T., and Zhu, W.-J. (2002). Bleu: a method for automatic evaluation of machine translation. In *Proceedings of the 40th Annual Meeting of the Association for Computational Linguistics*, pages 311–318, Philadelphia, Pennsylvania, USA. Association for Computational Linguistics.

Post, M. (2018). A call for clarity in reporting BLEU scores. In *Proceedings of the Third Conference on Machine Translation: Research Papers*, pages 186–191, Belgium, Brussels. Association for Computational Linguistics.

Richburg, A., Eskander, R., Muresan, S., and Carpuat, M. (2020). An evaluation of subword segmentation strategies for neural machine translation of morphologically rich languages. In *Proceedings of the The Fourth Widening Natural Language Processing Workshop*, pages 151–155, Seattle, USA. Association for Computational Linguistics.

Rios, A. (2016). A basic language technology toolkit for quechua. *Procesamiento del Lenguaje Natural*, 56:91–94.

Rios Gonzales, A. and Castro Mamani, R. A. (2014). Morphological disambiguation and text normalization for Southern Quechua varieties. In *Proceedings of the First Workshop on Applying NLP Tools to Similar Languages, Varieties and Dialects*, pages 39–47, Dublin, Ireland. Association for Computational Linguistics and Dublin City University.

Sennrich, R., Haddow, B., and Birch, A. (2015). Neural machine translation of rare words with subword units. *CoRR*, abs/1508.07909.

Tiedemann, J. (2012). Parallel data, tools and interfaces in OPUS. In *Proceedings of the Eighth International Conference on Language Resources and Evaluation (LREC'12)*, pages 2214–2218, Istanbul, Turkey. European Language Resources Association (ELRA).

Vaswani, A., Shazeer, N., Parmar, N., Uszkoreit, J., Jones, L., Gomez, A. N., Kaiser, L., and Polosukhin, I. (2017). Attention is all you need. *arXiv:1706.03762. Version 5.*

Wang, L., Cao, Z., Xia, Y., and De Melo, G. (2016). Morphological segmentation with window lstm neural networks. In *Proceedings of the AAAI Conference on Artificial Intelligence*, volume 30.

Zuters, J., Strazds, G., and Immers, K. (2018). Semi-automatic quasi-morphological word segmentation for neural machine translation. In Lupeikiene, A., Vasilecas, O., and Dzemyda, G., editors, *Databases and Information Systems*, pages 289–301, Cham. Springer International Publishing.

Active Learning for Massively Parallel Translation of Constrained Text into Low Resource Languages

Zhong Zhou zhongzhou@cmu.edu
Alex Waibel alex@waibel.com
Language Technology Institute, School of Computer Science, Carnegie Mellon University, 5000 Forbes Ave, Pittsburgh PA 15213

Abstract

We translate a closed text that is known in advance and available in many languages into a new and severely low resource language. Most human translation efforts adopt a portion-based approach to translate consecutive pages/chapters in order, which may not suit machine translation. We compare the portion-based approach that optimizes coherence of the text locally with the random sampling approach that increases coverage of the text globally. Our results show that the random sampling approach performs better. When training on a seed corpus of ~1,000 lines from the Bible and testing on the rest of the Bible (~30,000 lines), random sampling gives a performance gain of +11.0 BLEU using English as a simulated low resource language, and +4.9 BLEU using Eastern Pokomchi, a Mayan language. Furthermore, we compare three ways of updating machine translation models with increasing amount of human post-edited data through iterations. We find that adding newly post-edited data to training after vocabulary update without self-supervision performs the best. We propose an algorithm for human and machine to work together seamlessly to translate a closed text into a severely low resource language.

1 Introduction

Machine translation has flourished ever since the first computer was made (Hirschberg and Manning, 2015; Popel et al., 2020). Over the years, human translation is assisted by machine translation to remove human bias and translation capacity limitations (Koehn and Haddow, 2009; Li et al., 2014; Savoldi et al., 2021; Bowker, 2002; Bowker and Fisher, 2010; Koehn, 2009). By learning human translation taxonomy and post-editing styles, machine translation borrows many ideas from human translation to improve performance through active learning (Settles, 2012; Carl et al., 2011; Denkowski, 2015). We propose a workflow to bring human translation and machine translation to work together seamlessly in translation of a closed text into a severely low resource language as shown in Figure 1 and Algorithm 1.

Given a closed text that has many existing translations in different languages, we are interested in translating it into a severely low resource language well. Researchers recently have shown achievements in translation using very small seed parallel corpora in low resource languages (Lin et al., 2020; Qi et al., 2018; Zhou et al., 2018a). Construction methods of such seed corpora are therefore pivotal in translation performance. Historically, this is mostly determined by field linguists' experiential and intuitive discretion. Many human translators employ a portion-based strategy when translating large texts. For example, translation of the book "The Little Prince" may be divided into smaller tasks of translating 27 chapters, or even smaller translation units like a few consecutive pages. Each translation unit contains consecutive

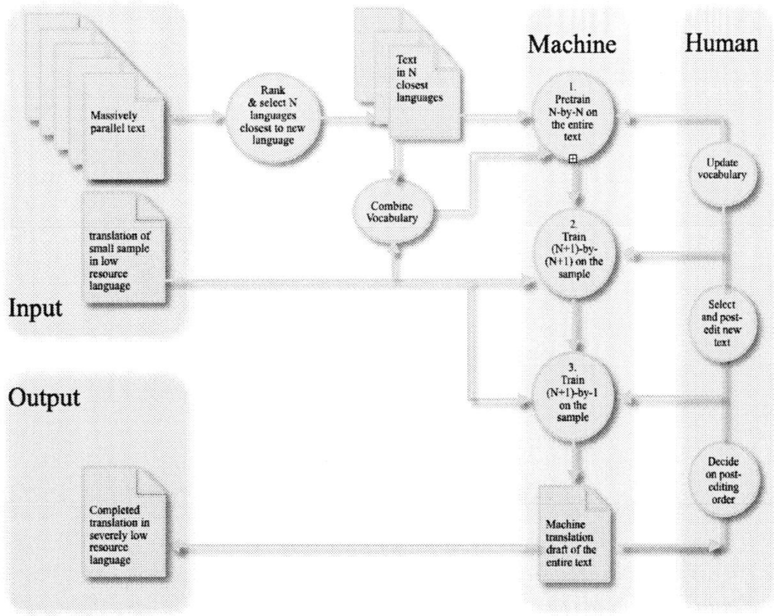

Figure 1: Proposed joint human machine translation sequence for a given closed text.

sentences. Consequently, machine translation often uses seed corpora that are chosen based on human translators' preferences, but may not be optimal for machine translation.

We propose to use a random sampling approach to build seed corpora when resources are extremely limited. In other words, when field linguists have limited time and resources, which lines would be given priority? Given a closed text, we propose that it would beneficial if field linguists translate randomly sampled ~1,000 lines first, getting the first machine translated draft of the whole text, and then post-edit to obtain final translation of each portion iteratively as shown in Algorithm 1. We recognize that the portion-based translation is very helpful in producing quality translation with formality, cohesion and contextual relevance. Thus, our proposed way is not to replace the portion-based approach, but instead, to get the best of both worlds and to expedite the translation process as shown in Figure 1.

The main difference of the two approaches is that the portion-based approach focuses on preserving coherence of the text locally, while the random-sampling approach focuses on increasing coverage of the text globally. Our results show that the random sampling approach performs better. When training on a seed corpus of ~1,000 lines from the Bible and testing on the rest of the Bible (~30,000 lines), random sampling beats the portion-based approach by +11.0 BLEU using English as a simulated low resource language on a family of languages ranked by distortion, and by +4.9 using a Mayan language, Eastern Pokomchi, training on a family of languages based on linguistic definition. Using random sampling, machine translation is able to produce an apt first draft of the whole text that expedites the subsequent translation iterations.

Moreover, we compare three different ways of incorporating incremental post-edited data during the translation process. We find that self-supervision using the whole translation draft affects performance adversely, and is best to be avoided. We also show that adding the newly post-edited text to training with vocabulary update performs the best.

Algorithm 1: Proposed joint human machine translation sequence for a given closed text.

Input: A text of N lines consisting multiple books/portions, parallel in L source languages
Output: A full translation in the target low resource language, l'
0. Initialize translation size, $n = 0$, vocabulary size, $v = 0$, vocabulary update size, $\triangle v = 0$;
1. Randomly sample S ($\sim$1,000) sentences with vocabulary size v_S for human translators to produce the seed corpus, update $n = S$, $v = v_S$;
2. Rank and pick a family of close-by languages by linguistic, distortion or performance metric ;
while $n < N$ **do**
  if $\triangle v > 0$ **then**
    3. Pretrain on the full texts of neighboring languages ;
  4. Train on the n sentences of all languages in multi-source multi-target configuration ;
  5. Train on the n sentences of all languages in multi-source single-target configuration ;
  6. Combine translations from all source languages using the centeredness measure ;
  7. Review all books/portions of the translation draft ;
  8. Pick a book/portion with n' lines and v' more vocabulary ;
  9. Complete human post-editing of the portion chosen, $v = v + v'$, $n = n + n'$, $\triangle v = v'$;
return full translation co-produced by human (Step 1, 7-9) and machine (Step 0, 2-6) translation ;

2 Related Works

2.1 Human Translation and Machine Translation

Machine translation began about the same time as the first computer (Hirschberg and Manning, 2015; Popel et al., 2020). Over the years, human translators have different reactions to machine translation advances, mixed with doubt or fear (Hutchins, 2001). Some researchers study human translation taxonomy for machine to better assist human translation and post-editing efforts (Carl et al., 2011; Denkowski, 2015). Human translators benefit from machine assistance as human individual bias and translation capacity limitations are compensated for by large-scale machine translation (Koehn and Haddow, 2009; Li et al., 2014; Savoldi et al., 2021; Bowker, 2002; Bowker and Fisher, 2010; Koehn, 2009). On the other hand, machine translation benefits from professional human translators' context-relevant and culturally-appropriate translation and post-editing efforts (Hutchins, 2001). Severely low resource translation is a fitting ground for close human machine collaboration (Zong, 2018; Carl et al., 2011; Martínez, 2003).

2.2 Severely Low Resource Text-based Translation

Many use multiple rich-resource languages to translate to a low resource language using multilingual methods (Johnson et al., 2017; Ha et al., 2016; Firat et al., 2016; Zoph and Knight, 2016; Zoph et al., 2016; Adams et al., 2017; Gillick et al., 2016; Zhou et al., 2018a,b). Some use data selection for active learning (Eck et al., 2005). Some use as few as $\sim$4,000 lines (Lin et al., 2020; Qi et al., 2018) and $\sim$1,000 lines (Zhou and Waibel, 2021) of data. Some do not use low resource data (Neubig and Hu, 2018; Karakanta et al., 2018).

2.3 Active Learning and Random Sampling

Active learning has long been used in machine translation (Settles, 2012; Ambati, 2012; Eck et al., 2005; Haffari and Sarkar, 2009; González-Rubio et al., 2012; Miura et al., 2016; Gangadharaiah et al., 2009). Random sampling and data selection has been successful (Kendall and Smith, 1938; Knuth, 1991; Clarkson and Shor, 1989; Sennrich et al., 2015; Hoang et al., 2018; He et al., 2016; Gu et al., 2018). The mathematician Donald Knuth uses the population of Menlo Park to illustrate the value of random sampling (Knuth, 1991).

Book	Author	Books	Chapters	Pages	Languages
The Bible	Multiple	66	1,189	1,281	689
The Little Prince	Antoine de Saint Exupéry	1	27	96	382
Dao De Jing	Laozi	1	81	~10	>250
COVID-19 Wiki Page	Multiple	1	1	~50	155
The Alchemist	Paulo Coelho	1	2	163	70
Harry Potter	J. K. Rowling	7	199	3,407	60
The Lord of the Rings	J. R. R. Tolkien	6	62	1,037	57
Frozen Movie Script	Jennifer Lee	1	112	~40	41
The Hand Washing Song	Multiple	1	1	1	28
Dream of the Red Chamber	Xueqin Cao	2	120	2500	23
Les Misérables	Victor Hugo	68	365	1,462	21

Table 1: Examples of different texts with the number of languages translated to date (UNESCO, 1932; Mayer and Cysouw, 2014; de Saint-Exupéry, 2019; Laozi, 2019; Fung et al., 2020; Coelho, 2015; Rowling, 2019; Tolkien, 2012; Lee, 2013; Thampi et al., 2020; Xueqin, 2016; Hugo, 1863).

3 Methodology

We train our models using a state-of-the-art multilingual transformer by adding language labels to each source sentence (Johnson et al., 2017; Ha et al., 2016; Zhou et al., 2018a,b). We borrow the order-preserving named entity translation method by replacing each named entity with `__NEs` (Zhou et al., 2018b) using a multilingual lexicon table that covers 124 source languages and 2,939 named entities (Zhou and Waibel, 2021). For example, the sentence "Somchai calls Juan" is transformed to "`__opt_src_en __opt_tgt_ca __NE0` calls `__NE1`" to translate to Chuj. We use families of close-by languages constructed by ranking 124 source languages by distortion measure (*FAMD*), performance measure (*FAMP*) and linguistic family (*FAMO*$^+$); the distortion measure ranks languages by decreasing probability of zero distortion, while the performance measure incorporates an additional probability of fertility equalling one (Zhou and Waibel, 2021). Using families constructed, we pretrain our model first on the whole text of nearby languages, then we train on the ~1,000 lines of low resource data and the corresponding lines in other languages in a multi-source multi-target fashion. We finally train on the ~1,000 lines in a multi-source single-target fashion (Zhou and Waibel, 2021).

We combine translations of all source languages into one. Let all N translations be $t_i, i = 1, \ldots, N$ and let similarity between translations t_i and t_j be S_{ij}. We rank all translations according to how centered it is with respect to other sentences by summing all its similarities to the rest through $\sum_j S_{ij}$ for $i = 1, \ldots, N$. We take the most centered translation for every sentence, $\max_i \sum_j S_{ij}$, to build the combined translation output. The expectation of the combined score is higher than that of any of the source languages (Zhou and Waibel, 2021).

Our work differs from the past research in that we put low resource translation into the broad collaborative scheme of human machine translation. We compare the portion-based approach with the random sampling approach in building seed corpora. We also compare three methods of updating models with increasing amount of human post-edited data. We add the newly post-edited data to training in three ways: with vocabulary update, without vocabulary update, or incorporating the whole translation draft in a self-supervised fashion additionally. For best performance, we build the seed corpus by random sampling, update vocabulary iteratively, and add newly post-edited data to training without self-supervision. We also have a larger test set, we test on ~30,000 lines rather than ~678 lines from existing research.

We propose a joint human machine translation workflow in Algorithm 1. After pretraining

Input Language Family														
By Linguistics					By Distortion					By Performance				
FAMO^{+}					*FAMD*					*FAMP*				
Training	*Luke*		*Rand*		Training	*Luke*		*Rand*		Training	*Luke*		*Rand*	
Testing	*Best*	*All*	*Best*	*All*	Testing	*Best*	*All*	*Best*	*All*	Testing	*Best*	*All*	*Best*	*All*
Combined	38.2	21.9	47.7	31.3	Combined	38.4	22.9	49.6	33.9	Combined	40.3	23.7	48.8	33.2
German	35.8	20.0	45.4	29.4	German	36.8	20.8	47.2	31.5	German	37.6	21.3	46.5	30.9
Danish	36.8	18.9	43.3	28.8	Danish	37.4	19.6	44.7	30.8	Danish	38.5	19.9	44.4	30.2
Dutch	36.2	20.3	45.3	29.9	Dutch	36.3	21.0	47.1	32.3	Dutch	37.8	21.6	46.3	31.6
Norwegian	36.6	20.2	45.1	29.7	Norwegian	36.9	20.9	46.5	31.7	Norwegian	37.6	21.2	46.1	31.2
Swedish	35.2	19.6	45.1	29.0	Afrikaans	38.4	22.2	48.0	33.1	Afrikaans	39.6	22.9	47.5	32.4
Spanish	36.8	21.6	45.1	30.3	Marshallese	35.3	21.6	47.1	31.5	Spanish	38.9	22.9	46.6	31.7
French	36.1	19.7	44.6	28.9	French	36.3	20.3	46.0	30.9	French	37.4	21.7	45.4	30.2
Italian	36.9	20.5	43.5	29.7	Italian	37.1	21.0	45.2	31.7	Italian	38.8	21.8	44.6	31.1
Portuguese	32.5	15.8	35.2	24.4	Portuguese	33.3	16.5	38.1	26.9	Portuguese	34.0	16.3	36.2	25.8
Romanian	34.9	19.3	43.0	28.8	Frisian	36.3	21.6	47.7	32.4	Frisian	38.0	22.3	47.4	31.8

Table 2: Performance training on 1,093 lines of Eastern Pokomchi data on *FAMO*$^{+}$, *FAMD* and *FAMP*. We train using the portion-based approach in *Luke*, and using random sampling in *Rand*. During testing, *Best* is the book with highest BLEU score, and *All* is the performance on $\sim$30,000 lines of test data.

on neighboring languages in Step 3, we iteratively train on the randomly sampled seed corpus of low resource data in Step 4 and 5. The reason we include both Step 4 and 5 in our algorithm is because training both steps iteratively performs better than training either one (Zhou and Waibel, 2021). Our model produces a translation draft of the whole text. Since the portion-based approach has the advantage with formality, cohesion and contextual relevance, human translators may pick and post-edit portion-by-portion iteratively. The newly post-edited data with updated vocabulary is feed back to the machine translation models without self-supervision. In this way, machine translation systems rely on quality parallel corpora that are incrementally produced by human translators. Human translators lean on machine translation for quality translation draft to expedite translation. This creates a synergistic collaboration between human and machine.

4 Data

We work on the Bible in 124 source languages (Mayer and Cysouw, 2014), and have experiments for English, a simulated language, and Eastern Pokomchi, a Mayan language. We train on $\sim$1,000 lines of low resource data and on full texts for all the other languages. We aim to translate the rest of the text ($\sim$30,000 lines) into the low resource language. In pretraining, we use 80%, 10%, 10% split for training, validation and testing. In training, we use 3.3%, 0.2%, 96.5% split for training, validation and testing. Our test size is >29 times of the training size. We use the book "Luke" for the portion-based approach as suggested by many human translators.

Training on $\sim$100 million parameters with Geforce RTX 2080 Ti, we employ a 6-layer encoder and a 6-layer decoder with 512 hidden states, 8 attention heads, 512 word vector size, 2,048 hidden units, 6,000 batch size, 0.1 label smoothing, 2.5 learning rate, 0.1 dropout and attention dropout, an early stopping patience of 5 after 190,000 steps, "BLEU" validation metric, "adam" optimizer and "noam" decay method (Klein et al., 2017; Papineni et al., 2002). We increase patience to 25 for larger data in the second stage of training in Figure 2a and 2b.

Input Language Family														
By Linguistics					By Distortion					By Performance				
FAMO$^+$					*FAMD*					*FAMP*				
Training	*Luke*		*Rand*		Training	*Luke*		*Rand*		Training	*Luke*		*Rand*	
Testing	*Best*	*All*	*Best*	*All*	Testing	*Best*	*All*	*Best*	*All*	Testing	*Best*	*All*	*Best*	*All*
Combined	23.1	8.6	24.4	13.5	Combined	23.2	8.5	22.7	12.6	Combined	22.2	7.2	20.3	10.9
Chuj	21.8	8.0	21.3	12.8	Chuj	21.9	8.5	20.2	12.0	Chuj	21.8	7.2	18.0	10.3
Cakchiquel	22.2	7.9	22.4	13.0	Cakchiquel	22.3	7.9	21.8	12.2	Cakchiquel	21.2	6.9	19.1	10.5
Guajajara	19.7	7.0	18.8	11.8	Guajajara	19.1	6.9	18.0	11.2	Guajajara	18.8	5.9	15.1	9.5
Mam	22.2	8.6	24.1	13.7	Russian	22.2	7.3	17.4	11.8	Mam	21.7	7.5	21.4	11.1
Kanjobal	21.8	8.1	22.3	13.1	Toba	21.9	8.3	21.8	12.5	Kanjobal	21.5	7.1	18.7	10.6
Cuzco	22.3	7.8	22.5	12.9	Myanmar	19.1	5.3	13.3	9.8	Thai	21.8	6.3	15.7	10.2
Ayacucho	21.6	7.6	23.3	12.8	Slovenský	22.1	7.5	18.5	12.0	Dadibi	19.9	6.2	17.8	9.8
Bolivian	22.2	7.8	22.3	12.9	Latin	21.9	7.8	20.4	12.2	Gumatj	19.1	3.8	11.7	4.7
Huallaga	22.2	7.7	22.7	12.8	Ilokano	22.6	8.4	22.4	12.5	Navajo	21.3	6.5	17.4	10.5
Aymara	21.4	7.5	23.0	12.7	Norwegian	22.6	8.3	22.0	12.6	Kim	21.6	7.0	17.5	10.7

Table 3: Performance training on 1,086 lines of Eastern Pokomchi data on *FAMO*$^+$, *FAMD* and *FAMP*. We train using the portion-based approach in *Luke*, and using random sampling in *Rand*. During testing, *Best* is the book with highest BLEU score, and *All* is the performance on $\sim$30,000 lines of test data.

5 Results

We observe that random sampling performs better than the portion-based approach. Random sampling gives a performance gain of +11.0 for English on FAMD and +4.9 for Eastern Pokomchi on FAMO$^+$ in Table 2 and 3. The performance gain for Eastern Pokomchi may be lower because Mayan languages are morphologically rich, complex, isolated and opaque (Aissen et al., 2017; Clemens et al., 2015; England, 2011). English is closely related to many languages due to colonization and globalization even though it is artificially constrained in size (Bird, 2020). This may explain why Eastern Pokomchi benefits less.

To simulate human translation efforts in Step 7 and 8 in Algorithm 1, we rank 66 books of the Bible by BLEU score on English's FAMD and Eastern Pokomchi's FAMO$^+$. We assume that BLEU ranking is available to us to simulate human judgment. In reality, this step is realized by human translators skimming through the translation draft and comparing performances of different books by intuition and experience. In Section 6, we will discuss the limitation of this assumption. Performance ranking of the simulated low resource language may differ from that of the actual low resource language. But the top few may coincide because of the nature of the text, independent of the language. In our results, we observe that the narrative books performs better than the philosophical or poetic books. The book "1 Chronicles" performs best for both English and Eastern Pokomchi, and the book "Philemon" performs worst for both languages. A possible explanation is that "1 Chronicles" is mainly narrative, and contains many named entities that are translated well by the order-preserving lexiconized model. If we compare BLEU scores of the best-performing book, random sampling outperforms the portion-based approach by +11.2 on English's FAMD, and by +1.3 on Eastern Pokomchi's FAMO$^+$.

In Table 4, we compare three different ways of updating the machine translation models by adding a newly post-edited book that human translators produced. We call the baseline without addition of the new book *Seed*. *Updated-Vocab* adds the new book to training with updated vocabulary while *Old-Vocab* skips the vocabulary update. *Self-Supervised* adds the whole translation draft of $\sim$30,000 lines to pretraining in addition to the new book. Self-supervision

Source	*Seed*	*Self-Supervised*	*Old-Vocab*	*Updated-Vocab*
Combined	33.9	29.4 (-4.5)	36.3 (+2.4)	36.7 (+2.8)
Danish	31.5	26.8 (-4.7)	33.1 (+1.6)	33.7 (+2.2)
Norwegian	30.8	27.6 (-3.2)	34.1 (+3.3)	34.7 (+3.9)
Italian	32.3	27.3 (-5.0)	34.1 (+1.8)	34.6 (+2.3)
Afrikaans	31.7	28.8 (-2.9)	35.6 (+3.9)	36.0 (+4.3)
Dutch	33.1	28.0 (-5.1)	34.6 (+1.5)	35.1 (+2.0)
Portuguese	31.5	23.6 (-7.9)	29.1 (-2.4)	29.8 (-0.7)
French	30.9	26.8 (-4.1)	33.3 (+2.4)	33.9 (+3.0)
German	31.7	27.4 (-4.3)	33.8 (+2.1)	34.4 (+2.7)
Marshallese	26.9	27.5 (+0.6)	33.8 (+6.9)	34.4 (+7.5)
Frisian	32.4	28.2 (-4.2)	34.7 (+2.3)	35.3 (+2.9)

Table 4: Comparing three ways of adding the newly post-edited book "1 Chronicles". *Seed* is the baseline of training on the seed corpus alone, *Old-Vocab* skips the vocabulary update while *Updated-Vocab* has vocabulary update. *Self-Supervised* adds the complete translation draft in addition to the new book.

refers to using the small seed corpus to translate the rest of the text which is subsequently used to train the model. We observe that the *Self-Supervised* performs the worst among the three. Indeed, *Self-Supervised* performs even worse than the baseline *Seed*. This shows that quality is much more important than quantity in severely low resource translation. It is better for us not to add the whole translation draft to the pretraining as it affects performance adversely.

On the other hand, we see that both *Updated-Vocab* and *Old-Vocab* performs better than *Seed* and *Self-Supervised*. *Updated-Vocab*'s performance is better than *Old-Vocab*. An explanation could be that *Updated-Vocab* has more expressive power with updated vocabulary. Therefore, in our proposed algorithm, we prefers vocabulary update in each iteration. If the vocabulary has not increased, we may skip pretraining to expedite the process.

We show how the algorithm is put into practice for English and Eastern Pokomchi in Figure 2a and 2b. We take the worst-performing 11 books as the held-out test set, and divide the other 55 books of the Bible into 5 portions. Each portion contains 11 books. We translate the text by using the randomly sampled $\sim$1,000 lines of seed corpus first, and then proceed with human machine translation in Algorithm 1 in 5 iterations with increasing number of post-edited portions. The red dotted line is the overall performance of the whole text excluding the seed corpus. We observe that the red dotted curve is steadily increasing for both languages. However, since we are interested in the test results of the held-out set, we evaluate only on the solid lines plotted.

For English, we observe that philosophical books like "Ecclesiastes" and poetry books like "Song of Solomon" perform very badly in the beginning, but begin to achieve above 90 BLEU scores after adding 33 books of training data. The high performance is due to the multilingual cross-lingual transfer and this is the main reason why we set up our problem as translation of a closed text that are available in many languages to the low resource language. However, some books like "Philemon", "Hebrews", "James", "Titus" remains difficult to translate even after adding 55 books of training data. This shows that adding data may benefit some books more than the others. A possible explanation is that there are multiple authors of the Bible, and books differ from each other in style and content. Some books are closely related to each other, and may benefit from translations of other books. But some may be very different and benefit much less.

For Eastern Pokomchi, even though the performance of the most difficult 11 books never reach the near perfect BLEU score of 90s like that of English experiments, all books has BLEU

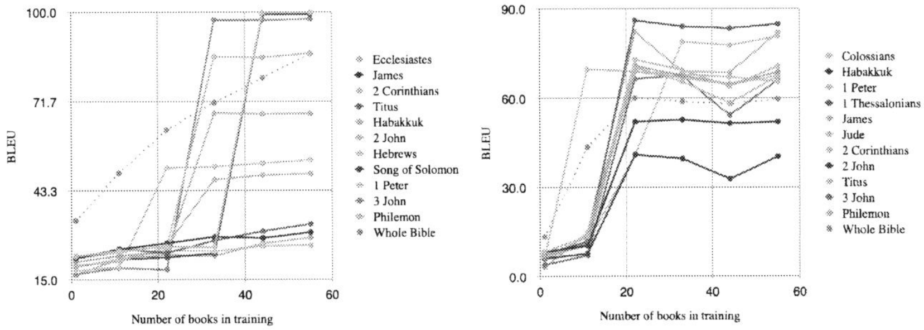

(a) English

(b) Eastern Pokomchi

Figure 2: Performance of the most difficult 11 books with increasing number of training books.

scores that are steadily increasing. Surprisingly, we observe good performance with the books that remain difficult with large training data in the English experiments. "Philemon", for example, increases to a BLEU score of 81.9 with 55 books of training data in Eastern Pokomchi while it has a BLEU score of 28.4 with 55 books of training data in English. This surprising result shows that what is difficult for simulated low resource languages may not be as difficult for real low resource languages. Even though Eastern Pokomchi gives a lower overall BLEU score than English, it has a better generalization to the most difficult book.

6 Conclusion

We propose to use random sampling to build seed parallel corpora instead of using the portion-based approach in severely low resource settings. Training on $\sim$1,000 lines, the random sampling approach outperforms the portion-based approach by +11.0 for English's FAMD, and by +4.9 for Eastern Pokomchi's FAMO^{+}. We also compare three different ways of updating the machine translation models by adding newly post-edited data iteratively. We find that vocabulary update is necessary, but self-supervision by pretraining with whole translation draft is best to be avoided.

One limitation of our work is that in real life scenarios, we do not have the reference text in low resource languages to produce the BLEU scores to decide the post-editing order. Consequently, field linguists need to skim through and decide the post-editing order based on intuition. However, computational models can still help. One potential way to tackle it is that we can train on $\sim$1,000 lines from another language with available text and test on the 66 books. Since our results show that the literary genre plays important role in the performance ranking, it would be reasonable to determine the order using a "held-out language" and then using that to determine order in the target low resource language. In the future, we would like to work with human translators who understand and speak low resource languages.

Another concern human translators may have is the creation of randomly sampled seed corpora. To gauge the amount of interest or inertia, we have interviewed some human translators and many are interested. However, it is unclear whether human translation quality of randomly sampled data differs from that of the traditional portion-based approach. We hope to work with human translators closely to determine whether the translation quality difference is manageable.

We are also curious how our model will perform with large literary works like "Lord of the Rings" and "Les Misérables". We would like to see whether it will translate well with philosophical depth and literary complexity. However, these books often have copyright issues and are not as easily available as the Bible data. We are interested in collaboration with teams who have multilingual data for large texts, especially multilingual COVID-19 data.

References

Adams, O., Makarucha, A., Neubig, G., Bird, S., and Cohn, T. (2017). Cross-lingual word embeddings for low-resource language modeling. In *Proceedings of the 15th Conference of the European Chapter of the Association for Computational Linguistics*, pages 937–947.

Aissen, J., England, N. C., and Maldonado, R. Z. (2017). *The Mayan languages*. Taylor & Francis.

Ambati, V. (2012). *Active learning and crowdsourcing for machine translation in low resource scenarios*. PhD thesis, Carnegie Mellon University.

Bird, S. (2020). Decolonising speech and language technology. In *Proceedings of the 28th International Conference on Computational Linguistics*, pages 3504–3519.

Bowker, L. (2002). *Computer-aided translation technology: A practical introduction*. University of Ottawa Press.

Bowker, L. and Fisher, D. (2010). Computer-aided translation. *Handbook of translation studies*, 1:60–65.

Carl, M., Dragsted, B., and Jakobsen, A. L. (2011). A taxonomy of human translation styles. *Translation journal*, 16(2):155–168.

Clarkson, K. L. and Shor, P. W. (1989). Applications of random sampling in computational geometry, ii. *Discrete & Computational Geometry*, 4(5):387–421.

Clemens, L. E., Coon, J., Pedro, P. M., Morgan, A. M., Polinsky, M., Tandet, G., and Wagers, M. (2015). Ergativity and the complexity of extraction: A view from mayan. *Natural Language & Linguistic Theory*, 33(2):417–467.

Coelho, P. (2015). *The alchemist*. HarperOne; 25th edition.

de Saint-Exupéry, A. (2019). *El Principito: The Little Prince*. Editorial Verbum.

Denkowski, M. (2015). Machine translation for human translators. *Unpublished doctoral dissertation, Carnegie Mellon University, Pittsburgh, Pennsylvania*.

Eck, M., Vogel, S., and Waibel, A. (2005). Low cost portability for statistical machine translation based on n-gram frequency and tf-idf. In *International Workshop on Spoken Language Translation*.

England, N. C. (2011). *A grammar of Mam, a Mayan language*. University of Texas Press.

Firat, O., Cho, K., and Bengio, Y. (2016). Multi-way, multilingual neural machine translation with a shared attention mechanism. In *Proceedings of the 15th Conference of the North American Chapter of the Association for Computational Linguistics on Human Language Technologies*, pages 866–875.

Fung, T. L. et al. (2020). COVID-19. `https://en.wikipedia.org/wiki/COVID-19`. [Online; accessed 24-May-2021].

Gangadharaiah, R., Brown, R. D., and Carbonell, J. G. (2009). Active learning in example-based machine translation. In *Proceedings of the 17th Nordic Conference of Computational Linguistics (NODALIDA 2009)*, pages 227–230.

Gillick, D., Brunk, C., Vinyals, O., and Subramanya, A. (2016). Multilingual language processing from bytes. In *Proceedings of the 15th Conference of the North American Chapter of the Association for Computational Linguistics on Human Language Technologies*, pages 1296–1306.

González-Rubio, J., Ortiz-Martínez, D., and Casacuberta, F. (2012). Active learning for interactive machine translation. In *Proceedings of the 13th Conference of the European Chapter of the Association for Computational Linguistics*, pages 245–254. Association for Computational Linguistics.

Gu, J., Wang, Y., Chen, Y., Cho, K., and Li, V. O. (2018). Meta-learning for low-resource neural machine translation. *arXiv preprint arXiv:1808.08437*.

Ha, T.-L., Niehues, J., and Waibel, A. (2016). Toward multilingual neural machine translation with universal encoder and decoder. *arXiv preprint arXiv:1611.04798*.

Haffari, G. and Sarkar, A. (2009). Active learning for multilingual statistical machine translation. In *Proceedings of the 47th Annual Meeting of the Association for Computational Linguistics*, pages 181–189. Association for Computational Linguistics.

He, D., Xia, Y., Qin, T., Wang, L., Yu, N., Liu, T.-Y., and Ma, W.-Y. (2016). Dual learning for machine translation. *Advances in neural information processing systems*, 29:820–828.

Hirschberg, J. and Manning, C. D. (2015). Advances in natural language processing. *Science*, 349(6245):261–266.

Hoang, V. C. D., Koehn, P., Haffari, G., and Cohn, T. (2018). Iterative back-translation for neural machine translation. In *Proceedings of the 2nd Workshop on Neural Machine Translation and Generation*, pages 18–24.

Hugo, V. (1863). *Les Miserables*. C. Lassalle.

Hutchins, J. (2001). Machine translation and human translation: in competition or in complementation. *International Journal of Translation*, 13(1-2):5–20.

Johnson, M., Schuster, M., Le, Q. V., Krikun, M., Wu, Y., Chen, Z., Thorat, N., Viégas, F., Wattenberg, M., Corrado, G., et al. (2017). Google's multilingual neural machine translation system: Enabling zero-shot translation. *Transactions of the Association for Computational Linguistics*, 5:339–351.

Karakanta, A., Dehdari, J., and van Genabith, J. (2018). Neural machine translation for low-resource languages without parallel corpora. *Machine Translation*, 32(1):167–189.

Kendall, M. G. and Smith, B. B. (1938). Randomness and random sampling numbers. *Journal of the royal Statistical Society*, 101(1):147–166.

Klein, G., Kim, Y., Deng, Y., Senellart, J., and Rush, A. (2017). Opennmt: Open-source toolkit for neural machine translation. *Proceedings of the 55th annual meeting of the Association for Computational Linguistics, System Demonstrations*, pages 67–72.

Knuth, D. E. (1991). *3: 16 Bible texts illuminated*. AR Editions, Inc.

Koehn, P. (2009). A process study of computer-aided translation. *Machine Translation*, 23(4):241–263.

Koehn, P. and Haddow, B. (2009). Interactive assistance to human translators using statistical machine translation methods. *MT Summit XII*.

Laozi (2019). *Dao de jing*. University of California Press.

Lee, J. (2013). Frozen.

Li, H., Graesser, A. C., and Cai, Z. (2014). Comparison of google translation with human translation. In *The Twenty-Seventh International Flairs Conference*.

Lin, Z., Pan, X., Wang, M., Qiu, X., Feng, J., Zhou, H., and Li, L. (2020). Pre-training multilingual neural machine translation by leveraging alignment information. *arXiv preprint arXiv:2010.03142*.

Martínez, L. G. (2003). *Human Translation Versuv Machine Translation and Full Post-editing of Raw Machine Translation Output*. Citeseer.

Mayer, T. and Cysouw, M. (2014). Creating a massively parallel bible corpus. *Oceania*, 135(273):40.

Miura, A., Neubig, G., Paul, M., and Nakamura, S. (2016). Selecting syntactic, non-redundant segments in active learning for machine translation. In *Proceedings of the 2016 Conference of the North American Chapter of the Association for Computational Linguistics: Human Language Technologies*, pages 20–29.

Neubig, G. and Hu, J. (2018). Rapid adaptation of neural machine translation to new languages. *arXiv preprint arXiv:1808.04189*.

Papineni, K., Roukos, S., Ward, T., and Zhu, W.-J. (2002). Bleu: a method for automatic evaluation of machine translation. In *Proceedings of the 40th annual meeting on association for computational linguistics*, pages 311–318. Association for Computational Linguistics.

Popel, M., Tomkova, M., Tomek, J., Kaiser, Ł., Uszkoreit, J., Bojar, O., and Žabokrtský, Z. (2020). Transforming machine translation: a deep learning system reaches news translation quality comparable to human professionals. *Nature communications*, 11(1):1–15.

Qi, Y., Sachan, D. S., Felix, M., Padmanabhan, S. J., and Neubig, G. (2018). When and why are pre-trained word embeddings useful for neural machine translation? *arXiv preprint arXiv:1804.06323*.

Rowling, J. (2019). Harry potter. *The 100 Greatest Literary Characters*, page 183.

Savoldi, B., Gaido, M., Bentivogli, L., Negri, M., and Turchi, M. (2021). Gender bias in machine translation. *arXiv preprint arXiv:2104.06001*.

Sennrich, R., Haddow, B., and Birch, A. (2015). Improving neural machine translation models with monolingual data. *arXiv preprint arXiv:1511.06709*.

Settles, B. (2012). Active learning. *Synthesis lectures on artificial intelligence and machine learning*, 6(1):1–114.

Thampi, N., Longtin, Y., Peters, A., Pittet, D., and Overy, K. (2020). It's in our hands: a rapid, international initiative to translate a hand hygiene song during the covid-19 pandemic. *Journal of Hospital Infection*, 105(3):574–576.

Tolkien, J. R. R. (2012). *The Lord of the Rings: One Volume*. Houghton Mifflin Harcourt.

UNESCO, I. T. (1932). World bibliography of translation.

Xueqin, C. (2016). *Dream of the Red Chamber*. Editorial Axioma.

Zhou, Z., Sperber, M., and Waibel, A. (2018a). Massively parallel cross-lingual learning in low-resource target language translation. In *Proceedings of the 3rd conference on Machine Translation Worshop of the 23rd Conference on Empirical Methods in Natural Language Processing*. Association for Computational Linguistics.

Zhou, Z., Sperber, M., and Waibel, A. (2018b). Paraphrases as foreign languages in multilingual neural machine translation. *Proceedings of the Student Research Workshop at the 56th Annual Meeting of the Association for Computational Linguistics*.

Zhou, Z. and Waibel, A. (2021). Family of origin and family of choice: Massively parallel lexiconized iterative pretraining for severely low resource text-based translation. *Proceedings of the 3rd Workshop on Research in Computational Typology and Multilingual NLP of the 20th Conference of the North American Chapter of the Association for Computational Linguistics on Human Language Technologies*.

Zong, Z. (2018). Research on the relations between machine translation and human translation. In *Journal of Physics: Conference Series*, page 062046. IOP Publishing.

Zoph, B. and Knight, K. (2016). Multi-source neural translation. In *Proceedings of the 15th Conference of the North American Chapter of the Association for Computational Linguistics on Human Language Technologies*, pages 30–34.

Zoph, B., Yuret, D., May, J., and Knight, K. (2016). Transfer learning for low-resource neural machine translation. In *Proceedings of the 21st Conference on Empirical Methods in Natural Language Processing*, pages 1568–1575.

Love Thy Neighbor: Combining Two Neighboring Low-Resource Languages for Translation

John E. Ortega jortega@cs.nyu.edu
New York University, New York, New York, USA

Richard Alexander Castro Mamani rcastro@hinant.in
Universidad Nacional de San Antonio Abad, Cusco, Perú

Jaime Rafael Montoya Samame jaime.montoya@pucp.edu.pe
Pontificia Universidad Católica del Perú, Lima, Perú

Abstract

Low-resource languages sometimes take on similar morphological and syntactic characteristics due to their geographic nearness and shared history. Two low-resource neighboring languages found in Peru, Quechua and Ashaninka, can be considered, at first glance, two languages that are morphologically similar. In order to translate the two languages, various approaches have been taken. For Quechua, neural machine transfer-learning has been used along with byte-pair encoding. For Ashaninka, the language of the two with fewer resources, a finite-state transducer is used to transform Ashaninka texts and its dialects for machine translation use. We evaluate and compare two approaches by attempting to use newly-formed Ashaninka corpora for neural machine translation. Our experiments show that combining the two neighboring languages, while similar in morphology, word sharing, and geographical location, improves Ashaninka–Spanish translation but degrades Quechua–Spanish translations.

1 Introduction

Low-resource languages (LRL) can be defined as languages that suffer from the presences of insufficient parallel source-target data. Until recently, in order to translate LRLs, rule-based (RBMT) or statistical-based machine translation (SMT) systems have been used with a combination of features and heuristic approaches to create a model that could predict target-side translations based on probability techniques given a source sentence (also known as a segment). With the rebirth of neural machine translation (NMT) in recent years thanks to higher-compute system availability, neural approaches have been used to jointly learn from several source and target segments (Zoph et al., 2016; Gu et al., 2018; Lakew et al., 2018b) avoiding the highly laborious process of creating rules and features to translate using previous RBMT and SMT systems. The majority of research that uses NMT for LRLs tends to show how the combining of two or more source-side languages to one target-side language can help translate low-resource languages by imputing word-level features from a higher-resource language to a lower-resource language.

One such case (Ortega et al., 2021) translates Quechua, a Peruvian LRL, to Spanish, an HRL, using Finnish, another HRL, in an approach called *BPE-Guided* based on glossary definitions found from suffixes on Wikipedia[1]. Their work which uses an NMT system based on byte-pair encoding (BPE) (Sennrich et al., 2015b) with a long short term memory (LSTM) (Graves, 2012) was found to outperform other systems measured according to human and system evaluations using BLEU (Papineni et al., 2002).

Research has also been performed by Ortega et al. (2020) on a neighboring Peruvian language called Ashaninka. Ashaninka has less resources than Quechua and is spoken by fewer people. There are nearly 70,000 native Ashaninka speakers (Gordon and Grimes, 2005) as compared to around 5 million native Quechua speakers[2] and both languages can be broken down into different dialects. The amount of resources available for Ashaninka is on the order of 8,000 sentences (or segments) whereas Quechua data is about 40,000 segments and growing. Ortega et al. (2020) dedicated their initial work on Ashaninka to language normalization by creating a finite-state transducer based on previous Quechua work (Rios, 2010). They left for future work the inclusion of Ashaninka in an NMT system.

In order to advance the work by Ortega et al. (2020, 2021), we use resources from their published articles available online[3] to extend their experiments which, in turn, marks the first time, to our knowledge, that an Ashaninka–Spanish machine translation (MT) system is introduced to the MT research community. Our hope is that, since Finnish and Quechua were found to be successful in previous work (Ortega and Pillaipakkamnatt, 2018) due to their highly-similar morphology, the addition of Ashaninka as source-side input should increase performance since Quechua and Ashaninka are from the same region, display similar morphological constructs, and even share loaned vocabulary words where higher-resource languages (Quechua and Spanish) are found in the lower-resource language (Ashaninka).

Our effort is a three-fold, novel, experimental introduction for the two Peruvian languages as seen below:

1. Introduce for the first time a Ashaninka–Spanish MT system.

2. Show how two neighboring South American languages with low resources perform when combined as training data for a NMT system.

3. Perform a micro-analysis on the morphology similarities and difference between Quechua and Ashaninka.

In order to realize the three points, we narrate the following. First, in Section 2, we describe related approaches not mentioned in Section 1. Next, we analyze Quechua and Ashaninka similarities and differences in Section 3. Our methodology and approach are detailed in Section 4 along with the experimental settings in Section 5. We then provide results in Section 6 that show how combining Quechua and Ashaninka together perform on both a Quechua and Ashaninka test set. Lastly, we conclude with an explanation on our findings and potential future research lines in Section 7.

2 Related Work

Ortega et al. (2020) present a system called *AshMorph* which is an approach for normalizing Ashaninkan text for machine translation use. Additionally, the corpus and MT system introduced by Ortega et al. (2021) are used. For more information on how they were used in our work, see Section 5. In this section, we describe other approaches that are similar to ours.

[1] `https://wikipedia.org`

[2] The native-speaker count includes all dialects for both languages

[3] `https://github.com/johneortega/mt_quechua_spanish` and `https://github.com/hinantin/AshMorph`

Pourdamghani and Knight (2017) use a deciphering approach which *relates* a high-resource language to a low-resource language through a character-level ciphering algorithm. Their work assumes that words are ordered similarly. We could not use this approach since, as discussed later in Section 3, word ordering is one of the key morphological differences between Quechua and Ashaninka.

Tantuğ and Adalı (2018) focus on agglutinating languages by using eight informal target-side, rule-based, edits. Their work can be considered similar to the work from Ortega et al. (2020) due to the way it handles morphology and knowledge transfer. However, they use discrete rules meant to work with a statistical disambiguation system for combining the source and target language. Our aim is to show that NMT could be used to learn similar rules without human intervention. Nonetheless, we feel that their work could be included for comparison in future iterations.

Bahdanau et al. (2014) use a neural machine translation system to first learn aligned words that form an encoded vector and then translate them. This work is similar to ours in its approach; however, our work is for an extremely low-resource language (Ashaninka) and depends on character-level differences not performed in their work.

We mirror Zoph et al. (2016)'s approach by using the "OpenNMT-LSTM" system mentioned in Ortega et al. (2021). Zoph et al. (2016)'s results show an increase of 5 BLEU when combining languages; our results are similar when using Quechua as the high-resource language.

Other work (Gu et al., 2018; Karakanta et al., 2018) tend to focus on the addition of several languages with high resources as was done by Ortega et al. (2021) with the inclusion of Finnish, a high-resource language. In this case, we are adding the lower-resource language, Ashaninka, with hopes to better the higher-resource language, Quechua. Additionally, other work (Lakew et al., 2018a) points out that bilingual NMT models may require adjustments when multilingual models perform better. Their work is considered helpful; but, at this early stage of investigation, we lean on the work from Zoph et al. (2016) for guidance.

3 Morphology

Quechua and Ashaninka are morphologically similar at first glance. However, the deeper differences explained here help to understand the results presented in Section 6. In this section, we provide an in-depth analysis of both languages based on previous work (Cerrón-Palomino, 1987; Mihas, 2015). The comparative analysis of the two language's grammatical makeup and morphology, to our knowledge, has not been taken into account by other research, specifically for machine translation.

Like many native North and South American languages, Ashaninka and Quechua are both *polysynthetic* and *agglutinating* (Bustamante et al., 2020), they add prefixes or suffixes to a root morpheme which expand or change a word's meaning. An example follows of the two languages agglutinating similarity.

"the child's hand"	
Quechua	**Ashaninka**
warmapa makin	irako eentsi
warma-**pa** maki-**n**	**ir**-ako eentsi
child-**GEN** hand-**3SG**	**3M**-hand child

At first glance, it is clear that the two languages form words by agglutination. Yet, Quechua and Ashaninka vastly differ when examined closer. This is seen with possessive noun phrases like "the child's hand" above where Quechua adds a suffix (–pa) for genitive (GEN) noun possession and adds a suffix for the possessive person (–n marks the third-person singular (3SG) for "maki" (hand)). While Quechua double marks possession, Ashaninka only marks the entity being possessed ("ako" (hand) is marked with the third-person masculine possessive (3M) prefix "ir") leaving the possessive person ("eentsi" (child)) unchanged. Additionally, it is worthwhile to note that ordering of words in Quechua is typically of type *possessor–possessed*, while in Ashaninka the order is reversed to *possessed–possessor*.

Verbal conjugation generally inflects and agglutinates in both languages. In Quechua, verbs use suffixes to express the present, past, or future tense. On the other hand, in Ashaninka, most verbs do not take tense inflection into account, instead they use a category called the "reality status" which distinguishes between two types of events: (1) past and present (*real*) events or (2) future (*unreal*) events. (Michael, 2014)

	"to come"	
Quechua	**Ashaninka**	**Conjugation**
hamu-ni	no-**pok**-i	"I come"
hamu-rqa-ni	no-**pok**-i	"I came"
hamu-saq	no-m-**pok**-e	"I will come"

Above, we see how the verb "to come" is conjugated for Quechua and Ashaninka. There is a clear distinction between present (hamuni), past (hamurqani), and future (hamusaq) tenses for the root Quechua morpheme **hamu**. Contrastingly, we see how Ashaninka uses the real/unreal method described, present and past (nopoki) are the same but the future (nompoke) is different for the root Ashaninka morpheme **pok**.

Other linguistic differences also exist with respect to suffixes and their order. More specifically, the phrasal order differs such that Quechua usually takes a subordinate clause proceeded by the verb while Ashaninka is the opposite. Additionally, the three languages (Quechua, Ashaninka, and Spanish) contain words in written texts that can be considered unknown, or *loaned*, words that are inherited from their higher-resource language where Quechua inherits from Spanish and Ashaninka inherits from both Quechua and Spanish. The overlapping words and other differences mentioned are found in the corpora from the work mentioned (Ortega et al., 2020, 2021) which contains normalized texts from corpora created in the past Mihas (2010); Cerrón-Palomino (2008).

4 Methodology

From the description in Section 3, it is clear that, while initially similar, the morphological makeup of Ashaninka is different than Quechua. Our experiments determine if it is better to use Ashaninka or Finnish as a language for transliteration in a NMT system when translating Quechua and Ashaninka to Spanish. The inclusion of Finnish as a source language in both Quechua and Ashaninka translations to Spanish is motivated by Ortega et al. (2021) which showed that neural machine translation was better when including Finnish as a source language during training.

Our experiments are based on previous work (Ortega et al., 2020, 2021) which experiments with Quechua[4], Finnish[4], and Ashaninka[5] as the source languages and Spanish as the target language. We use their translation and normalization approaches to compare the two neighboring language's (Quechua and Ashaninka) translations into Spanish using the NMT system described below.

The best performing system from Ortega et al. (2021)'s work is a NMT system first used

[4]Quechua and Finnish are the source languages in (Ortega et al., 2020).

[5]Ashaninka was not translated into another language in Ortega et al. (2021).

for development (called *OpenNMT-LSTM*) and later in testing (called *OpenNMT*).[6] We compare its performance by using Quechua, Finnish, and Ashaninka to train the NMT system in various combinations (see *Train Languages* in Table 1) with Spanish as the target language.

The results show the performance of the NMT system when using Ashaninka, a neighboring language (about 10 km away), and Finnish, a language that is of high geographic distance (about 8,000 km away), as source languages for translating Quechua to Spanish. Additionally, experiments are performed to show how well Quechua and Finnish perform as source languages when translating Ashaninka to Spanish. The implication is that since Finnish is agglutinative and polysynthetic and it has been shown to improve performance when translating Quechua to Spanish (Ortega et al., 2021), it should help when translating from both Quechua and Ashaninka to Spanish. The next section describes experimental settings for all languages.

5 Experimental Settings

Our experiments mirror previous experiments (Ortega et al., 2020, 2021) in terms of the corpora and NMT system used. Since we combine languages from both works, some of the corpora and languages used as NMT system input is different. In this section, we present those input changes and reiterate the similarities to previous work.

First, for Ashaninka text to be used as input into the NMT system, we transform it using the *AshMorph* (Ortega et al., 2020) normalization technique. For purposes of Ashaninka inclusion in the experiments, there are 521 Ashaninka training sentences (or segments), 111 development segments, and 111 test segments. They are used in three different *training* experiments: (1) Quechua+Finnish+Ashaninka, (2) Quechua+Ashaninka and (3) Ashaninka only; and, in one development and test direction (Ashaninka–Spanish). All of the corpora is randomly selected from the developoment corpora (Cushimariano Romano and Sebastián Q., 2008) used previously (Ortega et al., 2020).

Second, for Quechua normalization as input to the NMT system, a morphological normalizer (Rios and Castro-Mamani, 2014) from previous work (Ortega et al., 2021) is used. Quechua is used as a training language in all of our training experiments except for when Ashaninka is tested in isolation. The Quechua corpora consists of 17,500 training segments, 2,500 development segments, and 5585 test segments all randomly chosen from Ortega et al. (2021)'s experiments originated from the Opus corpus[7] (Tiedemann, 2012) and used in three different training settings: (1) Quechua+Finnish, (2) Quechua+Finnish+Ashaninka, and (3) Quechua+Ashaninka; and, in one development and test direction (Quechua–Spanish).

Third, Finnish and Spanish, both considered high-resource languages, are more plentiful. Like the work from Ortega et al. (2021), we use the JW300 corpus (Agić and Vulić, 2019). Since Spanish is the target language in all cases, Finnish is the only high-resource language included for training. We use 149,251 Finnish segments for training in two systems: (1) Quechua+Finnish and (2) Quechua+Finnish+Ashaninka. Spanish is used only for parallel development for testing with Quechua–Spanish and Ashaninka–Spanish language pairs.

All segments for all languages were tokenized and true-cased using Moses (Koehn et al., 2007) after normalization.

To summarize our validation technique for the neural MT system experiments, we use two source–target pairs: Quechua–Spanish and Ashaninka–Spanish. For example, for the *qu+fi+cni* system in Table 1 is used for translating Quechua to Spanish (*qu–es*). Its validation (or dev) data consists of 2500 parallel *qu–es* segments and test data is of 5585 *qu–es* segments. The Ashaninka to Spanish (*cni–es*) experiments consist of a dev and test set of 111 parallel *cni–es* segments.

[6]Details about the hyper parameters for both systems are found in Section 5.

[7]`http://opus.nlpl.eu/`

The NMT system used for all experiments is the system described in Ortega et al. (2021)'s dev phase called *OpenNMT-LSTM*. The system is trained for 100,000 epochs and it is a 2-layer LSTM model (Hochreiter and Schmidhuber, 1997) with 500 hidden units, dropout of 0.3, and uses stochastic gradient descent as the learning optimizer along with a batch size of 64. To evaluate the NMT system, we use BLEU (Papineni et al., 2002) like the work from Ortega et al. (2020, 2021).

The next section explains how previous work (Ortega et al., 2020, 2021) was used to test the neighboring Quechua and Ashaninka languages with the NMT system proposed.

6 Results

The experiments in Table 1 show the results of combining Quechua, Finnish, and Ashaninka. There are three main training scenarios along with one Ashaninka experiment in isolation. For each training scenario, there are two experiments performed, one with Quechua to Spanish (qu–es) and one with Ashaninka to Spanish (cni–es).

Our results are aligned with what has been discussed in Section 3 section at a high level – Ashaninka and Quechua appear similar in linguistic nature at first glance; however, at a deeper evaluation, the lack of resources and complex grammatical differences decrease *qu–es* translation performance. On the other hand, similar to work from Zoph et al. (2016), we have shown that by adding Quechua resources to Ashaninka, there is a gain of 4.6 BLEU. In all other cases where Ashaninka was combined with Quechua or Finnish, the performance degraded for *qu–es* translations and only very slightly (.2 BLEU) increased in one *cni–es* case.[8] Another interesting takeaway is that Finnish remains the better language to combine with Quechua when translating Quechua to Spanish. This is due to the large amount of Finnish training examples (149,251) compared to the small amount of Ashaninka training examples (521). In actuality, the BLEU score of the *qu+cni* trained system is the same as the BLEU score of using *qu+es* alone in training reported by Ortega et al. (2021). This leads us to believe that if there were more Ashaninka training examples the potential to outperform Finnish as the transfer-learning language is high.

Train Languages	Direction	Train Count	Dev Count	Test Count	BLEU
qu+fi	*qu–es*	166751	2500	5585	22.6
qu+fi	*cni–es*	166751	111	111	0.0
qu+fi+cni	*qu–es*	167272	2500	5585	17.0
qu+fi+cni	*cni–es*	167272	111	111	0.2
qu+cni	*qu–es*	18021	2500	5585	20.1
qu+cni	*cni–es*	18021	111	111	5.9
cni	*cni–es*	521	111	111	1.3

Table 1: Translating to Spanish (es) with Quechua (qu), Finnish (fi), and Ashaninka (cni) using a neural machine translation system.

7 Conclusion and Future Work

We have shown that while previous work combining languages may seem viable for low-resource languages, in some cases, while languages seem similar at first glance, results may differ. This is clear from our experiments with Quechua and Ashaninka that show performance loss when adding them together for transfer-based learning in an NMT system. Nonetheless, it would be advantageous to try other techniques such as back-translation (Poncelas et al., 2018;

[8]The higher resource pairs consist of 166,751 pairs of parallel data together of which the Finnish data is 149,251 parallel segments in total.

Karakanta et al., 2018; Sennrich et al., 2015a) to create more synthetic Ashaninka data since, at this point, Finnish provides more gain when combined with Quechua than Ashaninka does.

Future lines of investigation will include a supervised version of the **AshMorph** (Ortega et al., 2020) algorithm with the intent to automate sub-segment level selection. The plan is to improve Ashaninka to Spanish translations by first creating more human-evaluated training data and, second, experimenting with several other resources to create more synthetic data. Experimentation should also explore other similar languages since Quechua seems to help (not hurt) Ashaninka to Spanish translations.

References

Agić, Ž. and Vulić, I. (2019). JW300: A wide-coverage parallel corpus for low-resource languages. In *Proceedings of the 57th Annual Meeting of the Association for Computational Linguistics*, pages 3204–3210, Florence, Italy. Association for Computational Linguistics.

Bahdanau, D., Cho, K., and Bengio, Y. (2014). Neural machine translation by jointly learning to align and translate. *arXiv preprint arXiv:1409.0473*.

Bustamante, G., Oncevay, A., and Zariquiey, R. (2020). No data to crawl? monolingual corpus creation from pdf files of truly low-resource languages in peru. In *Proceedings of The 12th Language Resources and Evaluation Conference*, pages 2914–2923.

Cerrón-Palomino, R. (1987). *Lingüística quechua*. Centro de Estudios Rurales Andinos" Bartolomé de Las Casas".

Cerrón-Palomino, R. (2008). *Quechumara: Estructuras paralelas del quechua y del aimara*. Plural editores.

Cushimariano Romano, R. and Sebastián Q., R. C. (2008). Ñaantsipeta asháninkaki birakochaki. diccionario asháninka-castellano. versión preliminar. `http://www.lengamer.org/publicaciones/diccionarios/`. Visitado: 01/03/2013.

Gordon, R. G. and Grimes, B. F. (2005). Ethnologue : languages of the world.

Graves, A. (2012). Long short-term memory. In *Supervised sequence labelling with recurrent neural networks*, pages 37–45. Springer.

Gu, J., Hassan, H., Devlin, J., and Li, V. O. (2018). Universal neural machine translation for extremely low resource languages. *arXiv preprint arXiv:1802.05368*.

Hochreiter, S. and Schmidhuber, J. (1997). Long short-term memory. *Neural computation*, 9(8):1735–1780.

Karakanta, A., Dehdari, J., and van Genabith, J. (2018). Neural machine translation for low-resource languages without parallel corpora. *Machine Translation*, 32(1-2):167–189.

Koehn, P., Hoang, H., Birch, A., Callison-Burch, C., Federico, M., Bertoldi, N., Cowan, B., Shen, W.and Moran, C., Zens, R., Dyer, C., Bojar, O., Constantin, A., and Herbst, E. (2007). Moses: Open source toolkit for statistical machine translation. In *Proceedings of the 45th Annual Meeting of the Association for Computational Linguistics Companion Volume, Proceedings of the Demo and Poster Sessions*, pages 177–180, Prague, Czech Republic.

Lakew, S. M., Federico, M., Negri, M., and Turchi, M. (2018a). Multilingual neural machine translation for low-resource languages. *IJCoL. Italian Journal of Computational Linguistics*, 4(4-1):11–25.

Lakew, S. M., Lotito, Q. F., Negri, M., Turchi, M., and Federico, M. (2018b). Improving zero-shot translation of low-resource languages. *arXiv preprint arXiv:1811.01389.*

Michael, L. (2014). The nanti reality status system: Implications for the typological validity of the realis/irrealis contrast. *Linguistic Typology*, 18(2):251–288.

Mihas, E. (2010). *Essentials of Ashéninka Perené Grammar.* PhD thesis, The University of Wisconsin.

Mihas, E. (2015). *A grammar of Alto Perené (Arawak).* De Gruyter Mouton.

Ortega, J., Castro-Mamani, R. A., and Montoya Samame, J. R. (2020). Overcoming resistance: The normalization of an Amazonian tribal language. In *Proceedings of the 3rd Workshop on Technologies for MT of Low Resource Languages*, pages 1–13, Suzhou, China. Association for Computational Linguistics.

Ortega, J. and Pillaipakkamnatt, K. (2018). Using morphemes from agglutinative languages like quechua and finnish to aid in low-resource translation. In *Proceedings of the AMTA 2018 Workshop on Technologies for MT of Low Resource Languages (LoResMT 2018)*, pages 1–11.

Ortega, J. E., Mamani, R. C., and Cho, K. (2021). Neural machine translation with a polysynthetic low resource language. *Machine Translation*, pages 1–22.

Papineni, K., Roukos, S., Ward, T., and Zhu, W.-J. (2002). Bleu: a method for automatic evaluation of machine translation. In *Proceedings of the 40th annual meeting on association for computational linguistics*, pages 311–318. Association for Computational Linguistics.

Poncelas, A., Shterionov, D., Way, A., Wenniger, G. M. d. B., and Passban, P. (2018). Investigating backtranslation in neural machine translation. *arXiv preprint arXiv:1804.06189.*

Pourdamghani, N. and Knight, K. (2017). Deciphering related languages. In *Proceedings of the 2017 Conference on Empirical Methods in Natural Language Processing*, pages 2513–2518.

Rios, A. (2010). Applying finite-state techniques to a native american language: Quechua. *Institut für Computer Linguistik, Universitaät Zürich.*

Rios, A. and Castro-Mamani, R. (2014). Morphological disambiguation and text normalization for southern quechua varieties.

Sennrich, R., Haddow, B., and Birch, A. (2015a). Improving neural machine translation models with monolingual data. *arXiv preprint arXiv:1511.06709.*

Sennrich, R., Haddow, B., and Birch, A. (2015b). Neural machine translation of rare words with subword units. *arXiv preprint arXiv:1508.07909.*

Tantuğ, A. C. and Adalı, E. (2018). Machine translation between turkic languages. In *Turkish Natural Language Processing*, pages 237–254. Springer.

Tiedemann, J. (2012). Parallel data, tools and interfaces in opus. In *Lrec*, volume 2012, pages 2214–2218.

Zoph, B., Yuret, D., May, J., and Knight, K. (2016). Transfer learning for low-resource neural machine translation. *arXiv preprint arXiv:1604.02201.*

Structural Biases for Improving Transformers on Translation into Morphologically Rich Languages

Paul Soulos*[1], Sudha Rao[2], Caitlin Smith*[1], Eric Rosen*[1], Asli Celikyilmaz[2], R. Thomas McCoy*[1], Yichen Jiang*[3], Coleman Haley*[1], Roland Fernandez[2], Hamid Palangi[2], Jianfeng Gao[2], Paul Smolensky[1,2]
[1]Johns Hopkins University [2]Microsoft Research, Redmond [3]UNC Chapel Hill
{psoulos1, csmit372, erosen27, tom.mccoy, chaley7}@jhu.edu
{sudha.rao, aslicel, rfernand, hpalangi, jfgao, psmo}@microsoft.com
{yichenj}@cs.unc.edu

Abstract

Machine translation has seen rapid progress with the advent of Transformer-based models. These models have no explicit linguistic structure built into them, yet they may still implicitly learn structured relationships by attending to relevant tokens. We hypothesize that this structural learning could be made more robust by explicitly endowing Transformers with a structural bias, and we investigate two methods for building in such a bias. One method, the TP-Transformer, augments the traditional Transformer architecture to include an additional component to represent structure. The second method imbues structure at the data level by segmenting the data with morphological tokenization. We test these methods on translating from English into morphologically rich languages, Turkish and Inuktitut, and consider both automatic metrics and human evaluations. We find that each of these two approaches allows the network to achieve better performance, but this improvement is dependent on the size of the dataset. In sum, structural encoding methods make Transformers more sample-efficient, enabling them to perform better from smaller amounts of data.

1 Introduction

The task of machine translation has seen major progress in recent times with the advent of large-scale Transformer-based models (e.g., Vaswani et al., 2017; Dehghani et al., 2019; Liu et al., 2020a). However, there has been less progress on language pairs that specifically involve morphologically rich languages. Moreover, although there has been previous work that builds linguistic structure into translation models to deal with morphological complexity (Sennrich and Haddow, 2016; Dalvi et al., 2017; Matthews et al., 2018), to the best to our knowledge there has not been work that applies such strategies to large-scale Transformer-based models. We hypothesize that providing Transformers access to structured linguistic representations can significantly boost their performance on translation into languages with complex morphology that encodes linguistic structure.

In this work, we investigate two methods for introducing such structural bias into Transformer-based models. In the first method, we use the TP-Transformer (TPT) (Schlag et al., 2019), in which a traditional Transformer is augmented with Tensor Product Representations (TPRs) (Smolensky, 1990) (§ 2). At a high level, TPRs use a composition of *roles*

*Work partially done while at Microsoft Research.

English:	I want people to raise their hands who are in favour of the motion to report progress. (17)
Turkish:	Ilerleme raporunun talep edilmesinden yana olanların el kaldırmalarını istiyorum. (9)
Inuktitut:	isaaquvaksi taikkua nangmaksaqtut pigiaqtitausimajumut nuqqarumaliqtu. (5)

Table 1: Parallel sentence in English, Turkish, and Inuktitut. The number of words in each translation (marked in parentheses) is indicative of their information density and, hence, their morphological complexity.

and *fillers* where roles encode structural information (e.g., the part-of-speech of a word) and fillers encode the content (e.g., the meaning of a word). This enables learned internal structured representations. In the second method, we encode structure external to the model by segmenting training data using morphological tokenization (§3): morphological segmentation is done by existing parsers prior to training the Transformer. Since all neural models that operate over sequences tokenize the training data, through this method, we aim to answer the question of whether linguistically-informed tokenization that respects morphological structure can be helpful in processing morphologically-rich languages. Through the use of TPT, we aim to examine whether enabling a Transformer to learn its own structured *internal* representations will help it learn linguistic structure including structure which is encoded morphologically in morphologically-rich languages. Unlike the morphological tokenizer, the TPT architecture is language-agnostic and can be used on arbitrary datasets without feature engineering. We further investigate how the biases of these two approaches work together. We experiment on the task of translating from English into two morphologically rich languages: Turkish and Inukitut (Inuit; Eastern Canada). For Turkish, we train on several different dataset sizes from Open Subtitles (1.4M, 5M and 36M), a spoken-language domain, and also fine-tune on SETimes (200K), a news-wire domain. For Inuktitut, we train on the Nunavut Hansard Corpus (1.3M). We test models' performance using both an automatic metric and human evaluation (§5).

In the English to Turkish translation task, we find that the TP-Transformer beats the Transformer when evaluated for nuances such as morphology, word-order and subject/object-verb agreement. TPT provides a significant improvement on small datasets segmented with language agnostic BPE ($\sim$ 1 BLEU for Open Subtitles 1.4m and $\sim$ 2.5 BLEU for Hansard) and a more modest improvement on larger datasets (0.16 BLEU for Open Subtitles 5m and 0.36 BLEU for Open Subtitles 36m). Using morphologically segmented data helps substantially with models that are trained on small datasets. This is true for both pre-training (Open Subtitles 1.4m and Inuktitut Hansard), as well as models that are trained on large datasets and later finetuned using a smaller dataset (SETimes). This suggests that the method of encoding structure directly in the training data helps substantially with sample efficiency and transfer learning. When our two techniques are used together, we achieve an **8 BLEU** improvement over the state of the art on translation into Inuktitut (Joanis et al., 2020).

In order to better understand our models, we conduct detailed analysis, including error analysis, on sample outputs from different model variations (Appendix G). We also separate results out into different bins as defined by the morphological density of the target outputs to understand how results vary with morphological complexity §6. We find that morphological tokenization is strongly correlated with improved performance on complex sentences.

2 Using the TP-Transformer

The TP-Transformer (TPT) was introduced by Schlag et al. (2019) to improve performance on mathematical problem solving, a highly symbolic task. The model introduces an additional component to the attention mechanism which represents relational structure. In addition to the standard key K, query Q, and value V vectors used in attention, they introduce the role vector R.

Let the input for token $i \in 1, .., N$ at layer l be represented as X_i^l. For head h, the vectors are:

$$Q_i^{lh} = X_i^l W_q^{lh} + b_q^{lh} \qquad K_i^{lh} = X_i^l W_k^{lh} + b_k^{lh} \qquad V_i^{lh} = X_i^l W_v^{lh} + b_v^{lh} \qquad R_i^{lh} = X_i^l W_r^{lh} + b_r^{lh}$$

The output of soft attention $\bar{V}_i^{lh}$ is: $\bar{V}_i^{lh} = \sum_{t=1}^{N} \text{softmax}(\frac{Q_i^{lh} K_t^{lh}}{\sqrt{d_k}})^\top V_t^{lh}$

In a Tensor Product Representation, role vectors are bound to their corresponding filler vectors by the tensor product $\otimes$ or some compression of it: in the TPT, we use the compression of discarding the off-diagonal elements, resulting in the elementwise or Hadamard product $\odot$. The query Q_i^{lh} is interpreted as probing for a filler for the role R_i^{lh}, so the output of attention $\bar{V}_i^{lh}$ is taken to be the filler of that role; thus for the original TPT, this yielded: $Z_i^{lh} = \bar{V}_i^{lh} \odot R_i^{lh}$.

The role vector R is intended to act as a structural encoding independent of that structure's content (which is encoded in $\bar{V}$). We hypothesize that, by disentangling structure and content in this way, we can improve the model's ability to place familiar linguistic units in novel structures (e.g., using a suffix with a word stem that never had that suffix during training). Such structural flexibility is crucial for morphologically-rich languages.

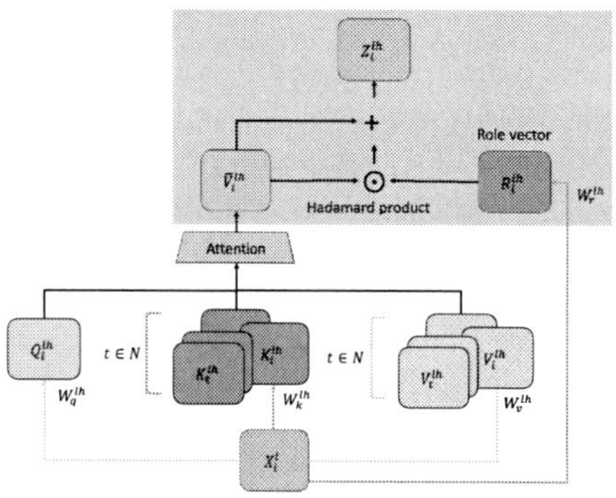

Figure 1: Architectural diagram of TPT attention mechanism. Highlighted section shows the additional components added to standard Transformer attention.

We make two modifications to the TPT used in Schlag et al. (2019)[1]. First, we use relative position embeddings (Shaw et al., 2018). We also use a residual connection to produce gradients that are not zero; $\bar{V} \odot R$ is a multiplicative interaction, so values of R near 0 will produce activation values and gradients of 0. This is similar to the model detail in Perez et al. (2017) Section 7.2. A schematic of our attention is shown in Figure 1. The rest of the architecture follows the standard residual connections and encoder-decoder architecture defined in Vaswani et al. (2017)

3 Using morphological segmentation

Our target languages, Turkish and Inuktitut, both exhibit a high degree of morphological complexity. Words in both languages consist of a root followed by potentially many suffixes, each of which may have multiple surface forms.

We used two methods of subword tokenization: one utilizing a type of character-level byte-pair encoding (Gage, 1994), and one incorporating morphological parsing plus byte-pair encoding. The first method (which we label 'BPE') used SentencePiece (Kudo and Richardson, 2018), a tokenizer that builds subword tokens using a combination of byte-pair encoding and unigram language modeling. BPE relies only on character frequencies and incorporates no morphological information.

Language	Segmented Word
Turkish	anla-t-ma-yacak
Gloss	understand-CAUS-NEG-FUT
English	will not tell
BPE	anlat-mayacak
Inuktitut	miv-vi-liar-uma-lauq-tur-uuq
Gloss	land-place-go-want-PAST-3S-say.3S
English	He said he wanted to go to the landing strip.
BPE	mivvi-lia-ruma-lau-qturuuq

Table 2: Morpheme breakdown, gloss, English, and BPE tokenization of Turkish and Inuktitut morphologically complex words

[1]Code available at `https://github.com/psoulos/tpt`

The second method (which we call 'morphological tokenization') incorporated morphological information by parsing all words (i.e. breaking them up into their composite morphemes) in our morphologically complex target languages before tokenizing them. For Turkish, we used the morphological parser from Zemberek (Akın and Akın, 2007), an open-source Turkish NLP toolkit. Zemberek uses sentence-level disambiguation to produce the most likely parse of each word given its sentential context. For Inuktitut, we used the morphological parsing method adopted by Joanis et al. (2020), incorporating a symbolic parser with a neural parser backoff. See Appendix D for implementational details on morphological segmentation.

The differences in how these tokenizers divide multi-morphemic Turkish and Inuktitut words into subwords are illustrated in Table 2. The boundaries determined by BPE do not reflect the internal morphological structure of these words.

4 Dataset description

4.1 English-Turkish data

For pretraining of the English-Turkish translation model, we used the Open Subtitles corpus (Lison and Tiedemann, 2016). This corpus consists of a large number of aligned pairs of subtitles from film and television. In order to test the effect of dataset size on model performance, we utilized three splits of this corpus: the full-size corpus, a sample of five million sentence pairs, and a sample of approximately one million sentence pairs. For fine-tuning of the English-Turkish model, we used the South-East European Parallel (SETimes) Corpus. SETimes is a collection of short written news stories in ten languages. For this task, we used the subset of this corpus that was used for the WMT 2018 English-Turkish shared translation task (Bojar et al., 2018).

4.2 English-Inuktitut data

Corpus	Training	Validation	Test
Open Subtitles 36m	28,694,211	3,586,776	3,586,777
Open Subtitles 5m	4,000,000	500,000	500,000
Open Subtitles 1.4m	1,300,000	65,000	65,000
SETimes	207,678	3,007	3,000
Nunavut Hansard	1,312,791	5,494	6,181

Table 3: Number of training, validation, and test samples in the different datasets.

Like Turkish, Inuktitut is a morphologically complex language. Words may consist of a root, a prefix, and potentially many suffixes. Table 2 contains an example of a multi-morphemic Inuktitut word. For training of the English-Inuktitut translation model, we used the Nunavut Hansard Inuktitut–English Parallel Corpus 3.0 (Joanis et al., 2020), the only sizable publicly available bilingual corpus. The dataset consists of over one million aligned sentence pairs from government proceedings. The size of the dataset splits are reported in Table 3.

5 Experimental Results

We aim to answer the following research questions (RQ) through our experimentation:

1. Do either or both of our structural methods improve translation?
2. If so, how does that advantage interact with:
   (a) Training data quantity?
   (b) Transfer learning?
   (c) Morphological richness of language?

As a baseline, we trained the standard Transformer model (Vaswani et al., 2017) with the addition of relative position embeddings (Shaw et al., 2018). Model training details and computing resources can be found in Section 1 and 2 of the supplementary materials. For each model, we used either byte pair encoding (BPE) (Sennrich et al., 2016) or morphological tokenization as described in §3. In order to see how our changes relate to sample efficiency, we vary the size of the subset of the Open Subtitles dataset used for training. We used the SETimes dataset to finetune these models to test whether either structural bias improves transfer learning. We also trained models on the Inuktitut dataset to compare the results from languages with differing morphological richness.

5.1 Automatic Metric Results

	Transformer	TP-Transformer
1.4m	7.5 ±.43	8.44 ±.25
1.4m morph	16.63 ±.19	16.89 ±.07
5m	18.70	18.86
5m morph	18.84	19.19
36m	20.95	21.31
36m morph	21.05	21.32

Table 4: BLEU scores on the test set of Open Subtitles separated by training set size and tokenization method. For the 1.4m runs, we show the mean and standard deviation of three randomly initialized models. The larger datasets only have one run each due to computational resource reasons.

Table 4 shows the test set BLEU[2] scores for the different size splits of the Open Subtitles dataset (Research Question RQ2a). For the smallest data split of 1.4m samples, TPT provides almost 1 BLEU improvement over a standard Transformer. Using a morphological tokenization provides an 8 BLEU improvement on the small split. Using TPT with morphologically tokenized data does not provide any additional benefit on the 1.4m split. For the two larger splits, TPT (across columns) and morphological parsing (across rows) provides minor improvements (0.1–0.36 BLEU), and this improvement becomes more modest when both are combined (top left cell to bottom right cell) (0.49 BLEU on the 5m split and 0.37 on the full 36m split). Next, in order to analyze whether either structural bias helps with transfer learning (RQ2b), we take the best performing models shown in Table 4 and finetune them on the SETimes dataset.

	Transformer	TP-Transformer
5m	14.19	14.25
5m morph	15.16	15.39
36m	16.77	17.01
36m morph	18.35	18.82

Table 5: BLEU scores on the test set of SETimes from models pretrained on OpenSubtitles (5m) and finetuned on SETimes (200K) divided by training set size and tokenization.

The BLEU scores for these finetuned models can be seen in Table 5. There is a large increase in BLEU score across rows between models that use either BPE encoding or morphological tokenization. This provides further evidence for the findings from the 1.4m split in Table 4 that morphological tokenization provides a large improvement in low data regimes. While morphological tokenization does not provide much of an improvement during large-scale pretraining, it is beneficial for transfer learning on a smaller domain.

	Transformer	TP-Transformer
BPE	18.56 ±1.92	21.12 ±.70
Morphological	26.05 ±.90	28.3 ±.50

Table 6: BLEU scores on the test set of Inuktitut divided by tokenization. We show the mean and standard deviation of three randomly initialized models.

In addition to Turkish, we trained models on the Inuktitut dataset described in §4.2 to understand the variance of model performance by the morphological richness of languages (RQ2c). We trained models using both data tokenized by BPE encoding as well as by an Inuktitut morphological parser. The results are shown in Table 6. As we saw on both the 1.4m Open Subtitles split and SETimes,

[2]We calculated BLEU using SacreBLEU (Post, 2018) and the signature is "BLEU+case.mixed+numrefs.1+smooth.exp+tok.13a+version.1.5.0". All models were also tested with CHRF (Popović, 2015) and the results can be found in Appendix E.

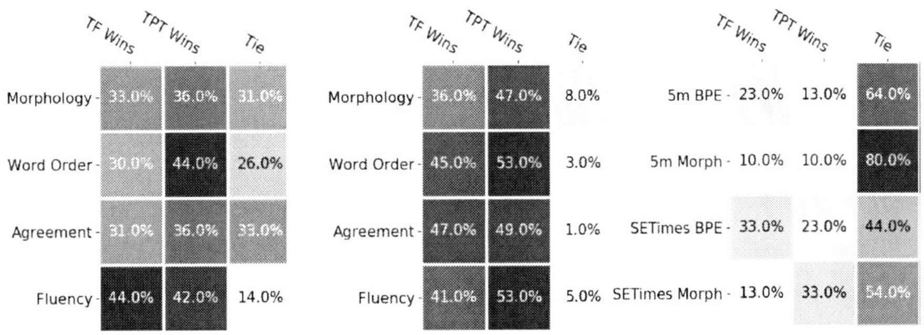

(a) (b) (c)

Figure 2: Human judgment results: (a) Comparison between Transformer (TF) and TPT on different criteria when trained on Open Subtitles (5m) using BPE encoding. (b) Comparison between Transformer and TPT when trained on Open Subtitles (5m) using morphologically segmented data. (c) Comparison between Transformer (TF) and TPT on meaning preservation when trained on different datasets.

morphological tokenization provides a huge improvement in BLEU. TPT provides a large average improvement regardless of the tokenization scheme, although the BPE Tranformer in particular has a high variance and is sensitive to random initialization. Inuktitut is more morphologically complex than Turkish across several measures of morphological complexity[3] and it is possible that TPT models perform better with more complex morphology. For example, compare the improvements from using TPT over a standard transformer for BPE on the Open Subtitles 1.4m split and Inuktitut. TPT provides $\sim$1 BLEU improvement on Turkish, and this improvement increases to $\sim$2.5 on Inuktitut. The previous state-of-the-art on the Hansard dataset is 20.3 BLEU on the test set (Joanis et al., 2020). Both methods proposed in this paper improve on that, and together they improve the state-of-the-art by 8 BLEU.

5.2 Human-based Evaluation Results

The BLEU scores in the previous section give us a single number summarizing the quality of our translations. We now evaluate some of the finer-grained characteristics of the outputs. We focus on four aspects of the output that are likely to benefit from more robust encodings of structure: morphology, word-order, subject-verb agreement and fluency.

We use Amazon Mechanical Turk to get human judgements. We perform a comparative study where we show annotators two Turkish translations from the transformer and the TPT models trained on the 5m Open Subtitles split. We do not show the English source sentence since the four criteria of evaluation in this study does not require looking at the source sentence. We collect three annotations per comparison and use only those instances where at least 2 out of the 3 annotators agree on the same answer. We collect annotations on 180 instances for each of the two comparative studies. See Appendix F for the questions asked to annotators.

Figure 2a shows the result of this comparison when we use BPE encoding to tokenize the data whereas Figure 2b shows the result of this comparison when we use morphological segmenter to tokenize the data. Under BPE encoding, we find that TPT has slightly less morphological and agreement errors and has significantly less word-order issues. This suggests that the structural bias introduced by the TPT helps in forming sentences that are overall morphologically better

[3]Using the parallel test sets from Mielke et al. (2019), we measured a type-token ratio of 0.42 for Inuktitut and 0.19 for Turkish, as well as a relative entropy of word structure of 1.75 for Inuktitut and 1.21 for Turkish

formed. On the other hand, annotators find translations from the Transformer to be slightly more fluent than those from the TPT. Under morphologically segmented data, annotators find translations from TPT are significantly better than the Transformers in morphological form and word-order and slightly better in subject-verb agreement, providing further evidence that the structural bias introduced by the TPT is helpful. Moreover, annotators also find translations from TPT in this case to be more fluent than those from the Transformer.

We perform an additional study to understand which of the two model translations best preserves the meaning of the English source sentence. We ask an expert, a linguistically-trained native Turkish speaker, to annotate 30 instances each from eight model outputs (5m Open Subtitles BPE & morphologically tokenized, SETimes BPE & morphologically tokenized for both Transformer and TPT). We show them the English sentence and two Turkish translations. We ask them "*Grammatical issues aside, which of the two translations better preserves the meaning of the English sentence?*" and let them choose from A, B or Both preserve equally. Figure 2c shows the results of this study. In the Open Subtitles dataset, we find the difference between Transformer and TPT performance is too small under both BPE encoding and morphological segmentation. In the SETimes dataset, we find the same trend under BPE encoding. Only under morphologically segmented data in SETimes, TPT significantly wins over Transformer. These results show that when we include the English source sentence, it is inconclusive if TPT or Transformer is better. This suggests that although TPT improves the ability to compose Turkish text (as found by the first study), it does not affect the ability to determine which Turkish output should go with a given English input.

6 Morphological density analysis

Given the rich morphology of the target languages, we are interested in whether either structural bias or morphological segmentation improves performance on more morphologically complex sentences. To answer this question, we used our Turkish morphological segmenter on sequences from the test set and binned sentences based on the average morphemes per word in a sentence. For example, a long sentence with simple words that are all a single morpheme would have an average morpheme per word of 1, whereas a sentence that is made of complex words would have a larger average morpheme per word. We then calculated the BLEU score for each of these buckets so that we could see if our models performed better on sentences that are morphologically complex.

The results are shown in Figure 3. On the 36m training set (top row), both of our methods provide an improvement at almost every morpheme density. Comparing TPT to a standard Transformer, Figure 3a shows a relatively consistent improvement of around 0.4 BLEU with a large increase for simple sentences. Comparing standard transformers with morphological parsing against BPE, Figure 3b shows that as the morphological complexity of sequences increases, the model using morphological tokenization improves over BPE tokenization. The same trend is visible when comparing TPT with morphological tokenization with a standard transformer using BPE tokenization (Figure 3c), except the magnitude of the increase is greater.

The morphological analysis on the 5m training set (bottom row) is less conclusive. TPT does not appear to have any impact as the morphological density increases (Figure 3d). Morphological tokenization shows a similar upward trend as on the 36m dataset, but this improvement disappears suddenly at 3.0 morphemes per word (Figure 3e). As the morphological density increases, the number of samples for each bucket on the test set decreases, so it is possible that the sudden drop is the result of too few samples.

Our results also show some correspondence with the overall morphological complexity of the dataset. We computed a modified version of the C_D measure (the "relative entropy of word structure") from Bentz et al. (2016), as we found it to be the most robust to the meaning

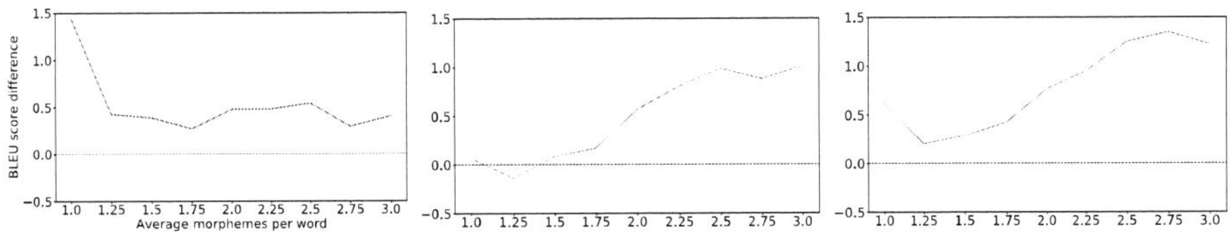

(a) 36m TPT BPE – Transformer BPE (b) 36m Transformer morph – Transformer BPE (c) 36m TPT morph – Transformer BPE

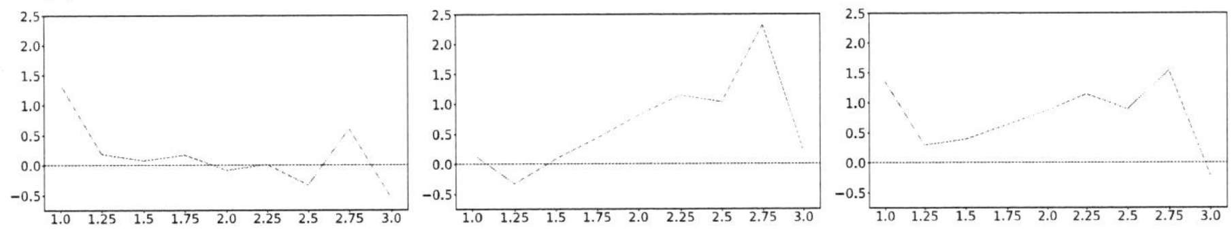

(d) 5m TPT BPE – Transformer BPE (e) 5m Transformer morph – Transformer BPE (f) 5m TPT morph – Transformer BPE

Figure 3: BLEU score differences between models on the Turkish Open Subtitles 36m (top row) and 5m (bottom row) training sets bucketed by morphological density (average number of morphemes per word in a sentence).

variations between corpora (Supplementary materials section 4). Higher values of this measure correspond to more regular structure/information in words, and thus, greater morphological complexity. We computed the measure over the first 100,000 characters of the test set of each dataset. We computed C_D as 1.89 for the Hansard dataset, while the Turkish datasets ranged from C_D 1.45-1.49. This corresponds to the relatively large increase in BLEU seen for Inuktitut.

7 Related Work

Translating into Morphologically-rich languages Previous work has leveraged morphology for translating into morphologically-rich languages. Turhan (1997) uses a recursive symbolic system to translate from English into Turkish including a morphological generator. Ataman et al. (2020) use hierarchical latent variable models to model both character and morpheme level statistics for translating into morphologically rich languages (Arabic, Czech, Turkish) with GRUs. Passban et al. (2018a) introduce a character-level neural machine translation model for translating into morphologically rich languages which incorporates a morphology lookup table into the decoder whereas Passban et al. (2018b) propose a subword-level model that uses separate embedding for stem and affix. Joanis et al. (2020) introduced the dataset that we use for Inuktitut and also explored using morphological segmentation for alignment as well as neural and statistical machine translation. This work was followed up by Knowles et al. (2020) who introduce additional methods techniques on the Inuktitut dataset. Roest et al. (2020) and Scherrer et al. (2020) also investigated morphological segmentation in Inuktitut in addition to data augmentation and pretraining.

Using Transformer-based models for translation In recent times, there have been several work that use variations of Transformer (Vaswani et al., 2017) model for the task of machine translation. Chen et al. (2018) combine the power of recurrent neural network and transformer. Dehghani et al. (2019) introduce universal transformers as a generalization of transformers whereas Deng et al. (2018) combine transformer architecture with several other techniques such as BPE, back translation, data selection, model ensembling and reranking. Bugliarello and Okazaki (2020) incorporate syntactic knowledge into transformer model to show improvements on English to German, Turkish and Japanese translation tasks. Currey and Heafield (2019) introduce two methods to incorporate English syntax when translating from English into other languages with Transformers. Liu et al. (2020b) introduce mBART, an auto-encoder pretrained on large-scale monolingual corpora and show gains on several languages.

Using TPRs TPRs have gained traction recently with the interest in neurosymbolic computation to achieve out-of-domain generalization. They have been used in a variety of domains, including mathematical problem solving (Schlag et al., 2019), reasoning (Schlag and Schmidhuber, 2018), image captioning (Huang et al., 2018), question-answering (Palangi et al., 2018), and program synthesis (Chen et al., 2020). A separate line of work uses TPRs as an interpretation tool to understand representations in networks that do not explicitly use TPRs (McCoy et al., 2019; Soulos et al., 2020).

8 Conclusion

We investigated two methods for improving translation into morphologically rich languages with Transformers. The TP-Transformer adds an additional component to Transformer attention to represent relational structure. This model had the largest improvement on smaller datasets and modest improvement on larger datasets. We also investigated morphological tokenization which had substantial improvements on small datasets and transfer learning. When used together, our methods improve on the state of the art for translation from English into Inuktitut by 8 BLEU. The models were analyzed by human evaluators to tease apart different dimensions along which our models excel; TP-Transformer had fewer morphological, word-order, and agreement issues. We analyzed the performance of our networks under varying morphological complexity and found that morphological tokenization provides a large benefit for more complex sentences.

References

Akın, A. A. and Akın, M. D. (2007). Zemberek, an open source NLP framework for Turkic languages. *Structure*, 10.

Ataman, D., Aziz, W., and Birch, A. (2020). A Latent Morphology Model for Open-Vocabulary Neural Machine Translation. In *ICLR 2020*.

Bentz, C., Ruzsics, T., Koplenig, A., and Samardžić, T. (2016). A comparison between morphological complexity measures: Typological data vs. language corpora. In *Proceedings of the Workshop on Computational Linguistics for Linguistic Complexity (CL4LC)*, pages 142–153, Osaka, Japan. The COLING 2016 Organizing Committee.

Bojar, O., Federmann, C., Fishel, M., Graham, Y., Haddow, B., Huck, M., Koehn, P., and Monz, C. (2018). Findings of the 2018 conference on machine translation (WMT18). In *Proceedings of the Third Conference on Machine Translation, Volume 2: Shared Task Papers*, pages 272–307, Belgium, Brussels. Association for Computational Linguistics.

Bugliarello, E. and Okazaki, N. (2020). Enhancing machine translation with dependency-aware self-attention. In *Proceedings of the 58th Annual Meeting of the Association for Computational Linguistics*, pages 1618–1627.

Chen, K., Huang, Q., Palangi, H., Smolensky, P., Forbus, K., and Gao, J. (2020). Mapping natural-language problems to formal-language solutions using structured neural representations. In III, H. D. and Singh, A., editors, *Proceedings of the 37th International Conference on Machine Learning*, volume 119 of *Proceedings of Machine Learning Research*, pages 1566–1575. PMLR.

Chen, M. X., Firat, O., Bapna, A., Johnson, M., Macherey, W., Foster, G., Jones, L., Schuster, M., Shazeer, N., Parmar, N., et al. (2018). The best of both worlds: Combining recent advances in neural machine translation. In *Proceedings of the 56th Annual Meeting of the Association for Computational Linguistics (Volume 1: Long Papers)*, pages 76–86.

Currey, A. and Heafield, K. (2019). Incorporating source syntax into transformer-based neural machine translation. In *Proceedings of the Fourth Conference on Machine Translation (Volume 1: Research Papers)*, pages 24–33, Florence, Italy. Association for Computational Linguistics.

Dalvi, F., Durrani, N., Sajjad, H., Belinkov, Y., and Vogel, S. (2017). Understanding and improving morphological learning in the neural machine translation decoder. In *Proceedings of the Eighth International Joint Conference on Natural Language Processing (Volume 1: Long Papers)*, pages 142–151, Taipei, Taiwan. Asian Federation of Natural Language Processing.

Dehghani, M., Gouws, S., Vinyals, O., Uszkoreit, J., and Kaiser, L. (2019). Universal transformers. In *International Conference on Learning Representations*.

Deng, Y., Cheng, S., Lu, J., Song, K., Wang, J., Wu, S., Yao, L., Zhang, G., Zhang, H., Zhang, P., et al. (2018). Alibaba's neural machine translation systems for wmt18. In *Proceedings of the Third Conference on Machine Translation: Shared Task Papers*, pages 368–376.

Gage, P. (1994). A new algorithm for data compression. *C Users J.*, 12(2):23–38.

Hausser, J. and Strimmer, K. (2009). Entropy inference and the james-stein estimator, with application to nonlinear gene association networks. *Journal of Machine Learning Research*, 10(50):1469–1484.

Huang, Q., Smolensky, P., He, X., Deng, L., and Wu, D. (2018). Tensor product generation networks for deep NLP modeling. In *Proceedings of the 2018 Conference of the North American Chapter of the Association for Computational Linguistics: Human Language Technologies, Volume 1 (Long Papers)*, pages 1263–1273, New Orleans, Louisiana. Association for Computational Linguistics.

Joanis, E., Knowles, R., Kuhn, R., Larkin, S., Littell, P., Lo, C.-k., Stewart, D., and Micher, J. (2020). The Nunavut hansard Inuktitut–English parallel corpus 3.0 with preliminary machine translation results. In *Proceedings of the 12th Language Resources and Evaluation Conference*, pages 2562–2572, Marseille, France. European Language Resources Association.

Knowles, R., Stewart, D., Larkin, S., and Littell, P. (2020). NRC systems for the 2020 Inuktitut-English news translation task. In *Proceedings of the Fifth Conference on Machine Translation*, pages 156–170, Online. Association for Computational Linguistics.

Kudo, T. and Richardson, J. (2018). SentencePiece: A simple and language independent subword tokenizer and detokenizer for Neural Text Processing. In *Proceedings of the 2018 Conference on Empirical Methods in Natural Language PRocessing (System Demonstrations)*, pages 66–71.

Lison, P. and Tiedemann, J. (2016). OpenSubtitles2016: Extracting large parallel corpora from movie and TV subtitles. In *Proceedings of the Tenth International Conference on Language Resources and Evaluation (LREC'16)*, pages 923–929, Portorož, Slovenia. European Language Resources Association (ELRA).

Liu, X., Duh, K., Liu, L., and Gao, J. (2020a). Very deep transformers for neural machine translation. In *arXiv:2008.07772 [cs]*.

Liu, Y., Gu, J., Goyal, N., Li, X., Edunov, S., Ghazvininejad, M., Lewis, M., and Zettlemoyer, L. (2020b). Multilingual denoising pre-training for neural machine translation. *Transactions of the Association for Computational Linguistics*, 8:726–742.

Matthews, A., Neubig, G., and Dyer, C. (2018). Using morphological knowledge in open-vocabulary neural language models. In *Proceedings of the 2018 Conference of the North American Chapter of the Association for Computational Linguistics: Human Language Technologies, Volume 1 (Long Papers)*, pages 1435–1445, New Orleans, Louisiana. Association for Computational Linguistics.

McCoy, R. T., Linzen, T., Dunbar, E., and Smolensky, P. (2019). RNNs implicitly implement tensor-product representations. In *International Conference on Learning Representations*.

Mielke, S. J., Cotterell, R., Gorman, K., Roark, B., and Eisner, J. (2019). What kind of language is hard to language-model? In *Proceedings of the 57th Annual Meeting of the Association for Computational Linguistics*, pages 4975–4989, Florence, Italy. Association for Computational Linguistics.

Palangi, H., Smolensky, P., He, X., and Deng, L. (2018). Question-answering with grammatically-interpretable representations. In *AAAI*.

Passban, P., Liu, Q., and Way, A. (2018a). Improving character-based decoding using target-side morphological information for neural machine translation. In *Proceedings of the 2018 Conference of the North American Chapter of the Association for Computational Linguistics: Human Language Technologies, Volume 1 (Long Papers)*, pages 58–68.

Passban, P., Way, A., and Liu, Q. (2018b). Tailoring neural architectures for translating from morphologically rich languages. In *Proceedings of the 27th International Conference on Computational Linguistics*, pages 3134–3145.

Perez, E., Strub, F., de Vries, H., Dumoulin, V., and Courville, A. C. (2017). Film: Visual reasoning with a general conditioning layer. *CoRR*, abs/1709.07871.

Popović, M. (2015). chrF: character n-gram F-score for automatic MT evaluation. In *Proceedings of the Tenth Workshop on Statistical Machine Translation*, pages 392–395, Lisbon, Portugal. Association for Computational Linguistics.

Post, M. (2018). A call for clarity in reporting BLEU scores. In *Proceedings of the Third Conference on Machine Translation: Research Papers*, pages 186–191, Belgium, Brussels. Association for Computational Linguistics.

Roest, C., Edman, L., Minnema, G., Kelly, K., Spenader, J., and Toral, A. (2020). Machine translation for English–Inuktitut with segmentation, data acquisition and pre-training. In *Proceedings of the Fifth Conference on Machine Translation*, pages 274–281, Online. Association for Computational Linguistics.

Scherrer, Y., Grönroos, S.-A., and Virpioja, S. (2020). The University of Helsinki and aalto university submissions to the WMT 2020 news and low-resource translation tasks. In *Proceedings of the Fifth Conference on Machine Translation*, pages 1129–1138, Online. Association for Computational Linguistics.

Schlag, I. and Schmidhuber, J. (2018). Learning to reason with third order tensor products. *Advances in neural information processing systems*, 31:9981–9993.

Schlag, I., Smolensky, P., Fernandez, R., Jojic, N., Schmidhuber, J., and Gao, J. (2019). Enhancing the transformer with explicit relational encoding for math problem solving. *arXiv preprint arXiv:1910.06611*.

Sennrich, R. and Haddow, B. (2016). Linguistic input features improve neural machine translation. In *Proceedings of the First Conference on Machine Translation: Volume 1, Research Papers*, pages 83–91, Berlin, Germany. Association for Computational Linguistics.

Sennrich, R., Haddow, B., and Birch, A. (2016). Neural machine translation of rare words with subword units. In *Proceedings of the 54th Annual Meeting of the Association for Computational Linguistics (Volume 1: Long Papers)*, pages 1715–1725, Berlin, Germany. Association for Computational Linguistics.

Shaw, P., Uszkoreit, J., and Vaswani, A. (2018). Self-attention with relative position representations. In *Proceedings of the 2018 Conference of the North American Chapter of the Association for Computational Linguistics: Human Language Technologies, Volume 2 (Short Papers)*, pages 464–468, New Orleans, Louisiana. Association for Computational Linguistics.

Shazeer, N. and Stern, M. (2018). Adafactor: Adaptive learning rates with sublinear memory cost. volume 80 of *Proceedings of Machine Learning Research*, pages 4596–4604, Stockholmsmässan, Stockholm Sweden. PMLR.

Smolensky, P. (1990). Tensor product variable binding and the representation of symbolic structures in connectionist systems. *Artificial intelligence*, 46(1-2):159–216.

Soulos, P., McCoy, R. T., Linzen, T., and Smolensky, P. (2020). Discovering the compositional structure of vector representations with role learning networks. In *Proceedings of the Third BlackboxNLP Workshop on Analyzing and Interpreting Neural Networks for NLP*, pages 238–254, Online. Association for Computational Linguistics.

Turhan, C. K. (1997). An english to turkish machine translation system using structural mapping. In *Proceedings of the Fifth Conference on Applied Natural Language Processing*, ANLC '97, page 320–323, USA. Association for Computational Linguistics.

Vaswani, A., Shazeer, N., Parmar, N., Uszkoreit, J., Jones, L., Gomez, A. N., Kaiser, L., and Polosukhin, I. (2017). Attention is all you need. *Advances in Neural Information Processing Systems*, abs/1706.03762.

Appendix

A Model Training Parameters

Both the standard Transformer and the TP-Transformer (TPT) use 6 layers and 8 heads per layer. TPT has key/value/query/role dimensions of 64, whereas the standard Transformer has key/value/query dimensions of 80. The reason for this increase is so that the resulting models match in terms of parameter count, and we add parameters are the most homologous area. The standard Transformer has 74,375,936 parameters, and the TP-Transformer has 74,385,152 parameters. Both networks use a token dimension of 512, a feedforward dimension of 2048, and 32 relative positioning buckets Shaw et al. (2018). The input vocabulary size is 50,000. We set a training batch size of 80 per GPU and used the Adafactor Shazeer and Stern (2018) optimizer with square root learning rate decay. Throughout the model, we used a commonly used dropout rate of .1.

B Computing Resources

The models were all trained with 8 Tesla V100 GPUs. The models trained on the small Hansard and Open Subtitles 1.4m datasets converged in about 8 hours. The larger Open Subtitles 5m models coverged in around 40 hours, and the Open Subtitles 32m models coverged in 15 days.

C Corpora Morphological Complexity

Studies have considered what corpus-based measures are correlated with linguistic measures of morphological complexity. Most notably, Bentz et al. (2016) found several corpus-based measures that correlate strongly with complex morphological typology. This measure computes the regularity of structure within words by taking the character-level entropy of the corpus and subtracting that from the entropy of a "masked" version of the corpus, where all non-whitespace characters have been replaced with random samples from the uniform distribution over the characters in the corpus. Rather than the approximation used in Bentz et al. (2016) for character-level entropy, we directly computed the character-level Shannon's entropy using a James-Stein shrinkage estimator as in Hausser and Strimmer (2009).

D Morphological parser process

For each target language, its parser was used to insert morpheme boundaries into all multi-morphemic words in the dataset. Due to the comparatively low level of morphological complexity of the English source data, no parsing of English words was conducted. From here, each SentencePiece tokenizer's vocabulary was built over a dataset's training data (both the source and target language) with a target size of 50,000 vocabulary items. SentencePiece allows the user to specify special characters that cannot be crossed when constructing subword tokens, both during training of the tokenizer and during tokenization of a sentence. The symbol used to represent morpheme boundaries was specified as such a special symbol. As a result, morpheme boundaries in Turkish and Inuktitut (as identified by their respective parsers) always served as subword token boundaries.

Each SentencePiece tokenizer's vocabulary was built over a dataset's training data (both source and target language) with a target size of 50,000 vocabulary items. This tokenization method (which we label simply 'BPE') relies only on character frequencies and incorporates no morphological information, so many multi-morphemic words may each be assigned to a single token, and there is no guarantee that a word's subword boundaries align with its morpheme boundaries.

E CHRF Results

The same models used to measure BLEU scores are also tested using CHRF (Popović, 2015). The results are shown in Tables 7, 8, and 9.

	Transformer	TP-Transformer
1.4m	.351 ±.005	.365 ±.004
1.4m morph	.438 ±.001	.440 ±.001
5m	.461	.463
5m morph	.467	.469
36m	.486	.488
36m morph	.490	.492

Table 7: CHRF scores on the test set of Open Subtitles separated by training set size and tokenization method. For the 1.4m runs, we show the mean and standard deviation of three randomly initialized models. The larger datasets only have one run each due to computational resource reasons.

	Transformer	TP-Transformer
5m	.502	.502
5m morph	.509	.514
36m	.532	.537
36m morph	.540	.543

Table 8: CHRF scores on the test set of SETimes from models pretrained on OpenSubtitles (5m) and finetuned on SETimes (200K) divided by training set size and tokenization.

F Annotator Questions

We ask annotators the following questions:
Morphology: *"Which of the two sentences has more morphological issues (i.e. incorrect suffixes)?"* and let annotators choose from A, B, Both or None.
Word-order: *"Which of the two sentences has word-order issues?"* and let annotators choose from A, B, Both or None.
Agreement: *"Which of the two sentences has more agreement errors between the subject/object and the verb (i.e. the suffixes for the verbs and/or the nouns do not agree with each other)?"* and let annotators choose from A, B, Both or None.
Fluency: *"Which of the two sentences is more fluent i.e. reads more like it was written by a native Turkish speaker?"* and let annotators choose from A, B, Both are equally fluent.

	Transformer	TP-Transformer
BPE	.498 ±.011	.513 ±.003
Morphological	.526 ±.007	.539 ±.006

Table 9: CHRF scores on the test set of Inuktitut divided by tokenization. We show the mean and standard deviation of three randomly initialized models.

G Output analysis

Here we present an error analysis of a few sample translations from Transformer and TPT models. We group errors according to the aspects used to perform human-based evaluation in §5.2. Table 10 shows the result of this analysis. Under fluency issues, Transformer introduces an unnecessary word 'zamaninda' making it less fluent compared to the TPT translation. Under meaning preservation, the translation by Transformer incorrectly suggests "in exchange for money" whereas TPT correctly preserves the meaning. Under agreement issues, TPT includes incorrect use of first person suffix whereas Transformer does not

	Fluency Issues
English	*"I want to carry on living," he said at the time of the CPJ award.*
Turkish Transformer	*CPJ ödülünün zamanında konuşan Jovanoviç, "Yaşamak istiyorum." dedi.*
Turkish TPT	*CPJ ödülünde konuşan bakan, "Yaşamayı sürdürmek istiyorum." dedi.*
Reason	unnecessary use of the word 'zamaninda'.
	Meaning Preservation
English	*Some say you chose Turkey for money.*
Turkish Transformer	*Bazıları Türkiye'yi para karşılığında seçtiğinizi söylüyor.*
Turkish TPT	*Bazıları, para için Türkiye'yi seçtiğinizi söylüyorlar.*
Reason	"para karşılığında" suggests 'in exchange for money'
	Subject to verb agreement Issues
English	*Maybe because I go to bed listening to the message you left, saying how much you liked missing me.*
Turkish Transformer	*Belki de yatağa gidip, beni özlemeyi ne kadar sevdiğini söyleyen mesajını dinlediğim için.*
Turkish TPT	*Belki de yatağa gidip bıraktığın mesajı dinleyip beni özlediğini söy-le-di-ğ-im için.*
Reason	incorrect use of first person ('-im') instead of second person ('-in')
	Morphology Issues
English	*So far we have not received any news nor found any clues.*
Turkish Transformer	*Şimdiye kadar hiçbir haber alamadık ve hiçbir ipucu bulamadık*
Turkish TPT	*Bugüne kadar ne haber aldık ne de ipucu bul-a-ma-dı-k*
Reason	Highlighted word has a double negative instead of the correct form bul-a-bil-di-k/bul-du-k.

Table 10: Sample outputs showing issues relating to fluency, meaning preservation, agreement and morphology from Transformer and TPT models.

have any subject to verb agreement issues. Under morphology issues, TPT incorrectly includes a negation suffix making the sentence a double negative whereas Transformer correctly translates the English sentence.

Table 11 includes analysis of some additional sample outputs from Transformer and TPT models. Under morphology issues, Transformer includes an unnecessary plural suffix. The TPT translation is okay but would have been better with the addition of the '-mu' suffix. Under meaning preservation, Transformer incorrectly translates "Bank of England" as "Bank of England", thus losing out on the meaning. Whereas TPT correctly translates that named entity into Turkish. Under tense issues, Transformer uses an incorrect past tense suffix whereas TPT correctly preserves the tense of the English sentence. Under repetition issues, Transformer repeats a word which is not required in written-language but might be okay in spoken-language.

	Morphology Issues
English	*First we have to decide if those lost six minutes will be coming out of game time, bathroom time or the pizza break.*
Turkish Transformer	*İlk önce, bu altı dakika kaybet-me-ler-i-n oyun zamanından mı yoksa banyo zamanından mı olacağına karar vermeliyiz.*
Turkish TPT	*İlk olarak, o 6 dakikanın maçtan, banyo saatinden veya pizza molasından [illegible] çıkıp çıkmayacağına karar vermeliyiz.*
Reason	Unnecessary plural suffix (-ler)
	Meaning Preservation
English	*Bank of England to keep interest rates at 0.25%*
Turkish Transformer	*Bank of England faiz oranlarını %0,25 oranında tutacak.*
Turkish TPT	*İngiltere Merkez Bankası faiz oranlarını %0,25 oranında tutacak.*
Reason	Incorrect translation of named entity
	Tense Issues
English	*Barely out of bed and already on the phone.*
Turkish Transformer	*Yataktan zar zor çıktım ve telefonla konuştum bile.*
Turkish TPT	*Yataktan zar zor çıktım ve telefondayım.*
Reason	Incorrect use of past tense suffix ('-tum') instead of present tense suffix ('yorum')
	Repetition Issues
English	*Specific criteria, such as an asteroid's size and collision angle, are the factors that would determine the depth of its crater and the damage that its impact would cause.*
Turkish Transformer	*Asteroidin büyüklüğü ve çarpışma açısı gibi belli kriterler, kraterin derinliğini belirleyecek ve etkisinin yaratacağı hasarı belirleyecek faktörler*
Turkish TPT	*Bir asteroidin büyüklüğü ve çarpışma açısı gibi belirli kriterler, kraterinin derinliğini ve etkisinin yol açacağı hasarı belirleyecek faktörler*
Reason	The word "belirleyecek" is repeated which is unnecessary in written-language but would be okay in spoken-language.

Table 11: Sample outputs from Transformer and TPT models showing issues relating to morphology, meaning preservation, tense and repetition.

A Comparison of Different NMT Approaches to Low-Resource Dutch-Albanian Machine Translation

Arbnor Rama rama.arbnor@gmail.com
Eva Vanmassenhove e.o.j.vanmassenhove@tilburguniversity.edu
Department of CSAI, Tilburg University, Tilburg, The Netherlands

Abstract

Low-resource languages can be understood as languages that are more scarce, less studied, less privileged, less commonly taught and for which there are less resources available (Singh, 2008; Cieri et al., 2016; Magueresse et al., 2020). Natural Language Processing (NLP) research and technology mainly focuses on those languages for which there are large data sets available. To illustrate differences in data availability: there are 6 million Wikipedia articles available for English, 2 million for Dutch, and merely 82 thousand for Albanian. The scarce data issue becomes increasingly apparent when large parallel data sets are required for applications such as Neural Machine Translation (NMT). In this work, we investigate to what extent translation between Albanian (SQ) and Dutch (NL) is possible comparing a one-to-one (SQ↔AL) model, a low-resource pivot-based approach (English (EN) as pivot) and a zero-shot translation (ZST) (Johnson et al., 2016; Mattoni et al., 2017) system. From our experiments, it results that the EN-pivot-model outperforms both the direct one-to-one and the ZST model. Since often, small amounts of parallel data are available for low-resource languages or settings, experiments were conducted using small sets of parallel NL↔SQ data. The ZST appeared to be the worst performing models. Even when the available parallel data (NL↔SQ) was added, i.e. in a few-shot setting (FST), it remained the worst performing system according to the automatic (BLEU and TER) and human evaluation.

Keywords: *Machine Translation (MT), Neural Machine Translation (NMT), zero-shot MT, pivot-based translation, Dutch-Albanian, NL–SQ, low-resource MT*

1 Introduction

There are more than 7000 languages worldwide, with over 40% of the languages being endangered with less than 1000 speakers. On the other hand, roughly 35% of the world population, close to 3 billion people, account for only 3 languages: English, Mandarin Chinese and Hindi (Eberhard et al., 2021). This language division results in an inequality in literary resources available per language. Languages with a significant amount of literature and speakers are known as high-resource languages in the field of Natural Language Processing (NLP), whilst languages that lack these resources are known as low-resource languages. Mattoni et al. (2017, p.2) define low-resource languages as "languages that have a low population density, are under-taught or have limited written resources or are endangered". These languages are, therefore, not properly represented through literary media, resulting in an insufficient amount of training data availability. One such low-resource language is Albanian.

Albanian is spoken by approximately 8 million people in the world, the majority of which reside in Albania and Kosovo where the language is native to (Kallulli, 2011; Pustina, 2016). The language, however, is not limited to Albania and Kosovo, but extends further into other parts of the Balkans, such as Montenegro, Macedonia and Italy as well as Switzerland, places where Albanian is recognized as a minority language (Kallulli, 2011; Prifti, 2008; Pustina, 2016). Both Prifti (2008) and Pustina (2016) discuss the impact of the Ottoman rule on Albanian literature, a period during which publications in Albanian were forbidden, resulting in little to no development of the written culture. As discussed by Prifti (2008, p.29), this led to a limited number of resources in Albanian, despite the vast number of speakers, books in Albanian were not commonplace until the late 19th century. The impact of which, bred a limited amount of Albanian sources adequately translated into other languages.

A lack of readily available Albanian training data makes developing Statistical MT (SMT) and NMT methods difficult, as these methods require significant amounts of parallel data between language pairs in order to create useful MT systems (Tapo et al., 2020). Additionally, parallel corpora are often times domain-specific, leading to poor performance when deploying MT models for translating material outside of the trained domain (Koehn and Knowles, 2017).

Access to knowledge is a key driver for developing countries to progress in terms of educational, scientific, and societal advancement (Psacharopoulos and Woodhall, 1993). As such, creating opportunities to acquire general knowledge in languages native to developing countries could accelerate the development of their population. One of the most commonly known contributors to online open-access knowledge is Wikipedia (Teplitskiy et al., 2017). However, in terms of accessibility there is a significant lack of articles in non-major languages. For example, there are over 6 million English articles and more than 2 million articles in Dutch, while articles written in Albanian only account for approximately 82 thousand articles.[1]

While the access to knowledge can depend on multiple factors such as, the ability to read and understand English, the access to a stable internet connection, the lack of Albanian training data for NMT models suggest that online literary resources in the language are scarce.[2] Being able to automatically translate Wikipedia articles to a low-resource language offers open-access knowledge to a wider array of people, while allowing these users to improve on the automatically generated translations. Consequently, these improvements can be propagated back to the NMT model, which can help translate future articles more accurately.

In this work, we compare a one-to-one NMT model and two low-resource NMT approaches to translation from Dutch (NL) to Albanian (SQ), a low-resource language pair. By automatically and manually evaluating the translations, we aim to provide insights into how accurately NL↔SQ models can translate. We furthermore explore how the addition of direct parallel NL↔SQ data affects the performance of the ZST model, since often small amounts of parallel data are available. The main research questions can be formulated as follows: (a) *"To what extent are low-resource direct one-to-one NL↔SQ, pivot-based and zero/few-shot NMT models able to accurately translate and how do they compare?"* and (b) *"How does adding parallel NL↔SQ data affect the performance of the ZST model?"*. The performance of the models is evaluated and compared using automatic metrics (BLEU and TER) as well by providing a more detailed human evaluation of 100 random sentences for all models evaluated by three native Albanian speakers.

2 Related Work

SMT and NMT require a significant amount of parallel data in order to produce accurate and fluent translations (Cheng et al., 2017). Advancements in hardware technologies, data augmen-

[1]https://meta.wikimedia.org/wiki/List_of_Wikipedias_by_language_group

[2]https://opus.nlpl.eu/

tation techniques, and deep neural networks, have led to the development of methods capable of translating low-resource languages, subsequently circumventing the need for copious amounts of parallel data (Tapo et al., 2020). As a result, low-resource MT models that use additional languages - also known as a pivot languages - to bypass parallel data between the source and target language have been introduced (Johnson et al., 2016; Ha et al., 2016; Tapo et al., 2020; Liu et al., 2018; Cheng et al., 2017). Traditionally, in the case of a lack of parallel resources, a translation pipeline would be constructed using an intermediate, high-resource pivot language. The pivot-based approach was widely used in the SMT method due to its "simplicity, effectiveness and minimum requirement of multilingual data" (Cheng et al., 2017, p. 3974). The challenge for NMT then, is the lack of large-scale parallel corpora available in order to create better translations.

Johnson et al. (2016) compare how implicit bridging functions in contrast to explicit bridging, for the sake of simplicity, implicit bridging will be referred to as ZST NMT and explicit bridging as pivot MT. Johnson et al. (2016) were the pioneers in showcasing the possibility of a ZST NMT without the use of a(n) (explicit) pivot language. The difference between implicit and explicit bridging is as follows, implicit language bridging allows a system to translate from a source to a target language without having prior training for a specific language pair (Johnson et al., 2016, p. 341). Whereas explicit language bridging requires an extra step where a source language is translated into a pivot language and then from the pivot is translated into the target language (Johnson et al., 2016). Some disadvantages of pivot MT are important to note, namely, a higher total translation time, and the potential for quality loss due to the translation to and from an intermediate language. Further, Johnson et al. (2016) use related languages to investigate the different types of multilingual NMTs, where this paper uses one pair of related languages and an unrelated language – Dutch and English classified as West Germanic languages and Albanian an Indo-European language yet classified as its own subdivision. For our experiments we use Transformers rather than Recurrent Neural Networks (RNN) (Johnson et al., 2016). As in Johnson et al. (2016), we use an additional token that displays the language of origin. A method which resembles Lakew et al. (2018)'s "language flag", where in the pre-processing step a token is embedded into the model so as to identify the target language a source is paired with.

3 Experimental Setup

3.1 Datasets

Parallel data for SQ↔EN, NL↔EN, and SQ↔NL is available in the OpenSubtitles 2018 corpus (Lison and Tiedemann, 2016) which contains movie and TV subtitles for 62 languages total.

Subtitles, from a linguistic perspective, are often referred to as "conversational domain" (Lison and Tiedemann, 2016; Lison et al., 2018). Lison et al. (2018) state that parallel subtitle corpora are used for a variety of NLP tasks, including translation research, conversation models and exploring properties of colloquial language.

Table 1, shows the amount of data files relating to each individual language available. It is important to note that between the OpenSubtitles 2016 and OpenSubtitles 2018 the amount of data increased by more than 25% for both English and Dutch subtitles (Lison et al., 2018). Where Albanian files saw an increase of less than 5%. This further confirms the idea of stagnant growth in availability for low-resource language data.

All data was preprocessed by: (i) removing special characters such as equal signs, dollar signs and pound signs for the sake of clarity they are exemplified here "$ € = ;#", (ii) filtering out long sentences (more than 150 characters), and (iii) tokenizing sentences on spaces and punctuation using the Moses tokenizer tool [3].

[3] https://github.com/moses-smt/mosesdecoder/blob/master/scripts/tokenizer/

Language	OpenSub2016	OpenSub2018	Increase (%)
Albanian (SQ)	3.0K	3.1K	+3.3%
Dutch (NL)	98.2K	125K	+27.3%
English (EN)	322K	447K	+38.8%

Table 1: Overview number of subtitle files for NL, EN and SQ in the OpenSubtitles 2016 and OpenSubtitles 2018 datasets, including the increase (%) of files.

Table 2 shows the tokens per language set. Table 2 shows the amount of parallel sentences obtained per language pair, and their corresponding number of tokens. In order to reduce the effect of differences in corpora sizes between high- and low-resource languages the Dutch-English pair was reduced to 2 million sentences from its original 37 million parallel sentences to match the English-Albanian corpora, as seen in Table 2. For the other language pairs (EN-SQ and NL-SQ), the maximum amount of data available was used. Additionally, the data was split 70/20/10 for training, development and testing. A batch of 100 NL-SQ sentences was sampled from the test set for human evaluation.

Language pair	Sentences	Tokens source	Tokens target
NL-SQ	1.6 M	12.4 M	13.2 M
EN-SQ	1.9 M	15.3 M	14.0 M
NL-EN	2.0 M	14.6 M	16.9 M

Table 2: Overview of the amount of parallel sentences and tokens available per language (pair).

3.2 Machine Translation Systems

Three Neural MT methods were trained and compared using the OpenNMT library (Klein et al., 2017): a one-to-one NL↔SQ model, a pivot translation model and a ZST/FST NMT model. For the implementation, we relied on the translation pipeline provided on GitHub by Shterionov (2018). For the Transformer systems we used OpenNMT-py.[4] The systems were trained for a maximum of 30K steps, saving an intermediate model every 1000 steps for 5 intermediate models. The options we used for the neural systems: number of layers *6*, size *256*, transformerff *2048*, number of heads *8*, dropout *0.1*, batch size *4096*, batch type *tokens*, learning optimizer *Adam* with $beta_2$=*0.998*, learning rate *2*. The Transformers have the learning rate decay enabled and the training data is distributed over a single Tesla P100-PCIE-16GB GPU powered by Google Colab. We use settings suggested by the OpenNMT community[5] as the optimal ones that lead to a quality on par with the original Transformer by Vaswani et al. (2017). Sub-word units (Sennrich et al., 2015) were used to build the vocabulary for the NMT systems, mitigating the out-of-vocabulary problem. We used BPE with 50k merging operation for all data sets.

The simplest model, i.e. the one-to-one NMT, is trained on the NL↔SQ data set. For the two-step pivot MT approach, two one-to-one models were trained: an NL↔EN model and an EN↔SQ model. The pivot approach requires two models for a one-way translation making it the least efficient approach. The final model ZST NMT is trained on the same data as the pivot approach but uses a single NMT model to translate between NL and SQ instead of two separate models as illustrated in Fig.1. Tokens indicating the translation direction per language (<2EN>, <2NL>, <2SQ>) are added to the training of the ZST model, allowing the specification of the

tokenizer.perl

[4]https://opennmt.net/OpenNMT-py/

[5]https://opennmt.net/OpenNMT-py/FAQ

desired target language at generation time.

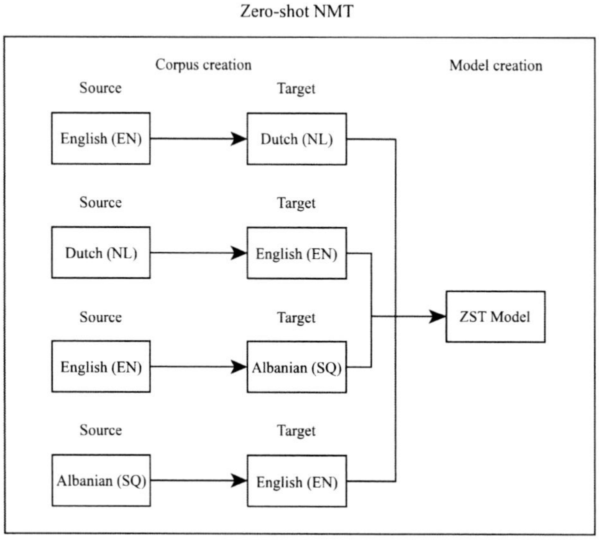

Figure 1: Zero-shot NL→EN NMT translation pipeline.

We additionally compare three ZST/FST models: ZST NMT, FST 50K NMT, and FST 150K NMT, where 50k and 150k of parallel NL→SQ data is added to the original ZST models, converting the system into a few-shot one. This way, we aim to measure the effect of adding the often limited available parallel.

3.3 Human evaluation

The human evaluation was conducted by three native Dutch and Albanian speakers that are also fluent in English. 100 sentences, varying in length, were sampled from the test sets of 1000 sentences. This evaluation serves as a supplement to the automatic evaluation methods, further analyzing bottlenecks missed by automatic evaluation metrics. The sentences were defined as either correct or incorrect. The correct section is divided into two categories: correct and correct without context. The correct without context section relates to generated translations being correct literal translations, or verbatim translations. These translations are highly dependent on the conversation topic, some translations can be considered accurate as they generate a sentence with the exact same wording as the source sentence. Yet, in some situations the generated translation may lack meaning as the context is not present in either the source, or the reference sentence. The incorrect section was divided into five error types: structural errors (word placement and sentence structure), missing words, incorrect word choice and incorrect language. The incorrect language category was introduced for analyzing the errors that occur during the transition of languages when using bridging methods.

4 Results

4.1 Automatic evaluation

As shown in Table 3, the highest performing model, according to the evaluation metrics, BLEU and TER, is the pivot model. Table 4 contains the results of the direct translations (NL→EN and EN→SQ). This table indicates how models perform on high-resource languages in comparison with low-resource languages. These values serve as a guideline to highlight how well the pivot MT performs on the basis of a low-resource language. As the pivot essentially combines the models in Table 4, into one model, it is beneficial to see how the performance is altered when running a pivot model from Dutch to Albanian, in contrast to the individual branches running directly.

Model	BLEU↑	TER↓
NL→SQ	13.68	0.65
pivot MT	**16.68**	**0.64**
ZST NMT	7.89	1.01
FST 50K NMT	10.98	0.96
FST 150K NMT	12.85	0.95

Table 3: Performance per model according to the automatic BLEU and TER metrics.

Model	BLEU↑	TER↓
NL→EN	33.41	0.46
EN→SQ	22.87	0.58

Table 4: BLEU and TER scores for the NL→EN & EN→SQ direct translations models.

As previously stated, this research compares three methods: one-to-one NMT, pivot MT, and ZST NMT. The pivot MT is the best performing method since both the NL→EN and EN→SQ (Table 3 and 4) achieve BLEU scores that indicate an acceptable translation quality.

While the ZST is the worst performing model, the addition of parallel data (50K and 150K) does increase its performance. However, this means that parallel data between the source and target language is necessary to produce acceptable results.

It is worth mentioning that while the pivot MT outperforms the one-to-one NL→SQ NMT by 3 points in terms of BLEU score, the TER score differs slightly. This matter could describe that while the NL→SQ produces less accurate sentences than the pivot MT, the number of edits required to transform the generated sentences into the reference sentences is close to equal.

4.2 Human evaluation

Table 5 gives an overview of the human evaluation in terms of correct/incorrect translations. Again, the pivot MT (NL→EN→SQ) appears to be the (overall) best performing system.

Model	Correct	Correct/Context	Total Correct
NL-SQ	62	8	70
pivot MT	63	13	76
ZST NMT	32	1	33
ZST 50K NMT	55	4	59
ZST 150K NMT	58	7	65

Table 5: Human Evaluation of 100 random sample sentences.

Table 6, shows the incorrect sentences from the human evaluation process. When it comes to spelling mistakes all models scored perfectly on this category and made no mistakes, this is due to the fact that the models base the spelling directly on the training data, meaning if there are no spelling mistakes in the dataset, the model will not make spelling mistakes on its

Models	Structure	Missing word	Word Choice	Language	Total Incorrect
NL-SQ	5	22	3	0	30
pivot MT	7	17	0	0	24
ZST NMT	5	34	9	19	67
FST 50K NMT	2	31	8	0	41
FST 150K NMT	4	28	3	0	35

Table 6: Overview of the detailed human evaluation, dividing the errors into different types: structure, missing words, word choice and language mistakes.

own. Incorrect language is only applicable to the ZST NMTs due to implicit bridging. In this situation the ZST model showed 19 incidents, within the selected 100 sentences, where words appeared in the wrong language, neither the source nor the target language, this issue is further discussed in the next section. This table also highlights the value of adding parallel corpora to the ZST model as it shows an overall improvement on the missing word error as well as the language choice error. Overall, the results strongly indicate to the pivot MT performing the best low-resource translation from Dutch to Albanian.

5 Discussion

According to the automatic and human evaluation, the pivot approach performs best, however, as evidenced in Table 4, adding parallel corpora to the ZST training data rapidly improves its performance. Low-resource languages often lack of training data and thus the ability to add parallel corpora may not always be present. Johnson et al. (2016), create a more promising analysis of a ZST model on low-resource languages, however, next to producing their own dataset, the amount of data available to Johnson et al. (2016) is far more substantial. Due to time constraints creating such a dataset and running it is out of the capabilities of this research. Additionally, Johnson et al. (2016) in contrast to this research, worked with single language pairs, operating with 255 million parameters per model, whereas this research operated on 55 million parameters per model, five times less the amount of Johnson et al. (2016).

A major point that requires addressing, is the difficulty of translating any language when the context is lacking. In this specific case the data used for the sentences came from movie translations, where context is inherently significant. Two examples that highlight the difficulty will be explored and discussed below.

NL Source	Het was verkeerd wat ze deden .
EN Translation	It was wrong what they did .
SQ Reference	Atë që kanë bër është gabim Valerie .
Pivot MT	Ishte gabim ajo që bënë ata.

Table 7: Translation generated by the pivot MT model for the Dutch sentence "Het was verkeerd wat ze deden."

Table 7 illustrates an example of a translation produced by the pivot MT model. The Dutch input sentence "Het was verkeerd wat ze deden." can be translated into English as "It was wrong what they did", a translation that closely reflects the word placement whilst capturing the message of the phrase. The SQ reference sentence provided, can be literally translated into English as "What they did was wrong Valerie.". The reference thus contains an additional word "Valerie" which is not present in the source. This could be due to the specific context in which this sentence was uttered. The translation generated by the pivot MT can be literally translated as "It was wrong what they did", a translation which not only follows the reference sentence verbatim but also carries forth the sentiment and message embedded in the sentence. This example illustrates some of the shortcomings of the automatic evaluation metrics while highlighting the importance of contextual cues and ambiguity in translation.

NL Source	Wat is oké ?
EN Translation	What is okay ?
SQ Reference	Çfarë është në rregull ? (EN: What is okay?)
One-To-One	Çfarë është ? (EN: What is?)
Pivot MT	Çfarë ke ? (EN: What's up?)
ZST MT	Çfarë është mirë ? (EN: What is okay?)

Table 8: Overview of translations generated by the one-to-one, pivot MT and ZST MT models for the Dutch sentence "What is oké"

This is, however, not the case for all sentences in a movie, as suggested by the examples in Table 8. This example highlights the importance of context in translation.

In Table 8, the ZST seems to generate the most accurate and fluent translation given the NL source sentence "What is oké?" (EN: "What is okay?"). The one-to-one model generates an incomplete translation while the pivot MT generated an incorrect translation. However, without any further context, and given the fact that the reference is rather vague, it is nearly impossibly to determine which one of those translations is the most accurate.

Finally, Table 6 presents the human evaluation of the models. In terms of the models this table reiterates the fact that the ZST model performed the worst in translating accurately. Furthermore, the ZST is the only model that made a language error, when translating from the reference to the generated sentence, some words came out in English rather than Albanian (see Appendix C: Sentence 13). This issue is explored in the Johnson et al. (2016) paper in relation to Japanese and Korean translation, by feeding a linear combination of the embedding vectors giving it a notation of 0 and 1. In the midst of the translation the model produces an output of 0.5, in some cases translating from Japanese to Korean, and in other instances with an output of 0.58 producing a mix of both languages resulting in an incoherent sentence, a situation that may be attributed to a difference in scripts. This investigation by Johnson et al. (2016) is relevant here as the multilingual ZST model used also resulted in some instances of mixed language outputs. In addition to the language error, the ZST model also performs the worst in terms of word choice in the generated translation, however, as posited in the second sub-question, adding parallel corpora improves the model accuracy. Overall, Table 6 restates the conclusion that the pivot-based NMT outperforms the other models when accurately translating Dutch to Albanian to the largest extent.

6 Conclusion

In this paper, three approaches to NL→SQ MT are explored: a one-to-one direct model and two approaches specific to low-resource settings, Pivot-NMT and ZST, including FST - where small amounts of parallel data was added to the ZST models. From our experiments it results that the pivot approach outperformed the others in terms of the automatic (BLEU & TER) and human assessment. Additional experiments were conducted where small amounts of parallel NL-SQ data was added to the ZST training data leading to improvements, approaching the results obtained using English as a pivot. Additionally, ZST/FST has some advantages over pivot-based MT in terms of efficiency as it only requires the training of one model. In future work, we would like to further explore how parallel data affects the performance of ZST models and experiment with different, morphologically richer pivot languages since English does not capture many of the specific linguistic properties of Albanian (gender, cases...).

References

Cheng, Y., Yang, Q., Liu, Y., Sun, M., and Xu, W. (2017). Joint training for pivot-based neural machine translation. In *Proceedings of the 26th International Joint Conference on Artificial Intelligence*, pages 3974–3980.

Cieri, C., Maxwell, M., Strassel, S., and Tracey, J. (2016). Selection criteria for low resource language programs. In *Proceedings of the Tenth International Conference on Language Resources and Evaluation (LREC'16)*, pages 4543–4549.

Eberhard, D. M., Simons, G. F., and Fennig, C. D. (2021). *Ethnologue: Languages of the World. Twenty-fourth edition.* Dallas, Texas: SIL International, Online version: http://www.ethnologue.com.

Ha, T.-L., Niehues, J., and Waibel, A. (2016). Toward multilingual neural machine translation with universal encoder and decoder. *Institute for Anthropomatics and Robotics*, 2(10.12):16.

Johnson, M., Schuster, M., Le, Q. V., Krikun, M., Wu, Y., Chen, Z., Thorat, N., Viégas, F., Wattenberg, M., Corrado, G., et al. (2016). Google's multilingual neural machine translation system: Enabling zero-shot translation. *Transactions of the Association for Computational Linguistics*, 5:339–351.

Kallulli, D. (2011). 9 albanian. In *The Languages and Linguistics of Europe*, pages 199–208. De Gruyter Mouton.

Klein, G., Kim, Y., Deng, Y., Senellart, J., and Rush, A. M. (2017). Opennmt: Open-source toolkit for neural machine translation. In *Proc. ACL*.

Koehn, P. and Knowles, R. (2017). Six challenges for neural machine translation. *ACL 2017*, page 28.

Lakew, S., Cettolo, M., and Federico, M. (2018). A comparison of transformer and recurrent neural networks on multilingual neural machine translation. In *27th International Conference on Computational Linguistics (COLING)*, pages 641–652.

Lison, P. and Tiedemann, J. (2016). Opensubtitles2016: Extracting large parallel corpora from movie and tv subtitles. In *Proceedings of the Tenth International Conference on Language Resources and Evaluation (LREC'16)*, pages 923–929.

Lison, P., Tiedemann, J., and Kouylekov, M. (2018). Opensubtitles2018: Statistical rescoring of sentence alignments in large, noisy parallel corpora. In *Proceedings of the Eleventh International Conference on Language Resources and Evaluation (LREC 2018)*.

Liu, C.-H., Silva, C. C., Wang, L., and Way, A. (2018). Pivot machine translation using chinese as pivot language. In *China Workshop on Machine Translation*, pages 74–85. Springer.

Magueresse, A., Carles, V., and Heetderks, E. (2020). Low-resource languages: A review of past work and future challenges. *arXiv preprint arXiv:2006.07264*.

Mattoni, G., Nagle, P., Collantes, C., and Shterionov, D. (2017). Zero-shot translation for indian languages with sparse data. *Proceedings of the 16th machine translation summit (MTSummit 2017)*, 2:1–10.

Prifti, P. R. (2008). Albanian literature. *Translation Review*, 76(1):29–31.

Psacharopoulos, G. and Woodhall, M. (1993). *Education for development*. Citeseer.

Pustina, B. (2016). Transmitting albanian cultural identity in the age of the internet. *New Review of Information Networking*, 21(1):24–36.

Sennrich, R., Haddow, B., and Birch, A. (2015). Neural machine translation of rare words with subword units. *arXiv preprint arXiv:1508.07909*.

Shterionov, D. (2018). Nmtscripts. `https://github.com/dimitarsh1/NMTScripts`.

Singh, A. K. (2008). Natural language processing for less privileged languages: Where do we come from? where are we going? In *Proceedings of the IJCNLP-08 Workshop on NLP for Less Privileged Languages*.

Tapo, A. A., Coulibaly, B., Diarra, S., Homan, C., Kreutzer, J., Luger, S., Nagashima, A., Zampieri, M., and Leventhal, M. (2020). Neural machine translation for extremely low-resource african languages: A case study on bambara. In *Proceedings of the 3rd Workshop on Technologies for MT of Low Resource Languages*, pages 23–32.

Teplitskiy, M., Lu, G., and Duede, E. (2017). Amplifying the impact of open access: Wikipedia and the diffusion of science. *Journal of the Association for Information Science and Technology*, 68(9):2116–2127.

Vaswani, A., Shazeer, N., Parmar, N., Uszkoreit, J., Jones, L., Gomez, A. N., Kaiser, Ł., and Polosukhin, I. (2017). Attention is all you need. In *Proceedings of the 31st International Conference on Neural Information Processing Systems*, pages 6000–6010.

Manipuri-English Machine Translation using Comparable Corpus

Lenin Laitonjam[1,2] lenin.lai@iitg.ac.in
Sanasam Ranbir Singh[1] ranbir@iitg.ac.in

[1]Department of Computer Science and Engineering, Indian Institute of Technology Guwahati, Assam, 781039, India
[2]Department of Computer Science and Engineering, National Institute of Technology Mizoram, 796012, India

Abstract

Unsupervised Machine Translation (MT) model, which has the ability to perform MT without parallel sentences using comparable corpora, is becoming a promising approach for developing MT in low-resource languages. However, majority of the studies in unsupervised MT have considered resource-rich language pairs with similar linguistic characteristics. In this paper, we investigate the effectiveness of unsupervised MT models over a Manipuri-English comparable corpus. Manipuri is a low-resource language having different linguistic characteristics from that of English. This paper focuses on identifying challenges in building unsupervised MT models over the comparable corpus. From various experimental observations, it is evident that the development of MT over comparable corpus using unsupervised methods is feasible. Further, the paper also identifies future directions of developing effective MT for Manipuri-English language pair under unsupervised scenarios.

1 Introduction

The performances of standard data-driven MT systems rely heavily on parallel sentences. Unfortunately, parallel resources are not readily available for most low-resource languages and specialized domains, as their generation is a very costly and time-consuming task. Manipuri[1], is a language spoken in the north-eastern states of India that lacks readily available large parallel sentences. Recently developed unsupervised MT models, called Unsupervised Statistical Machine Translation (USMT) (Lample et al., 2018; Artetxe et al., 2018c) and Unsupervised Neural Machine Translation (UNMT) (Song et al., 2019; Conneau and Lample, 2019), achieved remarkable results without using any parallel sentences. The ability to learn translation features without using parallel data will boost the progress of low-resource MT studies.

Despite the reported successes, the capability of the unsupervised MT to an actual low-resource scenario is still in question. Majorities of the previous unsupervised MT-related studies (Lample et al., 2018; Artetxe et al., 2018c; Conneau and Lample, 2019;

[1]Meitei Mayek is another script used for writing Manipuri. However, in this study, we are considering Manipuri texts in Bengali.

Song et al., 2019) are for combinations of high resource languages like English, German, French, etc. for which conventional MT works well and where quality monolingual corpora are also available in abundance. Studies in (Marchisio et al., 2020; Leng et al., 2019) have also reported that USMT and UNMT performances usually vary based on the similarity/difference of the source and the target language characteristics like quantity and quality of bilingual corpus, language branch, alphabet, morphology, etc. Not only Manipuri lacks a large-quality monolingual corpus, but the language is also highly agglutinative. It belongs to the Tibeto-Burman language group (Singh and Bandyopadhyay, 2010) and has a very complex morphological structure that is very different from English (Choudhury et al., 2004). The previous study related to unsupervised Manipuri-English MT has only exploited UNMT models (Singh and Singh, 2020). However, when considering resource-scarce languages, statistical machine translation (SMT) generally outperforms neural machine translation (NMT) (Dowling et al., 2018).

Motivated by the above reason, investigating the performances of both the USMT and UNMT models on the distant language pair is meaningful and challenging. To the best of our knowledge, this study is the first attempt to investigate the performance of the USMT model on Manipuri language. Empirical evaluation of the previous models show that USMT model outperforms UNMT models for the language pair. Monoses (Artetxe et al., 2018c), a popular USMT model, achieve the best BLEU score, followed by the UNMT model proposed in (Artetxe et al., 2017). However, more advance UNMT models, MASS (Song et al., 2019) and XLM (Conneau and Lample, 2019), fails miserably. Although the preliminary experimental results are encouraging, we observe that the direct adaptation of unsupervised MT methods on the language pair is associated with many critical issues. This study also provides an in-depth analysis of the previous USMT and UNMT models and investigates their strengths and weaknesses on the language pair. Furthermore, we also propose approaches that further improve the translation performance by (1) suffix segmenting Manipuri texts to alleviate the data sparsity due to its agglutinating nature, (2) weakly supervising the cross-lingual embeddings generation using transliteration pairs, and (3) generating phrase-table using transliteration models.

The rest of the paper is organized as follows. Section 2 discusses the related works. Section 3.1 and 3.2 provides a detailed description of the USMT and UNMT models respectively. Section 4 describe the proposed approaches. Our experimental setups are presented in the section 5 followed by the results and discussion in section 6. Section 8 conclude the study.

2 Related Studies

The majority of the previous studies that try to overcome the parallel sentences dependency problem exploited the monolingual data to enhanced the MT system trained on a few hundred thousand parallel sentences (Wu and Wang, 2007; Sennrich et al., 2016; Edunov et al., 2018; Rubino et al., 2020). As a result, apart from a few (Singh and Bandyopadhyay, 2010; Sing and Bandyopadhyay, 2010; Singh, 2013; Singh and Bandyopadhyay, 2011), MT studies for low-resource Manipur-English language pair is still in their inception. There are only a few thousands publicly available Manipuri-English parallel sentences (Jha, 2012; Bansal et al., 2013; Haddow and Kirefu, 2020), which are not sufficient for statistically motivated approaches.

Unsupervised MT has recently attracted lots of attention because of its ability to learn MT features from abundantly available non-parallel corpora. Unsupervised MT is motivated by the successes of word translation models developed based on the

Unsupervised Cross-lingual Embedding (UCLE) (Conneau et al., 2017; Artetxe et al., 2018b). UCLE forms the core of the unsupervised MT frameworks and is used for initializing the MT model. In this study, we systematically investigate whether the unsupervised MT methods apply to the distant Manipuri-English pair. Unsupervised MT can be approached by following either the SMT or NMT techniques. USMT (Artetxe et al., 2018c) follows the modular design comprising several models, whereas the UNMT methods (Conneau and Lample, 2019; Song et al., 2019) focus on training an end-to-end model. Each approach has its merits and demerits. A detailed description of the models is presented in the subsequent sections.

In the case of Manipuri unsupervised MT, to the best of our knowledge, study in (Singh and Singh, 2020) is the only available literature. The authors developed a UNMT for the Manipuri-English pair based on transformer with a shared encoder and language-specific decoders. They enhance the model by using a denoising autoencoder followed by a back-translation process, similar to the settings presented in (Artetxe et al., 2017). The models are fine-tuned using a few parallel sentences as a development set. However, in our study, we do not use any parallel sentences as we want to assess the applicability of the fully unsupervised models on the language pair.

3 Unsupervised MT models

This paper considers the following state-of-the-art unsupervised MT models.

3.1 Unsupervised Statistical MT

The USMT follows the standard statistical MT (Koehn et al., 2007) formulation of a log-linear combination of several models such as translation model, re-ordering model, word or phrase penalty, language model, etc., but in an unsupervised fashion. We consider the popular, Monoses (Artetxe et al., 2018c), as our USMT model representative as the other USMT models like (Lample et al., 2018; Artetxe et al., 2019) is also based on similar concept. Monoses follows a step-by-step training procedure. Firstly, a mapping between the source and target language embeddings is obtained by aligning the monolingual phrase embeddings to a common space using the Vecmap (Artetxe et al., 2018b). Secondly, an initial phrase-table is induced by using the cosine similarity of each source embedding with the mapped target embeddings. After the initial phrase-table induction, a preliminary phrase-based SMT model (PBSMT) (Koehn et al., 2007) is built by combining the initial phrase table, distortion penalty, and language model. Next, the initial PBSMT is then tuned by utilizing synthetic parallel data obtained from a non-parallel development dataset. Finally, the fine-tuned USMT model undergoes several rounds of iterative back-translation.

3.2 Unsupervised Neural MT

UNMT generally follows three main training steps: 1) Initialization, 2) Denoising Auto-Encoder, and 3) Back translation. Initialisation step, unlike the USMT, initialised the model itself following the NMT paradigm. Denoising auto-encoder improves the UNMT performance by introducing noise during learning phase. Then, the unsupervised features are finally fine-tuned by using iterative back-translation process. Initialization generally dictates the overall performance of the UNMT systems. Subsequently, various methods for effectively initializing the model has been proposed. Earlier UNMT studies relies on UCLE (Lample et al., 2018; Artetxe et al., 2017) for initialization of the word embedding layer in the encoder and the decoder. Later, they are succeeded by cross-lingual masked language models (CMLM) (Conneau and Lample, 2019;

Song et al., 2019). The CMLM initialised the entire the encoder and decoder of the UNMT. XLM (Conneau and Lample, 2019), motivated by BERT (Devlin et al., 2018) like pre-training, initialized both for the encoder and decoder, and achieved the previous state-of-the-art results on German-English unsupervised MT. Recently, authors in (Song et al., 2019) proposed a novel unsupervised model called MASS (MAsked Sequence to Sequence pre-training) that pre-trained the both the encoder and decoder jointly, enhancing the XLM model where encoder and decoder are pre-trained separately. In this study, we consider the UCLE-based UNMT model proposed in (Artetxe et al., 2017) and the CMLM-based UNMT models (XLM and MASS). The models performance are investigated on the distant Manipuri-English language pair.

4 Proposed Approaches for Handling Low-resource Scenarios

Majority of the studies considers bilingual dictionary between the target language pairs to generate cross-lingual embeddings (Artetxe et al., 2018a). Under a low-resource scenario, we may assume unavailability of such external resources. Motivated by this, this study exploits transliteration pairs of named-entities in place of bilingual dictionaries. The transliteration of named-entities is obtained using method proposed in (Laitonjam et al., 2018).

4.1 Weakly-supervised Cross-lingual Embeddings using Transliteration Pairs

The UCLEs in the Monoses are obtained by exploiting the intra-lingual similarity distribution of individually trained source and target language embeddings (Artetxe et al., 2018b). However, we approach the problem as a weakly-supervised by using the transliteration of named-entities to obtain the initial mapping between the source and target language embeddings. More specifically, we first learn two transformation matrices using the transliteration of named-entities as a dictionary to align the source language and target language embeddings into a shared embedding space and then iteratively refining them using the self-learning method (Artetxe et al., 2018a).

4.2 Phrase-table Generation using Transliteration Models

We investigate three different methods for generating the phrase-table in Monoses. Specifically, we re-score the phrase-translation and lexical probabilities using transliteration models (TMs)[2]. TMs enable the USMT to consider phonetic similarities between the source phrase embedding ($\overline{s}$) and the mapped target phrase embedding ($\overline{t}$).

1. *Re-score Lexical Weights(RS-lex)*: In this method, we introduce transliteration weights in place of lexical weights. The transliteration weights enable the model to exploit phonetic similarities, and are estimated using the TMs, as follows:

$$tns(\overline{t}|\overline{s}) = \prod_i max(\epsilon, max_j CA(t_i, TM_{S\to T}(s_j))) \quad (1)$$

Here, $TM_{S\to T}(x)$ is the transliterated word of the source word x using the source-to-target transliteration model (TM), and $CA(x,y)$ represents the character accuracy ([0,1]) between the word x and y. ϵ is a constant fixed at 0.3 (Artetxe et al., 2018c).

2. *Re-score phrase translation probabilities (RS-phrase)*: In this case, we modify the phrase translation probabilities ϕ_{ph} itself by incorporating the transliteration weights $tns(\overline{t}|\overline{s})$ as follows:

[2]Transliteration model converts a word from a source language to a target language by keeping the source language phonetic aspects intact.

Table 1: Manipuri-English News Domain Comparable Corpora. *Vocab* stands for vocabulary and *Seg-vocab* means vocabulary size on the segmented dataset.

Language	Documents	Words	Vocab	Seg-vocab
English	13408	5.79M	80855	80855
Manipuri	13177	5.62M	277406	165998

$$\phi_{ph}(\overline{t}|\overline{s}) = \frac{exp(cos(\overline{s}, \overline{t})/\tau)}{\sum_{\overline{t}'} exp(cos(\overline{s}, \overline{t}')/\tau)} * tns(\overline{t}|\overline{s}) \tag{2}$$

3. *Re-score both the phrase translation probabilities and lexical weights (RS-phrase-lex)*: In this method, we use the equation 2 for estimating the ϕ_{ph} and equation 1 for estimating the lexical weights alternative, the transliteration weights.

5 Experimental Setup

5.1 Manipuri Suffix Segmenter

Manipuri is highly agglutinative. Several new words can be formed by merely attaching prefixes and suffixes to a single root, leading to data sparsity. To normalize the agglutinative nature, we use a simple yet effective Manipuri suffix segmenter based on the popular unsupervised GRAph-based Stemmer (GRAS) (Paik et al., 2011) that segments Manipuri words into roots and suffixes before training the MT models. For example, words like ইম্ফালগী (for Imphal), ইম্ফালদগী (from Imphal), ইম্ফালদা (to Imphal), etc. are normalise by separating suffixes গী , দা and দগী from the root ইম্ফাল.

5.2 Dataset Description

We use a domain-aligned[3] Manipuri-English comparable corpus generated from news articles published on two of Manipur's leading newspapers: *Sangai Express*[4] and *Poknapham*[5]. The newspaper publishes dual edition in English and Manipuri. The articles from Sangai Express are published between January 2018 to November 2018, while the articles from the Poknapham are published between March 2017 to June 2020. The lower-cased English texts are tokenized by using the Moses Tokenizer[6], while a simple whitespace tokenization scheme[7] is use for Manipuri texts. A detailed description of the training dataset is presented in table 1. All the models are evaluated on a news domain Manipuri-English MT evaluation dataset, consisting of 1006 parallel sentences. The evaluation dataset is manually created by native speakers.

5.3 Transliteration Model Configurations

We consider the encoder-decoder based English-Manipuri transliteration model presented in the paper (Laitonjam et al., 2018) with attention mechanism (Bahdanau et al., 2015). The size of the hidden layer is fixed to 512 and embedding dimension to 256. The models are trained using the dataset presented in the study (Laitonjam et al., 2018). It consist of 4428 training transliteration pairs with 1000 development pairs.

[3]We consider the news domain.

[4]`https://www.thesangaiexpress.com/`

[5]`http://poknapham.in/`

[6]`https://github.com/moses-smt/mosesdecoder`

[7]Punctuation symbols are separated.

Table 2: Experimental results for preliminary experiments.

Methods	$En \rightarrow Mni$		$Mni \rightarrow En$	
	Non-segmented	Segmented	Non-segmented	Segmented
Conneau and Lample (2019) (XLM)	0	0.14	0	0.15
Song et al. (2019) (MASS)	0	0.18	0.44	0.23
Artetxe et al. (2017)	2.25	2.56	5.01	4.63
Artetxe et al. (2018c) (Monoses)	2.87	**3.13**	5.05	**6.37**

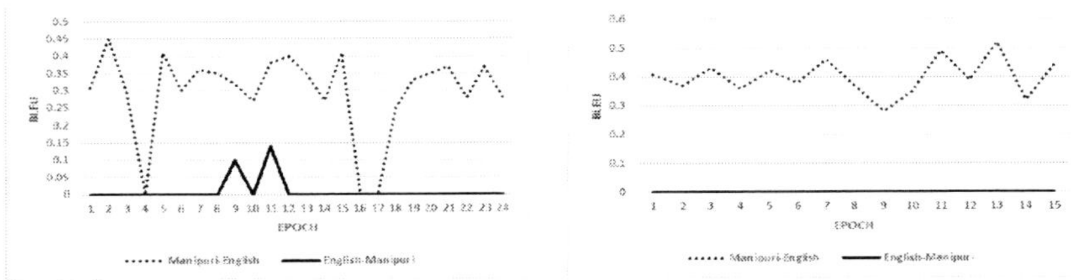

(a) Pre-training (b) Tuning

Figure 1: Training progress of the MASS on non-segmented dataset.

5.4 Unsupervised MT Configurations

For the UCLE-based UNMT model (Artetxe et al., 2017), we consider the original implementation[8] and default settings. We use the skip-gram model with ten negative samples to generate monolingual embeddings with size 300. Similarly, the hyperparameter of the XLM[9] and MASS[10] are set the same as in the studies (Conneau and Lample, 2019) and (Song et al., 2019) respectively. The embedding size is fixed to 1024. We jointly learn 60k sub-word units between source and target languages using BPE. However, unlike the studies (Song et al., 2019; Conneau and Lample, 2019) that uses multiple GPUs, we use only a single GPU with 12GB memory for training the model. In case of the USMT model, the Monoses[11], all model configuration settings are kept same as in the original work (Artetxe et al., 2018c).

6 Results and Discussion

Table 2 shows the translation results for our preliminary experiments. Here, *Segmented* represents the performance of the models on the segmented corpus. The segmentation is performed only on the Manipuri text using the segmenter presented in the section 5.1 to normalized the morphological infection issues of Manipuri language. Following the general practice, all the models are evaluated using BLEU scores (Papineni et al., 2002) as computed by the multi-bleu.perl[12] on the de-segmented outputs. It is evident from the experimental results that CMLM-based UNMT models (i.e., MASS and XLM) fail miserably for the language pair achieving less than 1% BLEU score on both the translation directions. Similar results were also previously reported in the study (Kim et al., 2020) for the distant English-Gujarati language pair. To further confirm CMLM-based UNMT models low performance, we evaluate the MASS at the end of each epoch during

[8] `https://github.com/artetxem/undreamt`

[9] `https://github.com/facebookresearch/XLM`

[10] `https://github.com/microsoft/MASS`

[11] `https://github.com/artetxem/monoses`

[12] `https://github.com/moses-smt/mosesdecoder/blob/master/scripts/generic/multi-bleu.perl`

Table 3: Experimental results of proposed models on segmented dataset.

Methods	$En \rightarrow Mni$	$Mni \rightarrow En$
Monoses	3.13	6.37
Monoses + Weakly Supervised	**3.50**	6.59
Monoses + RS-lex	3.37	6.41
Monoses + RS-phrase	3.29	6.35
Monoses + RS-phrase-lex	3.47	**6.69**

Table 4: Some translation examples. The first three rows shows the reference sentences. The final three rows represent the predicted outputs of the references.

	English	***Manipuri***
Reference 1	a charge sheet has been raised	চার্জ সিট থাঙ্গৎখ্রে
Reference 2	then prime minister , dr manmohan singh personally flew down to manipur	মতমদুগী প্রাইম মিনিষ্টর দাক্টর মনমোহন সিংহ মণিপুর দা লাকখি
Reference 3	academic career of the students	মহৈরোয় শিংগী একাডমিক কেরিয়ার
	$Mni \rightarrow En$	$En \rightarrow Mni$
Predicted 1	the charge sheet filed	অমা চার্জ সিতবু থাদোকউ
Predicted 2	the then prime minister dr manmohan singh put in manipur	অমুক হন্না প্রাইম মিনিস্তর , দাঃ মনমোহন সিংহ উনরগা flew তৌরগদি মণিপুর
Predicted 3	students and their academic career	মহৈরোয় শিংনা মহৈ তম্বগী

training. Figure 1 (a) and (b) shows the progress of the model in terms of BLEU score during pre-training and fine-tuning on the non-segmented dataset. It is found that the model never gets going. Apart from the distant language pair issues, the small training corpus size may also aid to this poor BLEU score. In previous studies, CMLM-based UNMT models are generally trained on very large corpora (in term of billions of words). However, such resources are currently not available for Manipuri. On the other hand, the UCLE-based UNMT model and the Monoses performs relatively better than the XLM and MASS. Monoses obtains the best BLEU score of 3.13 for En→Mni (English-to-Manipuri) and a score of 6.37 for Mni→En (Manipuri-English) outperforming the UNMT systems. Further, on comparing the performance of each models on *segmented* and *non-segmented* corpora to investigate the effectiveness of the suffix segmenter. It is observed that the BLEU score for both the translation directions increases on the segmented dataset in almost all the cases, except for the UCLE-based UNMT model and the MASS in $Mni \rightarrow En$, as shown in the table 2. This clearly shows that the segmenting Manipuri text significantly reduces the data spareness due to morphological inflections and improves the overall performance.

Table 3 shows the results observed after incorporating the proposed approaches presented in the section 4 to enhance the USMT model. We compare its performance with the original Monoses over the segmented corpus. It is evident from the results that for all the cases, except the *Monoses with RS-phrase* for Mni→En direction, the proposed methods outperform the baseline. Weakly supervising the cross-lingual embedding generation on Monoses using the transliteration pairs obtained the best result with 3.50 BLEU for En→Mni, while Monoses with RS-phrase-lex achieved the best BLEU score of 6.64 for the Mni→En. This shows that the proposed methods are able to exploit the phonetic similarity between the language pair.

Table 5: Monoses with RS-phrase-lex N-gram precisions along with corresponding BLEU scores

	BLEU	P_1	P_2	P_3	P_4
$Mni \rightarrow En$	6.69	33.8	9.1	3.7	1.7
$En \rightarrow Mni$	3.47	23.5	4.6	1.7	0.8

6.1 Error Analysis

To gain further insights, we perform an error analysis of one of the best performing model (*Monoses with RS-phrase-lex*) on the language pair. Table 4 shows some of the translation examples of the model. It is observed that the proposed model can generate unigram translations quite accurately. For instance, unigram translation pair (students, মহৈরোয়), as shown in table 4 (*Reference 3*), is correctly predicted for both the translation directions, as shown in *predicted 3* of table 4. Similarly, multi-word pairs like (prime minister, প্রাইম মিনিস্তর) are also correctly predicted. However, in most of the cases, the models fail to handle higher multi-gram translations, thereby leading to overall low BLEU score. The difference in BLEU score and the corresponding modified n-gram precisions P_n (n = *1,2,3,4*) for the model can also be seen in the table 5. The n-gram precision scores significantly decreases with increase in n. For instance, the uni-gram precision for $Mni \rightarrow En$ MT is 33.8%. However, the corresponding BLEU score is 6.69% only. We believe that difference in word order between the language pair is a major contributing factor to such a massive difference between the BLEU and n-gram precisions. English follows a Subject-Verb-Object (SVO) order in contrast to the Manipuri SOV order. As a result, the unsupervised model fails to handle the word order differences. For instance, in the $Mni \rightarrow En$ translation example, the order of the words *students* and *academic career*, shown in the reference 3 of table 4, gets interchange and is wrongly predicted as shown in the corresponding translation (predicted 3).

7 Future Research Directions

It is observed from the above observation that there is a potential for developing MT system for Manipuri-English language pair using comparable corpora, and may be a way forward to counter the challenges of creating sentence level parallel corpora. However, for developing such a system, we would need effective multi-lingual embedding techniques to develop effective bilingual dictionary, phrase-table, language modelling for post processing sentence correction etc. Further, we would also need to take care the dynamic writing styles followed in Manipuri. For instance, (জনুৱারী, জনুৱারি, জানুৱারী and জানুৱারি) are acceptable writing forms of the word *January*. Such a variation is inevitable for comparable corpora while the text are pooled specially from different sources.

In addition, from the P_1 performance in Table 5, it also evident that the translation performance can be further enhanced using post processing correction using methods like language modelling, NMT hybridization on the USMT model (Artetxe et al., 2019; Marie and Fujita, 2020), etc.

8 Conclusion

We develop a MT system for low-resource distant Manipuri-English language pair without using parallel sentences. Our study reveals that a relatively cheaper domain-aligned comparable corpora befit potential replacement of expensive parallel sentences for the language pair MT task. We also compare a popular USMT model with state-of-the-art UNMT models and found that the modular design of the USMT model is better suited for the language pair. Furthermore, this paper empirically shows that using a Manipuri suffix segmenter reduces the data sparseness issue due to the Manipuri text's agglutinative nature. Also, we found that weakly-supervising the USMT model using the transliteration pairs and transliteration models improves the translation performance. Though not with high performance, this work provides a stable MT baseline for the low-resource Manipuri-English language pair. We also offer several directions for future studies to encourage more research on this crucial problem.

References

Artetxe, M., Labaka, G., and Agirre, E. (2018a). Generalizing and improving bilingual word embedding mappings with a multi-step framework of linear transformations. In *Proceedings of the AAAI Conference on Artificial Intelligence*, volume 32.

Artetxe, M., Labaka, G., and Agirre, E. (2018b). A robust self-learning method for fully unsupervised cross-lingual mappings of word embeddings. *arXiv preprint arXiv:1805.06297.*

Artetxe, M., Labaka, G., and Agirre, E. (2018c). Unsupervised statistical machine translation. In *Proceedings of the 2018 Conference on Empirical Methods in Natural Language Processing*, pages 3632–3642.

Artetxe, M., Labaka, G., and Agirre, E. (2019). An effective approach to unsupervised machine translation. In *Proceedings of the 57th Annual Meeting of the Association for Computational Linguistics*, pages 194–203.

Artetxe, M., Labaka, G., Agirre, E., and Cho, K. (2017). Unsupervised neural machine translation. *arXiv preprint arXiv:1710.11041.*

Bahdanau, D., Cho, K., and Bengio, Y. (2015). Neural machine translation by jointly learning to align and translate. In *3rd International Conference on Learning Representations, ICLR 2015.*

Bansal, A., Banerjee, E., and Jha, G. N. (2013). Corpora creation for indian language technologies–the ilci project. In *the sixth Proceedings of Language Technology Conference (LTC '13).*

Choudhury, S. I., Singh, L. S., Borgohain, S., and Das, P. K. (2004). Morphological analyzer for manipuri: Design and implementation. In *Asian Applied Computing Conference*, pages 123–129. Springer.

Conneau, A. and Lample, G. (2019). Cross-lingual language model pretraining. In *Advances in Neural Information Processing Systems*, pages 7059–7069.

Conneau, A., Lample, G., Ranzato, M., Denoyer, L., and Jégou, H. (2017). Word translation without parallel data. *arXiv preprint arXiv:1710.04087.*

Devlin, J., Chang, M.-W., Lee, K., and Toutanova, K. (2018). Bert: Pre-training of deep bidirectional transformers for language understanding. *arXiv preprint arXiv:1810.04805.*

Dowling, M., Lynn, T., Poncelas, A., and Way, A. (2018). Smt versus nmt: Preliminary comparisons for irish. In *Proceedings of the AMTA 2018 Workshop on Technologies for MT of Low Resource Languages (LoResMT 2018)*, pages 12–20.

Edunov, S., Ott, M., Auli, M., and Grangier, D. (2018). Understanding back-translation at scale. In *Proceedings of the 2018 Conference on Empirical Methods in Natural Language Processing*, pages 489–500.

Haddow, B. and Kirefu, F. (2020). Pmindia–a collection of parallel corpora of languages of india. *arXiv preprint arXiv:2001.09907*.

Jha, G. N. (2012). The tdil program and the indian language corpora initiative. In *Language Resources and Evaluation Conference*.

Kim, Y., Graça, M., and Ney, H. (2020). When and why is unsupervised neural machine translation useless? *arXiv preprint arXiv:2004.10581*.

Koehn, P., Hoang, H., Birch, A., Callison-Burch, C., Federico, M., Bertoldi, N., Cowan, B., Shen, W., Moran, C., Zens, R., et al. (2007). Moses: Open source toolkit for statistical machine translation. In *Proceedings of the 45th annual meeting of the ACL on interactive poster and demonstration sessions*, pages 177–180. Association for Computational Linguistics.

Laitonjam, L., Singh, L. G., and Singh, S. R. (2018). Transliteration of english loanwords and named-entities to manipuri: Phoneme vs grapheme representation. In *2018 International Conference on Asian Language Processing (IALP)*, pages 255–260. IEEE.

Lample, G., Ott, M., Conneau, A., Denoyer, L., and Ranzato, M. (2018). Phrase-based & neural unsupervised machine translation. In *Proceedings of the 2018 Conference on Empirical Methods in Natural Language Processing*, pages 5039–5049.

Leng, Y., Tan, X., Qin, T., Li, X.-Y., and Liu, T.-Y. (2019). Unsupervised pivot translation for distant languages. In *Proceedings of the 57th Annual Meeting of the Association for Computational Linguistics*, pages 175–183.

Marchisio, K., Duh, K., and Koehn, P. (2020). When does unsupervised machine translation work? *arXiv preprint arXiv:2004.05516*.

Marie, B. and Fujita, A. (2020). Iterative training of unsupervised neural and statistical machine translation systems. *ACM Transactions on Asian and Low-Resource Language Information Processing (TALLIP)*, 19(5):1–21.

Paik, J. H., Mitra, M., Parui, S. K., and Järvelin, K. (2011). Gras: An effective and efficient stemming algorithm for information retrieval. *ACM Transactions on Information Systems (TOIS)*, 29(4):1–24.

Papineni, K., Roukos, S., Ward, T., and Zhu, W.-J. (2002). Bleu: a method for automatic evaluation of machine translation. In *Proceedings of the 40th annual meeting of the Association for Computational Linguistics*, pages 311–318.

Rubino, R., Marie, B., Dabre, R., Fujita, A., Utiyama, M., and Sumita, E. (2020). Extremely low-resource neural machine translation for asian languages. *Machine Translation*, 34(4):347–382.

Sennrich, R., Haddow, B., and Birch, A. (2016). Improving neural machine translation models with monolingual data. In *Proceedings of the 54th Annual Meeting of the Association for Computational Linguistics (Volume 1: Long Papers)*, pages 86–96.

Sing, T. D. and Bandyopadhyay, S. (2010). Statistical machine translation of english–manipuri using morpho-syntactic and semantic information. *Proceedings of the Association for Machine Translation in the Americas (AMTA 2010).*

Singh, S. M. and Singh, T. D. (2020). Unsupervised neural machine translation for english and manipuri. In *Proceedings of the 3rd Workshop on Technologies for MT of Low Resource Languages*, pages 69–78.

Singh, T. D. (2013). Taste of two different flavours: Which manipuri script works better for english-manipuri language pair smt systems? In *Proceedings of the Seventh Workshop on Syntax, Semantics and Structure in Statistical Translation*, pages 11–18.

Singh, T. D. and Bandyopadhyay, S. (2010). Manipuri-english bidirectional statistical machine translation systems using morphology and dependency relations. In *Proceedings of the 4th Workshop on Syntax and Structure in Statistical Translation*, pages 83–91.

Singh, T. D. and Bandyopadhyay, S. (2011). Integration of reduplicated multiword expressions and named entities in a phrase based statistical machine translation system. In *Proceedings of 5th International Joint Conference on Natural Language Processing*, pages 1304–1312.

Song, K., Tan, X., Qin, T., Lu, J., and Liu, T.-Y. (2019). Mass: Masked sequence to sequence pre-training for language generation. *arXiv preprint arXiv:1905.02450.*

Wu, H. and Wang, H. (2007). Pivot language approach for phrase-based statistical machine translation. *Machine Translation*, 21(3):165–181.

EnKhCorp1.0: An English–Khasi Corpus

Sahinur Rahman Laskar, Abdullah Faiz Ur Rahman Khilji
Darsh Kaushik, Partha Pakray, Sivaji Bandyopadhyay
Department of Computer Science and Engineering
National Institute of Technology Silchar
Assam, India
{sahinur_rs, abdullah_ug, darsh_ug, partha}@cse.nits.ac.in,
sivaji.cse.ju@gmail.com

Abstract

In machine translation, corpus preparation is one of the crucial tasks, particularly for low-resource pairs. In multilingual countries like India, machine translation plays a vital role in communication among people with various linguistic backgrounds. There are available online automatic translation systems by Google and Microsoft which include various languages which lack support for the Khasi language, which can hence be considered low-resource. This paper overviews the development of EnKhCorp1.0, a corpus for English–Khasi pair, and implemented baseline systems for English-to-Khasi and Khasi-to-English translation based on the neural machine translation approach.

1 Introduction

The Khasi language (also spelled Khasia, Khassee, Cossyah, or Kyi) is primarily spoken by people living in the region surrounding the Khasi and Jaintia Hills of Meghalaya state in India. It is a member of the Mon-Khmer linguistic branch of the Austroasiatic language family. Khasi is an associate official language[1] in Meghalaya since 2005. According to the 2011 census of India, there are around one million native speakers of Khasi[2]. Khasi has significant dialectal variation, some of them being Sohra Khasi, Mawlai Khasi, Pnar, Nongkrem Khasi, Mylliem Khasi, Bhoi Khasi Nonglung, War and Maram. Khasi has a subject-verb-object (SVO) sentence structure, similar to English but unlike most of the Indian languages Roberts (2005). Khasi contains several words borrowed from Indo-Aryan languages, mainly from Bengali and Hindi. In the past, the Khasi language had no script of its own. The Welsh missionary Thomas Jones[3], in 1841, wrote the language in the Latin script. As a result, the Latin alphabet of the language has a few similarities with the Welsh alphabet. Khasi in Latin script has a 23-letter alphabet.

1.1 Language Preservation

Every language is a unique perspective to comprehend the world by sharing its history, philosophy, and culture. Extinction of a language results in loss of historical, ecological, and cultural information and opinions. It may even affect its speakers' livelihood and existential mentality as they adopt the dominant languages to attain socio-economic benefit, tackle the scarcity of modern documentation and usage of the language, or mitigate the fear of discrimination. Therefore, the need to preserve such low-resource languages, including the Khasi language, is of significance. Machine translation (MT) helps in language preservation Bird and Chiang (2012). We have attempted to create a corpus and introduce it in an MT environment that helps document the Khasi language and preserve such minority languages by encouraging language usage and eliminating the linguistic barrier in communication.

1.2 Low-Resource Translation

In the domain of Natural Language Processing (NLP), MT deals with translation from one natural language to another. Further, Neural Machine Translation (NMT) is a state-of-the-art approach of incorporating artificial neural networks in MT systems. The data or resources for training the translation systems may include corpora from various online sources, native speakers, and

[1] https://www.indiacode.nic.in/bitstream/123456789/5467/1/the_meghalaya_state_language_act,_2005_(act_no._10_of_2005).pdf

[2] https://www.censusindia.gov.in/2011Census/Language-2011/Statement-1.pdf

[3] http://lisindia.ciil.org/Khasi/Khasi_script.html

computational resources. The Natural languages are categorized into three broad categories: high, medium, and low-resource. A language falls under the low-resource category when it has limited online resources Megerdoomian and Parvaz (2008); Probst et al. (2001). This categorization can also be made on the quantity of data required to train an NMT model Gu et al. (2018). According to Kocmi (2020), a language is considered a low-resource language if the number of training instances present in the corpus is below one million. Along with the corpus's size, the diversity of both language and structure is of importance too. Structurally, it must consist of all types of sentences, including short, medium, and long sentences. Different dialects of the same language might give rise to some inconsistency in translations. Therefore, the designation of a language as "low-resource" is not precise and requires consideration of many factors. Most world languages are categorized as low-resource on account of resource availability. In India, the limited MT works are performed on the northeastern region's low-resource languages, including Mizo Lalrempuii et al. (2021), Assamese Laskar et al. (2021b), Manipuri Singh and Singh (2020), and Khasi Thabah and Purkayastha (2021). We can consider the English–Khasi pair as a low-resource pair based on limited resources.

In this work, we have developed an English–Khasi corpus: EnKhCorp1.0 and built baseline systems based on NMT. There is no standard corpus available for the low-resource English–Khasi pair to the best of our knowledge. It is the hope of the authors that this resource fills that gap and leads to the development of more and better resources for the Khasi community.

The structure of the rest of the paper is as follows: Section 2 presents the overview of corpus preparation. Section 3 presents construction and evaluation of the baseline English–Khasi NMT system and conclude the paper in Section 4.

2 EnKhCorp1.0

This section overviews the corpus. Section 2.1 describes the contents of the corpus. Section 2.2 and 2.3 present the data extraction technique and domain coverage.

2.1 Details of Corpus

The available resource options for English–Khasi (En-Kha) parallel and monolingual data are limited. Therefore, we have explored different possible sources to prepare parallel and monolingual corpora. Table 1 presents some examples of sentences that were collected. The sources of data are reported below:

2.1.1 Parallel Corpus

- **Bible:** The Bible[4] is publicly available on the online in multiple languages, including Khasi. We have collected 26,086 parallel sentences from the Bible source using crawling technique.

- **Online Dictionary:** There are online dictionaries, namely, Glosbe[5], available in the multilingual form in which English–Khasi bilingual words and parallel examples are present. From Glosbe, we have collected 2,225 parallel sentences using crawling technique.

- **Learn-Khasi Website:** The website, namely, Learn Khasi online[6], is developed to teach essential words and daily usage sentences in the Khasi language. We have manually collected 120 parallel sentences from this website.

2.1.2 Monolingual Corpus

A standard monolingual corpus of English is available online: WMT16[7]. Therefore, we have focussed on the preparation of only Khasi monolingual corpus. We have collected 157,968 Khasi sentences from different web pages/blogs and added 25,836 Khasi sentences from the parallel data (train set) to increase the size of the monolingual corpus, totalling 183,804.

2.1.3 Corpus Analysis and Statistics

The collected raw data (both parallel and monolingual) are cleaned by removing unwanted symbols, URLs, many special characters (#####, ____, ..., $$$$), blank lines, etc. To keep the contextual meaning of the sentences, we did not remove punctuation marks. If we remove the punctuation marks, then it will alter the meaning of the sentence. Table 2 presents an example sentence having punctuation marks. In addition, long sentences

[4]https://www.bible.com/en-GB/bible/1865/GEN.1.KHASICLBSI

[5]https://glosbe.com/en/kha

[6]https://www.languageshome.com/English-Khasi.htm

[7]http://www.statmt.org/wmt16/translation-task.html

(more than 50 words) are split based on the punctuation marks (?.) at the end. It means a maximum sentence length of 50 words, we have considered. If the sentence length is greater than 50 words, then split it based on punctuation marks. Table 3 presents the overall data statistics. We have removed duplicate sentences from both parallel and monolingual corpora. After removing duplicates, the total parallel data reduced to 28,036 sentences. In order to do the experiment for the MT system, the parallel data needs to split into train, validation, and test set data. In Kunchukuttan et al. (2018), the English–Hindi parallel corpus was developed, and for the baseline system, they split the data by considering 99.79% data for the train set and <1% data for validation and test set. They considered most data for the training set and very few data for validation and test set. In our baseline system experiment, we have considered most data (92.15%) for the training set, 7.13% data for the validation and 0.71% for the test set. Table 4 presents the statistics of train, validation, and test set data. We have considered only 200 test data, since it is used for the baseline system. We will consider more test sentences in the future work. During the training process of a model, the train set is used for learning the parameters, and a validation set is required to verify the performance of a model to generate the optimum model. The unseen or test data is required to check the generated model.

Type	Sentences	Tokens	
		En	Kha
Train	25,836	664,385	830,393
Validation	2,000	42,725	67,474
Test	200	5,105	6,241

Table 4: Data statistics for training, validation and testing set

2.2 Data Extraction technique

We utilized Scrapy[8], an open-source framework for web crawling, to scrape the data from various online sources. The xpath of each element has undergone a certain degree of generalization coding to replicate multiple web pages. It helps to crawl numerous web pages and extract essential information. We first provide the URL of the web page. The Khasi raw text in the HTML files was extracted directly. The obtained Khasi monolingual data is kept as it is. However, the parallel data is aligned by separating them into source and target files. The process of alignment and verification took substantial human effort. Additionally, we collected parallel sentences manually from the : Learn-Khasi website.

2.3 Domain Coverage

The proposed corpus, EnKhCorp1.0 encompasses different domains, including religious material (the Bible), literature, daily usage, and common sentences.

3 Baseline System

In the area of MT, the NMT achieves a state-of-the-art approach for both high and low-resource language pairs Bahdanau et al. (2015); Pathak et al. (2018); Pathak and Pakray (2018); Laskar et al. (2019); Laskar et al. (2019, 2020b, 2021a). Therefore, we have chosen NMT to build the baseline system to estimate benchmark translation accuracy for both En-to-Kha and Kha-to-En translation.A sequence-to-sequence (seq2seq) model based encoder-decoder architecture is adopted for this work following the NMT baseline system of Laskar et al. (2020a); Kunchukuttan et al. (2018).

3.1 Experimental Setup

The OpenNMT-py[9] toolkit is employed to build two seq2seq models, namely RNN and BRNN. We have used two-layer long short term memory (LSTM), having 500 units in each layer with attention (Bahdanau et al., 2015). The default learning rate of 0.001 with Adam optimizer and 0.3 drop-outs are used. Moreover, GloVe[10] Pennington et al. (2014) pre-trained word vectors are used by utilizing the monolingual data. For English monolingual data, we have used 3 million sentences collected from WMT16.

3.2 Results

To evaluate baseline systems, we used the automatic evaluation metrics, namely, bilingual evaluation understudy (BLEU) Papineni et al. (2002), rank-based intuitive bilingual evaluation score (RIBES) Isozaki et al. (2010), translation edit rate (TER) Snover et al. (2006), word error rate (WER) Morris et al. (2004), metric for evaluation of translation with explicit ordering (METEOR)

[8] https://scrapy.org/

[9] https://github.com/OpenNMT/OpenNMT-py

[10] https://github.com/stanfordnlp/GloVe

Corpus	English	Khasi	Source
Parallel	After Jesus died, God restored him to life as a spirit person.	Hadien ba u Jisu u la ïap, U Blei u la ai biang ha u ïa ka jingim ba kynja mynsiem.	Bible
	We'll go to any length to send our child to a good university.	Ngin leh katba lah ban phah ia i khun jongngi sha ka iuniversity ba bha.	Glosbe
	How are you?	Kumno phi long?	Learn-Khasi website
Monolingual	-	Hynrei u wei na ki ba mynsaw u la khlad noh na ka daw ka jingmynsaw jur ha shwa ban poi sha Civil Hospital Shillong.	Web pages/Blogs
	-	Ha ka janmiet sngi nyngkong, ka kyhun ki pulit ka la hiar sha katei ka thain bad kem ïa kiba suba donkti ha ane ka jingjia shoh paidbhur ïa ki samla.	Web pages/Blogs

Table 1: Example sentences from various sources

English	Khasi
Jesus Christ himself said: "Do not marvel at this, because the hour is coming in which all those in the memorial tombs will hear his voice and come out."	U Jisu Krist da lade hi u la ong: "Wat sngew kyndit ia kane, namar ka por ka la jia, ha kaba kito kiba don ha ki jing tep kin ioh sngew ia ka jingpyrta jong u bad kin ia mih noh."

Table 2: Example sentence having punctuation marks

Corpus	Source	Sentences	Tokens	
			En	Kha
Parallel	Bible	26,086	684,090	866,326
	Glosbe	2,225	28,172	37,184
	Learn-Khasi	120	396	472
	Total Number of Sentences	28,431	712,658	903,982
Monolingual	Web Pages/Blogs/Bible/Glosbe	183,804	-	20,575,074

Table 3: Overall data statistics

Lavie and Denkowski (2009) and F-measure. For BLEU score evaluation, we have considered average scores up to trigram Laskar et al. (2020a). Table 5, 6 and 7 present the results of baseline systems.

Translation	BLEU		TER (%)	
	RNN	BRNN	RNN	BRNN
En-to-Kha	14.87	14.88	83.90	83.42
Kha-to-En	11.28	12.77	86.78	86.43

Table 5: BLEU and TER scores of baseline systems (higher the value of BLEU indicates better accuracy and lower the value of TER denotes better accuracy)

3.3 Analysis

From Table 5, 6 and 7, it is noticed that En-to-Kha translation accuracy is higher than Kha-to-En. It is because parallel data contains more Kha tokens than En, and thus, the model encodes a larger amount of token information and the decoder can produce a better translation in the case of En-to-Kha. Also, it is observed that the BRNN model outperforms the RNN model in both directions of translation. The BRNN model achieves BLEU, RIBES, METEOR and F-measure scores:(14.88, 12.77), (0.499622, 0.457185), (0.183745, 0.170957) and (0.433188, 0.392752) for En-to-Kha and Kha-to-En translation respectively. Also, the BRNN model attains better TER and WER scores: (83.42%, 86.43%), (83.59%, 90.30%) for both directions of translation. In the case of TER and WER, lower values indicate higher accuracy.

4 Conclusion and Future Work

This paper presents EnKhCorp1.0, where we have developed a parallel corpus of English–Khasi parallel and Khasi monolingual data. It can be used in various NLP tasks, including MT. The dataset will be publicly available here: `https://github.com/cnlp-nits/EnKhCorp1.0` along with necessary licence agreement. By utilizing this corpus, we have built NMT baseline systems for translation to and from Khasi. We will increase the corpus size in the future and perform more experiments with advanced deep learning techniques to improve translation accuracy.

Acknowledgement

We would like to thank Center for Natural Language Processing (CNLP) and Department of Computer Science and Engineering at National Institute of Technology, Silchar, India for providing the requisite support and infrastructure to execute this work.

Translation	RIBES		WER (%)	
	RNN	BRNN	RNN	BRNN
En-to-Kha	0.426957	0.499622	83.96	83.59
Kha-to-En	0.414650	0.457185	90.34	90.30

Table 6: RIBES and WER scores of baseline systems (higher the value of RIBES indicates better accuracy and lower the value of WER denotes better accuracy)

Translation	METEOR		F-measure	
	RNN	BRNN	RNN	BRNN
En-to-Kha	0.183013	0.183745	0.432489	0.433188
Kha-to-En	0.154466	0.170957	0.366319	0.392752

Table 7: METEOR and F-measure scores of baseline systems (higher the value of METEOR and F-measure indicate better accuracy

References

Dzmitry Bahdanau, Kyunghyun Cho, and Yoshua Bengio. 2015. Neural machine translation by jointly learning to align and translate. In *3rd International Conference on Learning Representations, ICLR 2015, San Diego, CA, USA, May 7-9, 2015, Conference Track Proceedings*.

Steven Bird and David Chiang. 2012. Machine translation for language preservation. In *Proceedings of COLING 2012: Posters*, pages 125–134, Mumbai, India. The COLING 2012 Organizing Committee.

Jiatao Gu, Hany Hassan, Jacob Devlin, and Victor O.K. Li. 2018. Universal neural machine translation for extremely low resource languages. In *Proceedings of the 2018 Conference of the North American Chapter of the Association for Computational Linguistics: Human Language Technologies, Volume 1 (Long Papers)*, pages 344–354, New Orleans, Louisiana. Association for Computational Linguistics.

Hideki Isozaki, Tsutomu Hirao, Kevin Duh, Katsuhito Sudoh, and Hajime Tsukada. 2010. Automatic evaluation of translation quality for distant language pairs. In *Proceedings of the 2010 Conference on Empirical Methods in Natural Language Processing*, pages 944–952.

Tom Kocmi. 2020. Exploring benefits of transfer learning in neural machine translation.

Anoop Kunchukuttan, Pratik Mehta, and Pushpak Bhattacharyya. 2018. The IIT Bombay English-Hindi parallel corpus. In *Proceedings of the Eleventh International Conference on Language Resources and Evaluation (LREC 2018)*, Miyazaki, Japan. European Language Resources Association (ELRA).

Candy Lalrempuii, Badal Soni, and Partha Pakray. 2021. An improved english-to-mizo neural machine translation. *Transactions on Asian and Low-Resource Language Information Processing*, 20(4):1–21.

S. R. Laskar, A. Dutta, P. Pakray, and S. Bandyopadhyay. 2019. Neural machine translation: English to hindi. In *2019 IEEE Conference on Information and Communication Technology*, pages 1–6.

Sahinur Rahman Laskar, Abdullah Faiz Ur Rahman Khilji, Partha Pakray, and Sivaji Bandyopadhyay. 2020a. Enascorp1. 0: English-assamese corpus. In *Proceedings of the 3rd Workshop on Technologies for MT of Low Resource Languages*, pages 62–68.

Sahinur Rahman Laskar, Abdullah Faiz Ur Rahman Khilji, Partha Pakray, and Sivaji Bandyopadhyay. 2020b. Hindi-Marathi cross lingual model. In *Proceedings of the Fifth Conference on Machine Translation*, pages 396–401, Online. Association for Computational Linguistics.

Sahinur Rahman Laskar, Partha Pakray, and Sivaji Bandyopadhyay. 2019. Neural machine translation: Hindi-Nepali. In *Proceedings of the Fourth Conference on Machine Translation (Volume 3: Shared Task Papers, Day 2)*, pages 202–207, Florence, Italy. Association for Computational Linguistics.

Sahinur Rahman Laskar, Partha Pakray, and Sivaji Bandyopadhyay. 2021a. Neural machine translation: Assamese–bengali. In *Modeling, Simulation and Optimization*, pages 571–579, Singapore. Springer Singapore.

Sahinur Rahman Laskar, Partha Pakray, and Sivaji Bandyopadhyay. 2021b. Neural machine translation for low resource assamese–english. In *Proceedings of the International Conference on Computing and Communication Systems: I3CS 2020, NEHU, Shillong, India*, volume 170, page 35. Springer.

Alon Lavie and Michael J. Denkowski. 2009. The meteor metric for automatic evaluation of machine translation. *Machine Translation*, 23(2–3):105–115.

Karine Megerdoomian and Dan Parvaz. 2008. Low-density language bootstrapping: the case of tajiki Persian. In *Proceedings of the Sixth International Conference on Language Resources and Evaluation*

(LREC'08), Marrakech, Morocco. European Language Resources Association (ELRA).

Andrew Cameron Morris, Viktoria Maier, and Phil Green. 2004. From wer and ril to mer and wil: improved evaluation measures for connected speech recognition. In *Eighth International Conference on Spoken Language Processing*.

Kishore Papineni, Salim Roukos, Todd Ward, and Wei-Jing Zhu. 2002. Bleu: A method for automatic evaluation of machine translation. In *Proceedings of the 40th Annual Meeting on Association for Computational Linguistics*, ACL '02, pages 311–318, Stroudsburg, PA, USA. Association for Computational Linguistics.

Amarnath Pathak and Partha Pakray. 2018. Neural machine translation for indian languages. *Journal of Intelligent Systems*, pages 1–13.

Amarnath Pathak, Partha Pakray, and Jereemi Bentham. 2018. English–mizo machine translation using neural and statistical approaches. *Neural Computing and Applications*, 30:1–17.

Jeffrey Pennington, Richard Socher, and Christopher D. Manning. 2014. Glove: Global vectors for word representation. In *Proceedings of the 2014 Conference on Empirical Methods in Natural Language Processing, EMNLP 2014, October 25-29, 2014, A meeting of SIGDAT, a Special Interest Group of the ACL*, pages 1532–1543, Doha, Qatar. ACL.

Katharina Probst, R. Brown, J. Carbonell, A. Lavie, Lori S. Levin, and Erik Peterson. 2001. Design and implementation of controlled elicitation for machine translation of low-density languages.

Hugh Roberts. 2005. *A grammar of the Khasi language*. Mittal publications.

Salam Michael Singh and Thoudam Doren Singh. 2020. Unsupervised neural machine translation for english and manipuri. In *Proceedings of the 3rd Workshop on Technologies for MT of Low Resource Languages*, pages 69–78.

Matthew Snover, Bonnie Dorr, Richard Schwartz, Linnea Micciulla, and John Makhoul. 2006. A study of translation edit rate with targeted human annotation. In *In Proceedings of Association for Machine Translation in the Americas*, pages 223–231.

N Donald Jefferson Thabah and Bipul Syam Purkayastha. 2021. Low resource neural machine translation from english to khasi: A transformer-based approach. In *Proceedings of the International Conference on Computing and Communication Systems: I3CS 2020, NEHU, Shillong, India*, volume 170, page 3. Springer.

Zero-Shot Neural Machine Translation with Self-Learning Cycle

Surafel M. Lakew[†] **Matteo Negri** **Marco Turchi**
[†]University of Trento, Fondazione Bruno Kessler, Trento, Italy
{lakew,negri,turchi}@fbk.eu

Abstract

Neural Machine Translation (NMT) approaches employing monolingual data are showing steady improvements in resource-rich conditions. However, evaluations using real-world low-resource languages still result in unsatisfactory performance. This work proposes a novel *zero-shot* NMT modeling approach that learns without the now-standard assumption of a *pivot* language sharing parallel data with the zero-shot *source* and *target* languages. Our approach is based on three stages: *initialization* from any pre-trained NMT model observing at least the target language, *augmentation* of source sides leveraging target monolingual data, and *learning* to optimize the initial model to the zero-shot pair, where the latter two constitute a self-learning cycle. Empirical findings involving four diverse (in terms of a language family, script and relatedness) zero-shot pairs show the effectiveness of our approach with up to +5.93 BLEU improvement against a supervised bilingual baseline. Compared to unsupervised NMT, consistent improvements are observed even in a domain-mismatch setting, attesting to the usability of our method.

1 Introduction

Since the introduction of NMT (Sutskever et al., 2014; Bahdanau et al., 2014), model learning using unlabeled (*monolingual*) data is increasingly gaining ground. Undoubtedly, the main motivating factor to explore beyond *supervised* learning is the lack of enough (*parallel*) examples, a performance bottleneck regardless of the underlying architecture (Koehn and Knowles, 2017). A fairly successful approach using monolingual data is the *semi-supervised* learning with back-translation (Sennrich et al., 2015), particularly if the initial supervised model is good enough for augmenting quality pseudo-bitext (Poncelas et al., 2018; Ott et al., 2018; Caswell et al., 2019). Moreover, back-translation showed to be a core element of new monolingual based approaches. These include zero-shot NMT (Lakew et al., 2017; Gu et al., 2019; Currey and Heafield, 2019), which relies on a multilingual model (Johnson et al., 2017; Ha et al., 2016) (Fig. 1b) and unsupervised NMT, which initializes from pre-trained embeddings (Lample et al., 2018; Artetxe et al., 2018) or cross-lingual language model (Lample and Conneau, 2019) (Fig. 1d). At least two observations can be made on the approaches that leverage monolingual data: *i*) they require high-quality and comparable monolingual examples, and *ii*) they show poor performance on real-world zero-resource language pairs (ZRPs)[1] (Neubig and Hu, 2018; Guzmán et al., 2019).

To overcome these problems, in this work we propose a zero-shot modeling approach (Fig. 1c) to translate from an unseen *source* language U to a *target* language T that has only been

[†]Work conducted when the author was at FBK.

[1]ZRP: a language pair with only monolingual data available, alternatively called Zero-Shot Pair (ZSP).

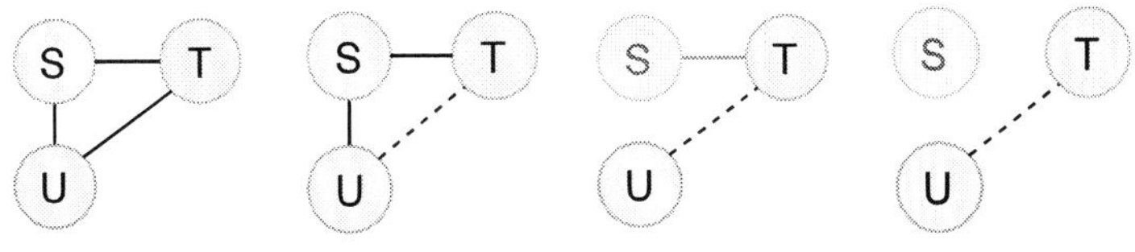

(a) Multilingual (b) Zero-Shot (c) Zero-Shot (d) Unsupervised

Figure 1: Proposed Zero-Shot (*c*) and existing NMT modeling approaches, using parallel (*solid line*) and monolingual (*broken line*) data.

observed by a model pre-trained on (S, T) parallel data (S being a different source language). In literature, zero-shot NMT has been investigated under the assumption that (U, P) and (P, T) parallel data involving a *pivot* language P are available for pre-training (Fig. 1b) (Johnson et al., 2017; Ha et al., 2016). However, most of the +7, 000 currently spoken languages do not exhibit any parallel data with a common P language. *This calls for new techniques to achieve zero-shot NMT by reducing the requirements of the pivoting-based method.*

To this aim, our approach follows a self-learning cycle, by first translating in the *primal* zero-shot direction $U \rightarrow T$ with a model pre-trained on (*S, T*) parallel data that has never seen U during training. Then, the generated translations are used as a pseudo-bitext to learn a model for the *dual* $T \rightarrow U$ translation direction. This inference-learning cycle is iterated, alternating the dual and primal zero-shot directions until convergence of the $U \leftrightarrow T$ zero-shot model.

Through experiments on data covering eight language directions, we demonstrate the effectiveness of our approach in the ZRP scenario. In particular, we report significant improvements compared to both a *supervised* model trained in low-resource conditions (up to $+5.93$ BLEU) and an *unsupervised* one exploiting large multilingual corpora (up to $+5.23$ BLEU).
Our contributions can be summarized as follows:

- We propose a new variant of zero-shot NMT, which reduces the requirements of previous pivoting-based methods. Our approach enables incorporating an unseen zero-resource language U, with no need of pre-training on parallel data involving U.
- We empirically evaluate our approach on diverse language directions and in a real-world zero-resource scenario, a testing condition disregarded in previous literature.
- We provide a rigorous comparison against unsupervised neural machine translation, by testing our models in an in-domain, out-of-domain, and source to target domain mismatch scenarios.

2 Zero-Shot Translation

From a broad perspective, ZST research is moving in three directions, (*i*) improving translation quality by employing ZST specific objectives (Chen et al., 2017; Lu et al., 2018; Blackwood et al., 2018; Al-Shedivat and Parikh, 2019; Arivazhagan et al., 2019a; Pham et al., 2019; Ji et al., 2019; Siddhant et al., 2020), (*ii*) training favorable large scale multilingual models for the ZST languages with lexically and linguistically similar languages (Aharoni et al., 2019; Arivazhagan et al., 2019b), and (*iii*) incrementally learning better model for the ZST directions with self-learning objectives (Lakew et al., 2017; Gu et al., 2019; Zhang et al., 2020). The common way of employing *self-supervised learning* in ZST modeling is iterative back-translation that generates the source from the monolingual target to construct a new parallel sentence pair. In terms of performance, while (*i*) and (*ii*) fall behind, (*iii*) either approaches or even outperforms the two-step *pivot translation* approach ($S \rightarrow P \rightarrow T$).

Despite these progresses, current approaches make identical assumptions, namely: *i) the* reliance on a multilingual model, and *ii)* observing both the U and T zero-shot languages paired with the P language(s). However, in a real-world setting these conditions are rarely satisfied, hindering the application of zero-shot NMT to the vast majority of ZRP. Moreover, conditioning ZST on P language(s) creates a performance ceiling that depends on the amount, domain, and quality of parallel data available for the $S-P$ and $P-T$ pairs.

To our knowledge, a zero-shot NMT modeling between an *unseen-U* and T zero-shot pair, and without the P language(s) criterion has not yet been explored, motivating this work.

2.1 Zero-Shot Translation with Self-Learning

We propose a new zero-shot NMT (zNMT) approach that expands the current definition of zero-shot to the extreme scenario, where we avoid the established assumption of observing the zero-shot (U, T) languages paired with the pivot (P) language(s). Instead, we consider only the availability of monolingual data for (U, T) and a pre-trained NMT observing only the T language – a scenario applicable to most zero-resource languages.

To this end, with the goal of learning a zero-shot model covering the primal ($U \rightarrow T$) and the dual ($T \rightarrow U$) directions, our zNMT approach consists of three stages: model initialization, incremental data augmentation, and model learning. The latter two steps can be iterated over time creating a *self-learning cycle* between the primal and dual zero-shot directions.

2.2 Model Initialization

Different from conventional ZST approaches, zNMT can be either initialized from a bilingual or a multilingual pre-trained system (Algorithm 1, *line* 2). The only assumption we consider is the availability of the zero-shot T side at pre-training time. Hence, our initialization introduces relaxation to model pre-training, a direct consequence of removing the P language premise. Considering that U has never been observed, we analyze different pre-training strategies to build a robust zero-shot system.

Algorithm 1: Proposed zNMT

1 Input;
$U_m, T_m \leftarrow$ monolingual data of the ZSP;
TM $\leftarrow$ pre-trained translation model;
$R \leftarrow$ maximum self-learning cyle;
2 zNMT^0, $\leftarrow$ TM;
3 $D_{Pr} = \emptyset$; $D_{Du} = \emptyset$;
4 $r \leftarrow 1$;
5 **for** r **to** R **do**
6 $\quad T^* \leftarrow Primal\_Infer$ (zNMT^0, U_m)
7 $\quad D_{Du} \leftarrow (T^*, U_m)$
8 $\quad$ zNMT^1 $\leftarrow$ Train (zNMT^0, $D_{Du} \cup D_{Pr}$)
9 $\quad D_{Pr} = \emptyset$
10 $\quad U^* \leftarrow Dual\_Infer$ (zNMT^1, T_m)
11 $\quad D_{Pr} \leftarrow (U^*, T_m)$
12 $\quad$ zNMT^2 $\leftarrow$ Train (zNMT^1, $D_{Pr} \cup D_{Du}$)
13 $\quad$ zNMT^0 $\leftarrow$ zNMT^2
14 $\quad D_{Du} = \emptyset$
end
15 **return** zNMT^0

2.3 Self-Learning Cycle

In our scenario, we have only access to monolingual data for both the U and T languages, and the pre-trained model did not leverage $U-T$ parallel data during training. In this setting, after the initialization, the very first task is a zero-shot inference for $U \rightarrow T$ (*line* 6), to which we refer as the *primal* ZST direction. The goal of this step is to acquire pseudo-bitexts to enhance the translation capability of the NMT system for the $T \rightarrow U$ direction.

To this aim, when the primal inference is concluded, a learning step is performed by reverting the generated pseudo-bitext data ($T \rightarrow U$). zNMT optimizes the same objective function (Eq. 1) as in the pre-training or Eq. 2 if zero-shot training is performed together with other supervised languages pairs (*co-learning*) as in (Johnson et al., 2017). The resulting model is then used to perform the $T \rightarrow U$ inference (*line* 10), to which we refer as the *dual* direction. The data generated by the dual process is then paired with the data produced by the primal one and used in a new leaning step. Assuming that at each inference step our algorithm generates better quality bi-texts, we replace the dual or primal data (D_{Du} and D_{Pr}) produced at the previous round with the ones generated in the current round. For instance, during the training at line 8, we use the D_{Du} generated at line 7, while we keep the D_{Pr} generated at line 11 of the previous round.

This sequential approach alternates the primal and dual inferences (*lines* 6, 10) with a learning phase in between (*lines* 8, 12). The goal of this procedure is two-fold, first to implement a self-learning strategy and then to acquire more and better pseudo-bitext pairs.

Unlike previous work on improving zero-shot translation (Lakew et al., 2017; Gu et al., 2019), we focus on learning only a model for the ZSP languages. However, for a better analysis and fair comparison with multilingual supervised approaches, we further show ZNMT performance by co-learning with language pairs with parallel data (*such as incorporating the $S - T$ pair while learning the zero-shot $U - T$*).

An important aspect for ZNMT is how close is U to S in terms of vocabulary and sentence structure. Our intuition is that the closer the two languages, the higher is the performance achieved by the ZNMT. This will be explored in §4.

3 Experimental Settings

To build an experimental ground that defines zero-shot translation without the pivot language, we selected a real-world low-resource languages benchmark. In other words, we considered the data to incorporate multiple and diverse languages, including parallel data for building strong baselines and monolingual data to evaluate ZNMT. Moreover, our choice is motivated by the findings of Neubig and Hu (2018) and Guzmán et al. (2019), showing that monolingual-based approaches under-perform when assessed with real-world zero-shot pairs (ZSPs).

3.1 Languages and Dataset

Due to their low-resource nature, we use Ted talks data (Cettolo et al., 2012; Qi et al., 2018) for Azerbaijani (Az), Belarussian (Be), Galician (Gl), and Slovak (Sk) paired with English (En). The four pairs come with train, dev, and test sets, with a max of $61k$ and as few as $4.5k$ examples, creating an ideal scenario of low-resource pair (LRP). The parallel data of the LRP is used to build baseline models in isolation and in a multilingual settings. The same dataset has been also used in recent works in an extremely low-resource scenario (Neubig and Hu, 2018; Xia et al., 2019; Lakew et al., 2019).

For the approaches utilizing monolingual data, we take the non-En side for each of the four LRP languages as in-domain (IND) monolingual examples. For the En monolingual data, segments are collected from the target side of the respective $S-T(En)$ pairs. However, to avoid the presence of comparable sentences in the U and T sides of the ZSP, we discard segments of monolingual En if the $T(En)$ side of the $U - T$ and $S - T$ are overlapping.

For out-of-domain (OOD) monolingual data we extract segments from Wikipedia dumps, similar to Xia et al. (2019).[2] The collected data are de-duplicated and overlapping segments with the IND monolingual are removed. To create a practical real-world scenario that represents most of the ZRP languages, we take only the top 2×10^6 segments, aligning with the maximum number of samples that are available for the non-En languages in this benchmark. Statistics about the data are shown in Table 1.

[2]Wikipedia: https://dumps.wikimedia.org/

		Domain	Az-En	Be-En	Gl-En	Sk-En
		IND	5.9k	4.5K	10.0k	61.5k
	Parallel (Train/Dev/Test)	IND	671	248	682	2271
Sample Size		IND	903	664	1007	2445
	Monolingual	IND	5.9k, 174k	4.5k, 201k	10K, 174K	61.5k, 58.6
		OOD	1.85M, 2M	1.67M, 2M	1.9M, 2M	1.8M, 2M
U Language Property	Family/Script		Turkic/Latin	Slavic/Cyrillic	Romance/Latin	Slavic/Latin

Table 1: Languages and data statistics for parallel in-domain (IND) LRP, monolingual IND and out-domain (OOD).

3.2 Models

To test the ZNMT strategy and compare it against other approaches, we train the following models:

- **NMT**: trained with *supervised* objective using parallel IND data of each LRP.
- **sNMT** (semi-supervised NMT): trained with *semi-supervised* objective (Sennrich et al., 2015) with back-translation leveraging OOD monolingual data.
- **MNMT** (multilingual NMT): trained with *supervised* objective aggregating 116 directions IND parallel data (Johnson et al., 2017).[3]
- **uNMT** (unsupervised NMT): trained with *unsupervised* objectives (Lample and Conneau, 2019) leveraging IND and OOD data.
- **zNMT** (zeros-shot NMT): trained with proposed *zero-shot* modeling leveraging IND and OOD monolingual data.

3.3 Pre-Training Objectives

UNMT leverages a cross-lingual masked language model pre-training (MLM). We train the MLM following the (Lample and Conneau, 2019) settings, using both OOD and IND monolingual data of each ZSP language. Although ZNMT can be initialized from any pre-trained NMT model as long as the T language of the ZSP is observed (see §2.1), we devise three types of pre-training strategies for a rigorous evaluation and based on data availability:

- BITM – four bilingual translation models trained with $S \leftrightarrow En$ parallel data.[4]
- MUTM100 – a multilingual NMT model with 100 translation directions from the TED talks data, excluding the four ZSP and the pairs used for BITM.
- MUTM108 – a similar multilingual model with MUTM100, however, including additional 8 directions used for the BITM models.

The idea behind the MUTM100 and MUTM108 strategies is to check to what extent the presence of close languages to the $unseen\text{-}U$ in the pre-trained model can support the ZNMT approach. Note that, unlike in the MLM, all the pre-training for ZNMT utilized only in-domain[5]

[3] List of languages can be found in the Appendix.

[4] S is a related language to the $unseen\text{-}U$. The $S/unseen\text{-}U$ combinations are: Az/Turkish(Tr), Be/Russian(Ru), Gl/Portuguese(Pt), and Sk/Czech(Cs).

[5] Utilizing OOD monolingual data for NMT pre-training could be an advantageous and interesting direction to investigate, however, for this work we constrain to utilizing only IND data.

Id	Model	Pre-Train	Scen.	Az-En	En-Az	Be-En	En-Be	Gl-En	En-Gl	Sk-En	En-Sk
1	Supervised (NMT)	-	IND	3.60	2.07	5.20	3.40	19.53	15.52	27.24	20.91
2	Semi-Supervised (SNMT)	-	IOD	3.74	1.92	5.74	4.03	22.08	17.27	**27.85**	**21.24**
3	Unsupervised (UNMT)	MLM	IND	1.97	1.56	4.61	1.47	13.93	5.89	15.70	11.91
4			OOD	3.26	2.55	5.69	3.73	16.71	14.90	10.62	7.62
5			I-OD	0.88	1.18	0.82	0.90	5.06	2.78	6.39	7.28
6			IOD	3.97	2.57	5.57	3.78	20.23	17.07	13.77	11.43
7	Zero-Shot (ZNMT)	BITM	IND	8.86	4.87	4.42	3.45	23.57	18.17	17.89	14.08
8			OOD	6.76	4.45	5.75	5.16	17.28	16.97	9.13	6.74
9			I-OD	2.63	3.96	1.20	2.23	14.96	16.23	9.10	11.35
10			IOD	**11.38**	**6.28**	**7.36**	**6.35**	**25.46**	**21.09**	19.43	14.70

Table 2: Results from low-resource supervised and semi-supervised, and our monolingual based ZNMT in comparison with UNMT (Lample and Conneau, 2019) across the four training scenarios.

3.4 Training Scenarios

We define four model training criteria based on a real-world scenario for a ZSP, that is the availability and characteristics (*such as domain and size*) of monolingual data.

- **IND**: in-domain data is used both on the U and T zero-shot sides.
- **OOD**: out-of-domain data are used both in the U and T sides of the ZSP.
- **I-OD**: a scenario where we create a domain mismatch between the U and T side of the ZSP, by replacing the T IND with OOD data.
- **IOD**: a the mix of IND and relatively large OOD data is used on both U and T sides.

3.5 Training Pipeline

Data Preparation: we collect the IND Ted talks data provided by Qi et al. (2018) and OOD Wikipedia[6] data, and then segment them into sub-word units. We use SentencePiece (Kudo and Richardson, 2018)[7] to learn BPE with 32k merge operations using the IND training data, whereas for UNMT we also use OOD monolingual data.

Model Settings: all experiments use Transformer (Vaswani et al., 2017). UNMT is trained using the XLM tool (Lample and Conneau, 2019)[8], while for the rest we utilize OpenNMT (Klein et al., 2017).[9] Models are configured with 512 dimension, 8 headed 6 self-attention layers, and 2048 feed-forward dimension. Additional configuration details are provided in the Appendix.

Evaluation: we use the BLEU score (Papineni et al., 2002)[10] for assessing models' performance. Scores are computed on detokenized (*hypothesis*, *reference*) pairs. The checkpoints with best BLEU on the dev set are used for the final evaluations.

4 Results and Analysis

In Table 2, we asses the quality of various NMT systems featuring different model types (§3.2), training scenarios (§3.4) using bilingual BITM for ZNMT and MLM for UNMT pre-training.

[6]WikiExtractor: https://github.com/attardi/wikiextractor
[7]SentencePiece: https://github.com/google/sentencepiece
[8]XLM: https://github.com/facebookresearch/XLM
[9]OpenNMT: https://github.com/OpenNMT
[10]Moses Toolkit: http://www.statmt.org/moses

Id	Model	Pre-Train	Scen.	Az-En	En-Az	Be-En	En-Be	Gl-En	En-Gl	Sk-En	En-Sk
1	Supervised (MNMT)	-	IND	**11.37**	**4.98**	**18.36**	10.06	29.77	25.44	27.49	**22.72**
2	Zero-Shot (ZNMT)	MUTM100	I-OD	1.04	2.55	7.31	7.14	22.91	22.93	12.33	11.81
3			IOD	2.51	1.55	16.20	10.30	32.14	26.68	23.52	16.60
4		MUTM108	I-OD	4.14	2.38	10.18	9.00	26.45	25.34	20.26	19.69
5			IOD	9.19	2.75	17.26	**10.95**	**32.83**	**27.49**	**28.94**	21.53

Table 3: ZNMT when initialized from multilingual pre-trained models, in comparison with supervised MNMT.

We then show the effect of leveraging massive multilingual pre-training on the ZNMT performance (Table 3). Finally, we expand our analysis to co-learning ZNMT with supervised NMT (Table 4). A preliminary assessment of the experimental choices adopted for ZNMT can be found in the Appendix.

4.1 Bilingual Pre-Training

The first two rows of Table 2 confirm the results of (Sennrich et al., 2015) showing that semi-supervised approaches, which leverage back-translation, outperform supervised NMT systems. Moreover, the performance of both approaches strongly relates to the quantity of the available training data ($Gl - En \gg Be - En$).

In the **in-domain** training scenario (IND), our ZNMT approach outperforms the supervised low-resource NMT, except for $Sk \leftrightarrow En$ and $Be \rightarrow En$ ($rows$ 1, 7), demonstrating the effectiveness of our proposal in leveraging monolingual data. The advantage of ZNMT is further confirmed when comparing it with UNMT. In this case, ZNMT outperforms UNMT in 7 out of 8 language directions and it is on par on the $Be \rightarrow En$ language pair.

In the **out-of-domain** training scenario (OOD), despite the fact that UNMT utilizes $\times 10$ more OOD segments than ZNMT, our approach surprisingly achieves better performance than UNMT, except for $Sk - En$ ($rows$ 4, 8). Fig. 2 shows the effect of varying the amount of monolingual data during pre-training (BITM, MLM). We observe that UNMT is significantly affected by decreasing the size of the monolingual data and, when using the same quantity applied in ZNMT (200k), it achieves much worse performance (-10 BLEU points). Our findings clearly show the effectiveness of ZNMT in learning better with small monolingual data, a case applicable for most LRP and ZSP.

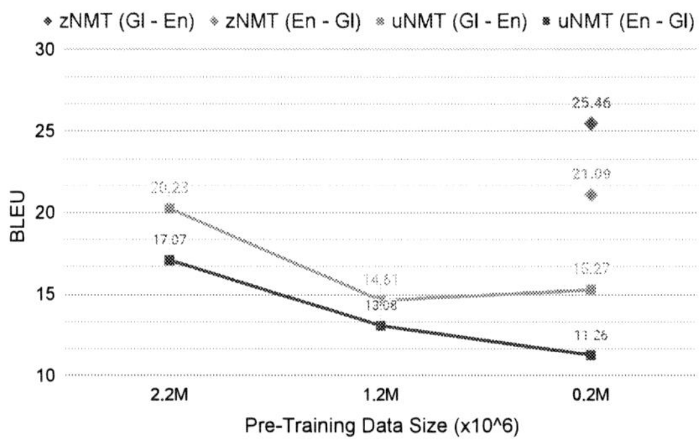

Figure 2: Effect of pre-training data size.

The **domain mismatch** scenario (I-OD) is the most realistic representation for ZSP and LRP settings, as it does not count on access to comparable monolingual data. Both ZNMT and UNMT show drastic performance drops in all directions (*rows* 5, 9), confirming the findings of Kim et al. (2020). Besides the performance drop, ZNMT shows higher robustness to domain shifts, resulting in higher scores. UNMT, in contrast, is susceptible to the domain divergence and requires comparable monolingual data that is hard to acquire for ZRP.

In the **mixed domain** scenario (IOD), ZNMT prevails over UNMT by a larger margin

Id	Model	Pre-Train	Scen.	Az-En	En-Az	Be-En	En-Be	Gl-En	En-Gl	Sk-En	En-Sk
1	MASSIVE	-	IND	12.78	5.06	21.73	**10.72**	30.65	26.59	29.54	24.52
2	DYNADAPT	MUTM108	IND	15.33	-	23.80	-	**34.18**	-	**32.48**	-
3	AUGADAPT	MUTM108	IOD	**15.74**	-	**24.51**	-	33.16	-	32.17	-
4	ZNMT + CO-LEARNING	MUTM108	IND	8.56	2.25	16.34	9.16	32.75	26.75	28.84	22.34
5			IOD	11.01	2.28	18.05	10.38	33.26	**27.64**	29.94	22.26

Table 4: Performance of ZNMT with co-Learning in comparison with the supervised MASSIVE (Aharoni et al., 2019) and DYNADAPT (Lakew et al., 2019), and semi-supervised AUGADAPT (Xia et al., 2019).

(*rows* 6, 10) ranging from +1.79 $(Az - En)$ to +7.41 $(Be - En)$ BLEU. This is a similar trend to the IND, OOD, and I-OD scenarios, validating the superiority of the proposed ZNMT learning approach. A more interesting aspect is that, except for $Sk - En$ (*rows* 2, 10), ZNMT also outperforms semi-supervised NMT. This shows that a stronger model can be learned exploiting as few as $200k$ monolingual data with our ZNMT learning principles, in comparison with a LRP performance (such as $Az - En$ with $5.9k$, and $Gl - En$ with 10k parallel data).

In sum, the results in Table 2 show that, for low-resource language pairs, ZNMT leveraging BITM can in most of the cases outperform supervised NMT trained on language-specific parallel data. Moreover, ZNMT is robust towards domain shifts from the pre-training and across $U - T$ ZSP, outperforming unsupervised NMT in all training scenarios.

4.2 Multilingual Pre-Training

To test the capability of ZNMT to leverage universal representation from the pre-trained model, we built two massive multilingual systems: MUTM100 that excludes the pairs used for BITM and MUTM108 that assumes a favorable condition by also including the BITM pairs.

Besides the initialization from the universal models, we train the best ZNMT scenario (IOD) and the most challenging one (I-OD) from Table 2 by only using the $U - T$ monolingual data. Table 3 (*row* 1) shows that the supervised MNMT benefits from the multilingual corpus (i.e., trained with 116 directions data including the zero-shot pairs), and, as expected, obtains improvements over the bilingual supervised models in Table 2.

In the **domain mismatch** scenario (I-OD), the use of BITM leads to large drops in performance compared to the IND or IOD scenario (Table 2, *row* 9). This is also confirmed when leveraging the MUTM* pre-training (*rows* 2, 4). However, the robust multilingual pre-training shows improvements compared with the initialization from BITM. For instance, the $Gl \to En$ with BITM drops -10.5 (from 25.46 with IOD to 14.96 with I-OD), while MUTM108 degrades only by 6.38 BLEU points.

Our approach leveraging the **mixed domain** (IOD) monolingual data with MUTM108 achieves the best performance in most of the language directions and is on par or even better with the supervised multilingual (*rows* 1, 3, and 5). This is a remarkable result because the ZNMT systems do not leverage any language-specific parallel data.

The advantage of using a **robust pre-training** can be ascribed to the availability of multiple languages that maximizes the lexical and linguistic similarity with the ZSP. Looking at the IOD scenario MUTM* in Table 3 (*rows* 3, 5), we notice an overall improvement over BITM pre-training (Table 2, *row* 10). A comparison against the best supervised SNMT model (Table 2) using low-resource parallel data shows better performance of ZNMT with MUTM108 up to (+10.75 $\leftrightarrow$ +10.22) for $Gl - En$. However, as for the BITM, it is not always the case to find closely related $S - T$ pair(s) to the $U - T$ ZSP for pre-training. Hence, it is rather more interesting to observe that ZNMT can learn even better with MUTM100 without observing the most related languages as in BITM.

With respect to the BITM, $Az-En$ is the only ZSP that do not benefit from the multilingual pre-training. One possible reason is the absence of related language pairs, which makes the pre-training representation dominated by other pairs. This becomes more evident (lower BLEU) when using MUTM100, a pre-training that excludes the closest $S-T$ pair to $Az-En$.

In sum, our approach shows significant improvements when leveraging universal pre-trained models. This is demonstrated by the large gains in performance in all the scenarios over the BITM pre-training. The fact that our method is able to approach the performance of the multilingual supervised settings, and in some cases to overcome them, makes it a valuable solution for ZSP languages.

4.3 Co-Learning with Supervised Directions

To test the complementary of ZNMT and supervised NMT, we add the parallel data of the latter only at the learning stage. Although it is possible to leverage multilingual parallel data, in this experiments we only utilize a single $S-T$ parallel pair from the BITM for the zero-shot co-learning stage of $U-T$.

We compare our co-learning system with three state-of-the-art approaches: MASSIVE trains a many-to-many system on all ($116 \leftrightarrow 116$) available pairs (Aharoni et al., 2019), DYNADAPT (Lakew et al., 2019) uses an IND criterion to adapt MUTM108 pre-trained model by first tailoring the vocabulary and embeddings to the LRP and AUGADAPT (Xia et al., 2019) generates pseudo-bitext from OOD monolingual and adapts MUTM108 together with the IOD data. The latter two utilize a similar co-learning strategy during the adaptation of the universal model with the parallel data, and reported results only when the target is En. Similar to MASSIVE, DYNADAPT, and AUGADAPT, we focused on IND and IOD training scenarios.

Table 4 reports the performance of these approaches and of ZNMT with co-learning using in the IND and IOD scenarios. Comparing ZNMT + CO-LEARNING (*rows* 5) with ZNMT in Table 3 (*row* 5), the results show that *co-learning* generally leads to better performance. However, when the target language is non-En, the differences are marginal and the two approaches can be considered comparable. This is directly associated with the fact that we have more En segments, from the aggregation of the $S-T(En)$ and $U-T(En)$ pairs. DYNADAPT and AUGADAPT are the two best performing supervised techniques on the this benchmark, but ZNMT with co-learning achieves competitive performance approaching them both in the IND and IOD scenarios.

Overall, these findings show that our approach makes it possible to extend zero-shot NMT to an unseen language U. In particular, leveraging a universal pre-training model and co-learning with supervised task allows our approach to learn a better NMT model from monolingual data.

5 Conclusion

We presented a new zero-shot NMT modeling variant, specifically targeting languages that have never been observed in a pre-trained NMT. We showed limitations of current approaches with the pivot language premise and zero-shot translation only between observed languages, and proposed a relaxation to zero-shot NMT to incorporate unseen languages. Our approach includes initialization, augmentation, and training stages to construct a self-learning cycle to incrementally correct the primal and dual zero-shot translation quality. We empirically demonstrated the effectiveness of the proposed approach using diverse real-world zero-resource languages in in-domain, out-of-domain, domain-mismatch, and mixed domain scenarios. Results both from bilingual and multilingual initialization not only revealed the possibility of extending zero-shot NMT for unseen languages but also improved performance over unsupervised, low-resource supervised and semi-supervised NMT.

References

Aharoni, R., Johnson, M., and Firat, O. (2019). Massively Multilingual Neural Machine Translation. In *Proceedings of the 2019 Conference of the North American Chapter of the Association for Computational Linguistics: Human Language Technologies, Volume 1 (Long and Short Papers)*, pages 3874–3884, Minneapolis, Minnesota. Association for Computational Linguistics.

Al-Shedivat, M. and Parikh, A. P. (2019). Consistency by agreement in zero-shot neural machine translation. *arXiv preprint arXiv:1904.02338.*

Arivazhagan, N., Bapna, A., Firat, O., Aharoni, R., Johnson, M., and Macherey, W. (2019a). The missing ingredient in zero-shot neural machine translation. *arXiv preprint arXiv:1903.07091.*

Arivazhagan, N., Bapna, A., Firat, O., Lepikhin, D., Johnson, M., Krikun, M., Chen, M. X., Cao, Y., Foster, G., Cherry, C., et al. (2019b). Massively multilingual neural machine translation in the wild: Findings and challenges. *arXiv preprint arXiv:1907.05019.*

Artetxe, M., Labaka, G., Agirre, E., and Cho, K. (2018). Unsupervised neural machine translation. In *Proceedings of the 6th International Conference on Learning Representations.*

Artetxe, M., Ruder, S., Yogatama, D., Labaka, G., and Agirre, E. (2020). A call for more rigor in unsupervised cross-lingual learning. *arXiv preprint arXiv:2004.14958.*

Bahdanau, D., Cho, K., and Bengio, Y. (2014). Neural machine translation by jointly learning to align and translate. *arXiv preprint arXiv:1409.0473.*

Bertoldi, N. and Federico, M. (2009). Domain adaptation for statistical machine translation with monolingual resources. In *Proceedings of the fourth workshop on statistical machine translation*, pages 182–189. Association for Computational Linguistics.

Blackwood, G., Ballesteros, M., and Ward, T. (2018). Multilingual neural machine translation with task-specific attention. *arXiv preprint arXiv:1806.03280.*

Bojar, O. and Tamchyna, A. (2011). Improving translation model by monolingual data. In *Proceedings of the Sixth Workshop on Statistical Machine Translation*, pages 330–336. Association for Computational Linguistics.

Caswell, I., Chelba, C., and Grangier, D. (2019). Tagged back-translation. *arXiv preprint arXiv:1906.06442.*

Cettolo, M., Girardi, C., and Federico, M. (2012). Wit3: Web inventory of transcribed and translated talks. In *Proceedings of the 16th Conference of the European Association for Machine Translation (EAMT)*, volume 261, page 268.

Chen, Y., Liu, Y., Cheng, Y., and Li, V. O. (2017). A teacher-student framework for zero-resource neural machine translation. *arXiv preprint arXiv:1705.00753.*

Cho, K., Van Merriënboer, B., Gulcehre, C., Bahdanau, D., Bougares, F., Schwenk, H., and Bengio, Y. (2014). Learning phrase representations using rnn encoder-decoder for statistical machine translation. *arXiv preprint arXiv:1406.1078.*

Currey, A. and Heafield, K. (2019). Zero-resource neural machine translation with monolingual pivot data. In *Proceedings of the 3rd Workshop on Neural Generation and Translation*, pages 99–107.

Dong, D., Wu, H., He, W., Yu, D., and Wang, H. (2015). Multi-task learning for multiple language translation. In *ACL (1)*, pages 1723–1732.

Firat, O., Cho, K., and Bengio, Y. (2016a). Multi-way, multilingual neural machine translation with a shared attention mechanism. *arXiv preprint arXiv:1601.01073*.

Firat, O., Sankaran, B., Al-Onaizan, Y., Vural, F. T. Y., and Cho, K. (2016b). Zero-resource translation with multi-lingual neural machine translation. *arXiv preprint arXiv:1606.04164*.

Gehring, J., Auli, M., Grangier, D., Yarats, D., and Dauphin, Y. N. (2017). Convolutional sequence to sequence learning. In *Proceedings of the 34th International Conference on Machine Learning-Volume 70*, pages 1243–1252. JMLR. org.

Gu, J., Wang, Y., Cho, K., and Li, V. O. (2019). Improved zero-shot neural machine translation via ignoring spurious correlations. *arXiv preprint arXiv:1906.01181*.

Guzmán, F., Chen, P.-J., Ott, M., Pino, J., Lample, G., Koehn, P., Chaudhary, V., and Ranzato, M. (2019). Two new evaluation datasets for low-resource machine translation: Nepali-english and sinhala-english. *arXiv preprint arXiv:1902.01382*.

Ha, T.-L., Niehues, J., and Waibel, A. (2016). Toward multilingual neural machine translation with universal encoder and decoder. *arXiv preprint arXiv:1611.04798*.

Ji, B., Zhang, Z., Duan, X., Zhang, M., Chen, B., and Luo, W. (2019). Cross-lingual pre-training based transfer for zero-shot neural machine translation. *arXiv preprint arXiv:1912.01214*.

Johnson, M., Schuster, M., Le, Q. V., Krikun, M., Wu, Y., Chen, Z., Thorat, N., Viégas, F., Wattenberg, M., Corrado, G., Hughes, M., and Dean, J. (2017). Google's multilingual neural machine translation system: Enabling zero-shot translation. *Transactions of the Association for Computational Linguistic*, 5:339–351.

Kalchbrenner, N. and Blunsom, P. (2013). Recurrent continuous translation models. In *Proceedings of the 2013 Conference on Empirical Methods in Natural Language Processing*, pages 1700–1709.

Kim, Y., Graça, M., and Ney, H. (2020). When and why is unsupervised neural machine translation useless? *arXiv preprint arXiv:2004.10581*.

Kim, Y., Petrov, P., Petrushkov, P., Khadivi, S., and Ney, H. (2019). Pivot-based transfer learning for neural machine translation between non-english languages. *arXiv preprint arXiv:1909.09524*.

Kingma, D. and Ba, J. (2014). Adam: A method for stochastic optimization. *arXiv preprint arXiv:1412.6980*.

Klein, G., Kim, Y., Deng, Y., Senellart, J., and Rush, A. M. (2017). Opennmt: Open-source toolkit for neural machine translation. *arXiv preprint arXiv:1701.02810*.

Kocmi, T. and Bojar, O. (2018). Trivial transfer learning for low-resource neural machine translation. *arXiv preprint arXiv:1809.00357*.

Koehn, P. and Knowles, R. (2017). Six challenges for neural machine translation. *arXiv preprint arXiv:1706.03872*.

Kudo, T. and Richardson, J. (2018). Sentencepiece: A simple and language independent subword tokenizer and detokenizer for neural text processing. *arXiv preprint arXiv:1808.06226*.

Lakew, S. M., Erofeeva, A., Negri, M., Federico, M., and Turchi, M. (2018). "Transfer Learning in Multilingual Neural Machine Translation with Dynamic Vocabulary". In *15th International Workshop on Spoken Language Translation (IWSLT)*, Bruges, Belgium.

Lakew, S. M., Karakanta, A., Federico, M., Negri, M., and Turchi, M. (2019). "Adapting Multilingual Neural Machine Translation to Unseen Languages". In *16th International Workshop on Spoken Language Translation (IWSLT)*, Hong Kong.

Lakew, S. M., Lotito, Q. F., Matteo, N., Marco, T., and Marcello, F. (2017). Improving zero-shot translation of low-resource languages. In *14th International Workshop on Spoken Language Translation.*

Lample, G. and Conneau, A. (2019). Cross-lingual language model pretraining. *arXiv preprint arXiv:1901.07291.*

Lample, G., Denoyer, L., and Ranzato, M. (2018). Unsupervised machine translation using monolingual corpora only. In *Proceedings of the 6th International Conference on Learning Representations.*

Lu, Y., Keung, P., Ladhak, F., Bhardwaj, V., Zhang, S., and Sun, J. (2018). A neural interlingua for multilingual machine translation. *arXiv preprint arXiv:1804.08198.*

Luong, M.-T., Le, Q. V., Sutskever, I., Vinyals, O., and Kaiser, L. (2015). Multi-task sequence to sequence learning. *arXiv preprint arXiv:1511.06114.*

Neubig, G. and Hu, J. (2018). Rapid adaptation of neural machine translation to new languages. In *Proceedings of the 2018 Conference on Empirical Methods in Natural Language Processing*, pages 875–880. Association for Computational Linguistics.

Nguyen, T. Q. and Chiang, D. (2017). Transfer learning across low-resource, related languages for neural machine translation. *arXiv preprint arXiv:1708.09803.*

Ott, M., Edunov, S., Grangier, D., and Auli, M. (2018). Scaling neural machine translation. *arXiv preprint arXiv:1806.00187.*

Papineni, K., Roukos, S., Ward, T., and Zhu, W.-J. (2002). Bleu: a method for automatic evaluation of machine translation. In *Proceedings of the 40th annual meeting on association for computational linguistics*, pages 311–318. Association for Computational Linguistics.

Pham, N.-Q., Niehues, J., Ha, T.-L., and Waibel, A. (2019). Improving zero-shot translation with language-independent constraints. *arXiv preprint arXiv:1906.08584.*

Poncelas, A., Shterionov, D., Way, A., Wenniger, G. M. d. B., and Passban, P. (2018). Investigating backtranslation in neural machine translation. *arXiv preprint arXiv:1804.06189.*

Press, O. and Wolf, L. (2016). Using the output embedding to improve language models. *arXiv preprint arXiv:1608.05859.*

Qi, Y., Sachan, D. S., Felix, M., Padmanabhan, S. J., and Neubig, G. (2018). When and why are pre-trained word embeddings useful for neural machine translation? In *Proceedings of NAACL-HLT 2018*, pages 529–535. Association for Computational Linguistics.

Sennrich, R., Haddow, B., and Birch, A. (2015). Improving neural machine translation models with monolingual data. *arXiv preprint arXiv:1511.06709.*

Sestorain, L., Ciaramita, M., Buck, C., and Hofmann, T. (2018). Zero-shot dual machine translation. *arXiv preprint arXiv:1805.10338.*

Siddhant, A., Bapna, A., Cao, Y., Firat, O., Chen, M., Kudugunta, S., Arivazhagan, N., and Wu, Y. (2020). Leveraging monolingual data with self-supervision for multilingual neural machine translation. *arXiv preprint arXiv:2005.04816.*

Sutskever, I., Vinyals, O., and Le, Q. V. (2014). Sequence to sequence learning with neural networks. In *Advances in neural information processing systems*, pages 3104–3112.

Vaswani, A., Shazeer, N., Parmar, N., Uszkoreit, J., Jones, L., Gomez, A. N., Kaiser, Ł., and Polosukhin, I. (2017). Attention is all you need. In *Advances in Neural Information Processing Systems*, pages 6000–6010.

Xia, M., Kong, X., Anastasopoulos, A., and Neubig, G. (2019). Generalized data augmentation for low-resource translation. *arXiv preprint arXiv:1906.03785.*

Xia, Y., He, D., Qin, T., Wang, L., Yu, N., Liu, T., and Ma, W. (2016). Dual learning for machine translation. *CoRR*, abs/1611.00179.

Zhang, B., Williams, P., Titov, I., and Sennrich, R. (2020). Improving massively multilingual neural machine translation and zero-shot translation. *arXiv preprint arXiv:2004.11867.*

Zoph, B., Yuret, D., May, J., and Knight, K. (2016). Transfer learning for low-resource neural machine translation. In *Proceedings of the 2016 Conference on Empirical Methods in Natural Language Processing*, pages 1568–1575. Association for Computational Linguistics.

Appendices

A Background and Motivation

For an S and T language pair, a standard NMT model is learned by mapping (s, t) example pairs with an encoder-decoder network (Kalchbrenner and Blunsom, 2013; Sutskever et al., 2014) such as Recurrent (Bahdanau et al., 2014; Cho et al., 2014), Convolutional (Gehring et al., 2017), and Transformer (Vaswani et al., 2017). Despite the varied architectural choices, the objective of NMT is to minimize the loss,

$$L_{\hat{\theta}}(s,t) = \sum_{i=1}^{|t|+1} logp(t_i|s,\hat{\theta}) \tag{1}$$

$\hat{\theta}$ is the parameterization of the network, s is the source sentence, and t is the predicted sentence. Reserved tokens $\langle bos \rangle$ at $i = 0$ and $\langle eos \rangle$ at $i = |t| + 1$ defines the beginning and end of t.

Training Paradigms

Semi-Supervised learning leverages monolingual data and has been used to improve supervised phrase-based models (Bertoldi and Federico, 2009; Bojar and Tamchyna, 2011). In NMT the procedure is commonly called – *back-translation* (Sennrich et al., 2015); to enhance $S \rightarrow T$ direction additional pseudo-bitext is utilized by augmenting the S side from T monolingual segments with a reverse $T \rightarrow S$ model. Back-translation became a core module in approaches that leverage monolingual data, such as dual-learning (Xia et al., 2016; Sestorain et al., 2018), zero-shot (Firat et al., 2016b; Lakew et al., 2017; Gu et al., 2019; Currey and Heafield, 2019; Zhang et al., 2020), and unsupervised (Lample et al., 2018; Artetxe et al., 2018) translation.

Unsupervised learning considers only monolingual data of S and T languages. Initialization from pre-trained embeddings (Artetxe et al., 2018; Lample et al., 2018) or cross-lingual language model (Lample and Conneau, 2019), denoising auto-encoder and iterative back-translation are commonly employed learning objectives. Despite being a rapidly growing research area, findings show failures in an unsupervised NMT when using real-world ZRP (Neubig and Hu, 2018), distant languages (Guzmán et al., 2019) in a domain-mismatched scenario (Kim et al., 2020; Artetxe et al., 2020). Given the similarity in leveraging monolingual data, we directly compare our zero-shot NMT with unsupervised NMT.

Multilingual modeling extends Eq. 1 objective to multiple language pairs. Although early work dedicates network components per language (Dong et al., 2015; Luong et al., 2015; Firat et al., 2016a), the most effective way utilizes "*language-id*" to share a single encoder-decoder model across multiple language pairs (Johnson et al., 2017; Ha et al., 2016). For L languages, a model learns to maximize the likelihood over all the available language pairs (max of $N = L(L-1)$) parallel data. For each language pair $S, T \in N$ and $S \neq T$, Eq. 1 can be written as,

$$L^T_{\hat{\theta}}(s^S, t^T) = \sum_{i=1}^{|t|+1} logp(t^T_i|s^S,\hat{\theta}) \tag{2}$$

Where the *language-id* (i.e. $\langle 2T \rangle$) is explicitly inserted at i=1 of the source (s^T). Most importantly, multilingual modeling enables translation between language pairs without an actual training data ($S, T \notin N$), exploiting an implicit transfer-learning from pairs with training data – also known as *Zero-Shot Translation* (ZST) (Johnson et al., 2017).

Transfer Learning across NMT models (i.e, *parent-to-child*) (Zoph et al., 2016), have been shown to work effectively with a shared vocabulary across related (Nguyen and Chiang, 2017) and even distant (Kocmi and Bojar, 2018) languages, by pre-training multilingual models (Neubig and Hu, 2018), by updating parent vocabularies with child (Lakew et al., 2018), and for a ZST with a pivot language (Kim et al., 2019). In this work, we leverage for the first time pre-trained models for zero-shot translation without the pivot language assumption.

B Preliminary Assessment

We summarize the motivation for certain experimental design choices in our zero-shot NMT (zNMT) modeling, analyzing model pre-training type (such as bilingual (BiTM) and multilingual (MuTM*)) and effective utilization of the in-domain (IND), out-of-domain (OOD), mixed domain (IOD) monolingual data. The $Gl - En$ zero-shot pair (ZSP) is used for our assessment.

Pre-Trained NMT Variant
Unlike previous work in zero-shot NMT, our zNMT aims to leverage both bilingual and multilingual pre-trainings. Fig. 3 shows zNMT improves better if initialized from multilingual pre-training (MuTM100). This is despite MuTM100 not observing the closest language pair ($Pt - En$) to the ZSP ($Gl - En$), while BiTM is trained using only $Pt - En$. Hence, the gain by initializing from MuTM100 shows the robustness of pre-training with multiple languages and its positive effect on zNMT. However, these results signal MuTM* importance for zNMT modeling, for further verification and better comparison with the bilingual supervised and unsupervised approaches our main experimental setup first focuses on utilizing BiTM.

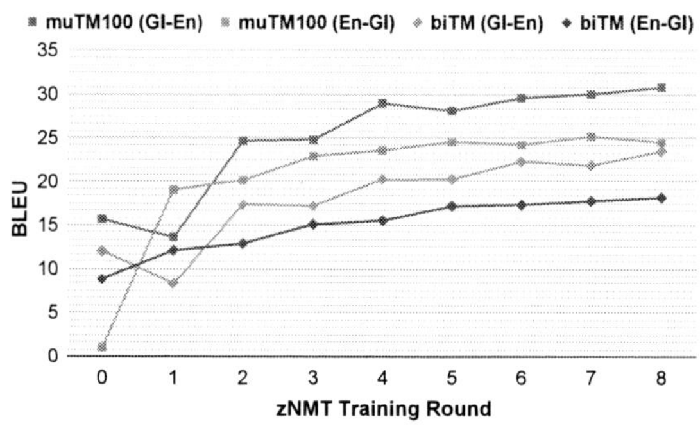

Figure 3: Performance of zNMT using bilingual (BiTM) and multilingual (MuTM100) pre-trainings.

Data Size and Domain
For the training scenarios involving IND and OOD data, Fig. 4 shows if available using all IND segments (All:All) is better than taking equal proportion (1:1) of the U and T sides of the ZSP. In a parallel experiment for IOD scenario, however, we observed that balancing the OOD segments with IND lead to a comparable or better performance. In other words, we select OOD proportionally ($\approx 200k$) to the largest IND side of the ZSP. We noted a similar trend for semi-supervised (sNMT) low-resource model, that shows better performance when using $\approx 200k$ OOD leading to

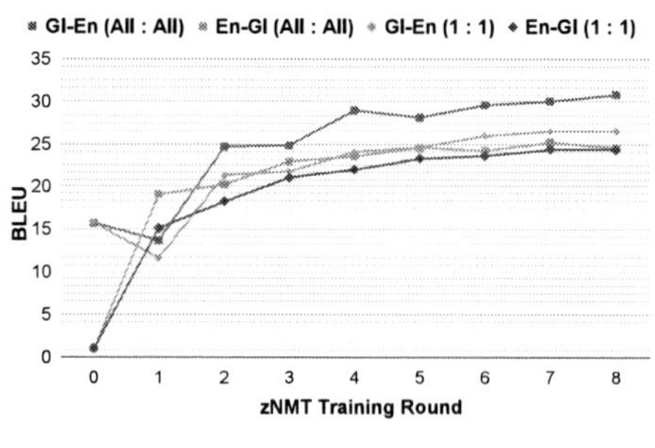

Figure 4: Performance of zNMT by varying monolingual data size ratio between U and T.

$22.08 \leftrightarrow 17.27$ ($Gl \leftrightarrow En$) than using $\approx 2M$ segments that degrades to $20.86 \leftrightarrow 16.44$ BLEU. However, for UNMT it is a common knowledge where more monolingual data leads to better performance (Lample and Conneau, 2019). We confirmed this by reducing the OOD to $200k$ as in ZNMT and SNMT, where we observed a 5 BLEU drop in UNMT performance in both $Gl \leftrightarrow En$ directions. For this reason, we train UNMT models using all the available IND and $\approx 2M$ OOD segments. In other words, the unsupervised models consume all the available IND and OOD monolingual data, that is $\times 10$ more than the SNMT baseline and our ZNMT utilized. In sum, this shows the efficiency of our approach to reach to a better performance with less resources. Detail comparisons are provided in the main experimental section.

Lastly, Fig. 5 shows an effective strategy of utilizing the IND and OOD data for ZNMT in a mixed domain (IOD) scenario. The test settings show first learning ZNMT with the IND and progressively incorporating OOD data (IND $>$ IOD) is the best approach, in comparison with (OOD $>$ IOD), or utilizing (IOD) from the beginning. Considering pre-trained models for ZNMT utilizes IND data (except for the unseen U), the finding is expected and leads to a better performance. Applying a similar (IND $>$ IOD) strategy for UNMT, however, resulted in a drop of up to 7 BLEU for $En \rightarrow Gl$, compared to training with the mixed domain (IOD) from the beginning. This is likely due to the fact that the the pre-training for UNMT observes both ID and OD data of $U - T$ ZSP and leading to a better learning when using IOD. In our main experimental setup we choose the best strategy for each of the approaches.

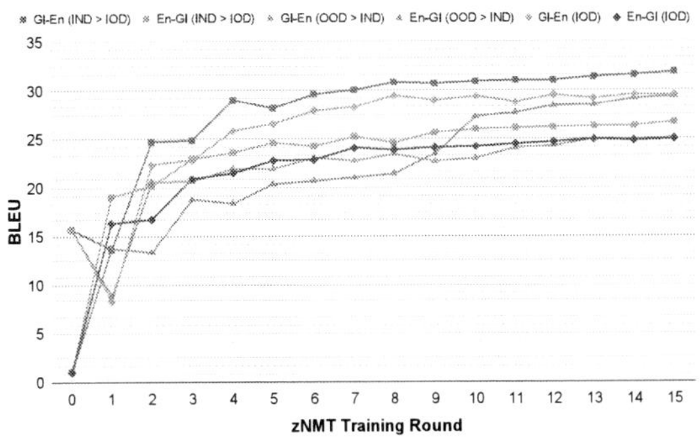

Figure 5: Training strategies to best utilize in-domain (IND) and out-of-domain (OOD) monolingual data.

C Model Configuration and Parameters

Model	Initialization	Params ($\times 10^6$)	Layers
MLM	-	41	6
BITM	-	53	6
MUTM*	-	69	6
NMT	-	38	4
SNMT	-	38	4
MNMT	-	69	6
UNMT	MLM	86	6
ZNMT	BITM	53	6
ZNMT	MUTM*	69	6

Table 5: Model, parameter size, and number of self-attention layers. MUTM* represents both MU100 and MU108.

To tackle over-fitting in the bilingual baseline supervised and semi-supervised NMT models we employ a dropout rate of 0.1 on the attention and 0.3 on all the other layers. Whereas the dropout rate for all the other models are set uniformly to 0.1. We use source and target tied embeddings (Press and Wolf, 2016). Samples exceeding 100 sub-word counts are discarded at time of training. Model training is done on a single V100 GPU with batch-size of $4,096$ tokens. Adam is used as an optimizer (Kingma and Ba, 2014) with a learning rate of 10^{-4}.

Details about model parameter are provided in Table 5. At time of training all models have shown to converge. While ZNMT shows the fastest learning curve within $15-20$ epochs, UNMT run up to 100 epochs to reach convergence.

D Languages and Data

Table 6 lists the languages and examples size from the TED talks data.

Language	Lang. Id	Train	Dev	Test
Arabic	ar	214111	4714	5953
Azerbaijani	az	5946	671	903
Belarusian	be	4509	248	664
Bulgarian	bg	174444	4082	5060
Bengali	bn	4649	896	216
Bosnian	bs	5664	474	463
Czech	cs	103093	3462	3831
Danish	da	44940	1694	1683
German	de	167888	4148	4491
Greek	el	134327	3344	4431
Esperanto	eo	6535	495	758
Spanish	es	196026	4231	5571
Estonian	et	10738	740	1087
Basque	eu	5182	318	379
Persian	fa	150965	3930	4490
Finnish	fi	24222	981	1301
French-Canadian	fr-ca	19870	838	1611
French	fr	192304	4320	4866
Galician	gl	10017	682	1007
Hebrew	he	211819	4515	5508
Hindi	hi	18798	854	1243
Croatian	hr	122091	3333	4881
Hungarian	hu	147219	3725	4981
Armenian	hy	21360	739	1567
Indonesian	id	87406	2677	3179
Italian	it	204503	4547	5625
Japanese	ja	204090	4429	5565
Georgian	ka	13193	654	943
Kazakh	kk	3317	938	775
Korean	ko	205640	4441	5637
Kurdish	ku	10371	265	766
Lithuanian	lt	41919	1791	1791
Macedonian	mk	25335	640	438
Mongolian	mn	7607	372	414
Marathi	mr	9840	767	1090
Malay	ms	5220	539	260
Burmese	my	21497	741	1504
Norwegian	nb	15825	826	806
Dutch	nl	183767	4459	5006
Polish	pl	176169	4108	5010
Portuguese-Brazilian	pt-br	184755	4035	4855
Portuguese	pt	51785	1193	1803
Romanian	ro	180484	3904	4631
Russian	ru	208458	4814	5483
Slovak	sk	61470	2271	2445
Slovenian	sl	19831	1068	1251
Albanian	sq	44525	1556	2443
Serbian	sr	136898	3798	4634
Swedish	sv	56647	1729	2283
Tamil	ta	6224	447	832
Thai	th	98064	2989	3713
Turkish	tr	182470	4045	5029
Ukrainian	uk	108495	3060	3751
Urdu	ur	5977	508	1006
Vietnamese	vi	171995	4645	4391
Chinese-China	zh-cn	199855	4558	5251
Chinese	zh	5534	547	494
Chinese-Taiwan	zh-tw	202646	4583	5377

Table 6: Languages and the parallel number of segments paired with English from the the TED Talks data (Qi et al., 2018). The four languages used as an unseen (U) source are highlighted.

Findings of the LoResMT 2021 Shared Task on COVID and Sign Language for Low-resource Languages

Atul Kr. Ojha[1,2] atulkumar.ojha@insight-centre.org
Chao-Hong Liu[3] ch.liu@acm.org
Katharina Kann[4] katharina.kann@colorado.edu
John Ortega[5] jortega@cs.nyu.edu
Sheetal Shatam[2] panlingua@outlook.com
Theodorus Fransen[1] theodorus.fransen@insight-centre.org
[1]Data Science Institute, NUIG, Galway
[2]Panlingua Language Processing LLP, New Delhi
[3]Potamu Research Ltd
[4]University of Colorado at Boulder
[5]New York University

Abstract

We present the findings of the LoResMT 2021 shared task which focuses on machine translation (MT) of COVID-19 data for both low-resource spoken and sign languages. The organization of this task was conducted as part of the fourth workshop on technologies for machine translation of low resource languages (LoResMT). Parallel corpora is presented and publicly available which includes the following directions: English↔Irish, English↔Marathi, and Taiwanese Sign language↔Traditional Chinese. Training data consists of 8112, 20933 and 128608 segments, respectively. There are additional monolingual data sets for Marathi and English that consist of 21901 segments. The results presented here are based on entries from a total of eight teams. Three teams submitted systems for English↔Irish while five teams submitted systems for English↔Marathi. Unfortunately, there were no systems submissions for the Taiwanese Sign language↔Traditional Chinese task. Maximum system performance was computed using BLEU and follow as 36.0 for English–Irish, 34.6 for Irish–English, 24.2 for English–Marathi, and 31.3 for Marathi–English.

1 Introduction

The workshop on technologies for machine translation of low resource languages (LoResMT)[1] is a yearly workshop which focuses on scientific research topics and technological resources for machine translation (MT) using low-resource languages. Based on the success of its three predecessors (Liu, 2018; Karakanta et al., 2019, 2020), the fourth LoResMT workshop intoduces a shared task section based on COVID-19 and sign language data as part of its research objectives. The hope is to provide assistance with translation for low-resource languages where it could be needed most during the COVID-19 pandemic.

[1]https://sites.google.com/view/loresmt/

To provide a trajectory of the LoResMT shared task success, a summary of the previous tasks follows. The first LoResMT shared task (Karakanta et al., 2019) took place in 2019. There, monolingual and parallel corpora for Bhojpuri, Magahi, Sindhi, and Latvian were provided as training data for two types of machine translation systems: neural and statistical. As an extension to the first shared task, a second shared task (Ojha et al., 2020) was presented in 2020 which focused on zero-shot approaches for MT systems.

This year, the shared task introduces a new objective focused on MT systems for COVID-related texts and sign language. Participants for this shared task were asked to submit novel MT systems for the following language pairs:

- English↔Irish
- English↔Marathi
- Taiwanese Sign Language↔Traditional Chinese

The low-resource languages presented in this shared task were found to be sufficient data for baseline systems to perform translation on the latest COVID-related texts and sign language. Irish, Marathi, and Taiwanese Sign Language can be considered low-resource languages and are translated to either English or traditional Chinese – their high-resource counterpart.

The rest of our work is organized as follows. Section 2 presents the setup and schedule of the shared task. Section 3 presents the data set used for the competition. Section 4 describes the approaches used by participants in the competition and Section 5 presents and analyzes the results obtained by the competitors. Lastly, in Section 6 a conclusion is presented along with potential future work.

2 Shared task setup and schedule

This section describes how the shared task was organized along with the systems. Registered participants were sent links to the training, development, and/or monolingual data (refer to Section 3 for more details). They were allowed to use additional data to train their system with the condition that any additional data used should be made publicly available. Participants were moreover allowed to use pre-trained word embeddings and linguistic models that are publicly available. As a manner of detecting which data sets were used during training, participants were given the following markers for denotation:

- *"-a"* - Only provided development, training and monolingual corpora.
- *"-b"*- Any provided corpora, plus publicly available language's corpora and pre-trained/linguistic model (e.g. systems used pre-trained word2vec, UDPipe, etc. model).
- *"-c"* - Any provided corpora, plus any publicly external monolingual corpora.

Each team was allowed to submit any number of systems for evaluation and their best 3 systems were included in the final ranking presented in this report. Each submitted system was evaluated on standard automatic MT evaluation metrics; BLEU (Papineni et al., 2002), CHRF (Popović, 2015) and TER (Post, 2018).

The schedule for deliver of training data and release of test data along with notification and submission can be found in Table 1.

Date	Event
May 10, 2021	Release of training data
July 01, 2021	Release of test data
July 13, 2021	Submission of the systems
July 20, 2021	Notification of results
July 27, 2021	Submission of shared task papers
August 01, 2021	Camera-ready

Table 1: LoResMT 2021 Shared Task programming

3 Languages and data sets

In this section, we present background information about the languages and data sets featured in the shared task along with a itemized view of the linguistic families and number of segments in Table 2.

3.1 Training data set

- **English↔Irish** Irish (also known as Gaeilge) has around 170,000 L1 speakers and "1.85 million (37%) people across the island (of Ireland) claim to be at least somewhat proficient with the language". In the Republic of Ireland, it is the national and first official language. It is also one of the official languages of the European Union and a recognized minority language in Northern Ireland with the ISO *ga* code.[2]

  English-Irish bilingual COVID sentences/documents were extracted and aligned from the following sources: (a) Gov.ie[3] - Search for services or information , (b) Ireland's Health Services[4] - HSE.ie , (c) Revenue Irish Taxes and Customs[5] and (d) Europe Union[6]. In addition, the Irish bilingual training data was built from monolingual data using back translation (Sennrich et al., 2016). English and Irish monolingual data was compiled from Wikipedia pages and newspapers such as The Irish Times[7], RTE[8] and COVID-19 pandemic in the Republic of Ireland[9]. Back-translated and crawled data were cross-validated for accuracy by language experts leaving approximately 8,112 Irish parallel sentences for the training data set.

- **English↔Marathi** Marathi, which has the ISO code *mr*, is dominantly spoken in India's Maharashtra state. It has around 83,026,680 speakers.[10] It belongs to the Indo-Aryan language family.

  English–Marathi parallel COVID sentences were extracted from the Government of India website and online newspapers such as PMIndia[11], myGOV[12], Lokasatta[13], BBC

[2] https://cloud.dfki.de/owncloud/index.php/s/sAs23JKXRwEEacn
[3] www.gov.ie
[4] https://www.hse.ie/
[5] https://www.revenue.ie/
[6] https://europa.eu
[7] https://www.irishtimes.com/
[8] https://www.rte.ie/news/ & https://www.rte.ie/gaeilge/
[9] https://en.wikipedia.org/wiki/COVID-19_pandemic_in_the_Republic_of_Ireland
[10] https://censusindia.gov.in/2011Census/C-16_25062018_NEW.pdf
[11] https://www.pmindia.gov.in/
[12] https://www.mygov.in/
[13] https://www.loksatta.com/

Marathi and English[14]. After pre-processing and manual validation, approximately 20,993 parallel training sentences were left. Additionally, English and Marathi monolingual sentences were crawled from the online newspapers and Wikipedia (see Table 2).

- **Taiwanese Sign Language ↔ Traditional Chinese** According to UN, there are "72 million deaf people worldwide... they use more than 300 different sign languages."[15] In Taiwan, Taiwanese Sign Language is a recognized national language, with a population of less than thirty thousand "speakers". Taiwanese Sign Language (and Korean Sign Language) evolved from Japanese Sign Language and share about 60% of "words" between them.
  The sign language data set is prepared from press conferences for COVID-19 response, which were held daily or weekly depending on the pandemic situation in Taiwan. Fig. 1 shows a sample video of sign language and its translations in Traditional Chinese (excerpted from the corpus) and English.

Figure 1: Sample of a sign language video in frames (excerpted from C00207_711.mp4 in the corpus; Translations in Traditional Chinese: "4.1吧或4.5 大概是這樣的一個比例", and English: "The ratio is approximately 4.1 or 4.5")

[14] `https://www.bbc.com/marathi` & `https://www.bbc.com/`

[15] `https://www.un.org/en/observances/sign-languages-day`

3.2 Development and test data sets

Similar to the training data, English-Irish and English-Marathi language pair's dev and test data sets were crawled from bilingual and/or monolingual websites. Additionally, some parallel segments and terminology were taken from the Translation Initiative for COVID-19 (Anastasopoulos et al., 2020), a manually translated and validated data set created by professional translators and native speakers of the target languages. The participants of the shared task were provided with the manual translations of which 502 Irish and 500 Marathi development segments were used while 250 (Irish-English), 500 (English-Irish), 500 (English-Marathi) and 500 (Marathi-English) manually translated segments were used for testing. Taiwanese Sign Language ↔ Traditional Chinese language pair's participants were provided with 3071 segments and videos for development and 7,053 videos for sign language testing.

The detailed statistics of the data set in each language is provided in Table2. The complete shared task data sets are available publicly[16].

Language	Code	Family	Train	Dev	Monolingual	Test
English	en	Indo-Germanic	-	-	8,826	-
Irish	ga	Celtic	8112	502	-	750
Marathi	mr	Indo-Aryan	20,933	500	21,902	1,000
TSign	sgTW	Japanese Sign Language	128,608	3,071	-	7,053
TChinese	zhTW	Mandarin Chinese	128,608	3,071	-	7,053

Table 2: Statistics of the Shared task data (TSign refers to Taiwanese Sign Language and TChinese refers to Traditional Chinese)

4 Participants and methodology

A total of 12 teams registered for the shared task: 5 teams registered to participate for all language pairs, 5 teams registered to participate only for English↔Marathi, one team registered for Taiwanese↔Mandarin (Traditional Chinese) sign language and one team registered for English↔Irish. Out of these, a total of 6 teams submitted their systems on COVID while none of them submitted a system for sign language. Out of the submitted systems, two teams participated for the English↔Irish and English↔Marathi tasks, one team participated for English-Irish and three teams participated for English↔Marathi (see Table 3). All the teams who submitted their systems were invited to submit system description papers describing their experiments. Table 3 identifies the participating teams and their language choices.

Team	English–Irish	English–Marathi	TSign–TChinese	System Description Paper
IIITT	en2ga & ga2en	en2mr & mr2en	—	(Puranik et al., 2021)
oneNLP-IIITH	—	en2mr & mr2en	—	(Mujadia and Sharma, 2021)
A3108	—	en2mr & mr2en	—	(Yadav and Shrivastava, 2021)
CFILT-IITBombay	—	en2mr & mr2en	—	(Jain et al., 2021)
UCF	en2ga & ga2en	en2mr & mr2en	—	(Chen and Fazio, 2021)
adapt_dcu	en2ga	—	—	(Lankford et al., 2021)
Total	**3**	**5**	**0**	**6**

Table 3: Details of the teams and submitted systems for the LoResMT 2021 Shared Task.

Next, we give a short description of the approaches used by each team to build their systems. More details about the approaches can be found in the papers by respective teams in the accompanying proceeding.

[16] https://github.com/loresmt/loresmt-2021

- **IIITT** (Puranik et al., 2021) used a fairseq pre-trained model Indictrans for English-Marathi. It consists of two models that can translate from Indic to English and vice-versa. The model can perform 11 languages: Assamese, Bengali, Gujarati, Hindi, Kannada, Malayalam, Marathi, Oriya, Punjabi, Tamil, Telugu pre-trained on the Samanantar data set, the largest data set for Indic languages during the time of submission. The model is fine-tuned on the training data set provided by the organizers and a parallel bible corpus for Marathi. The team used the parallel bible parallel corpus from a previous task (MultiIndicMT task in WAT 2020). After conducting various experiments, the best checkpoint was recorded and predicted upon. For Irish, the team fine-tuned an Opus MT model from Helsinki NLP on the training data set, and then predicted results after recording. After careful experimentation, the team observed that the Opus MT model outperformed the other models giving it the highest scoring model award.
- **oneNLP-IIITH** (Mujadia and Sharma, 2021) used a sequence to sequence neural model with a transformer network (4 to 8 layers) with label smoothing and dropouts to reduce overfitting with English-Marathi and Marathi-English. The team explored the use of different linguistic features like part-of-speech and morphology on sub-word units for both directions. In addition, the team explored forward and backward translation using web-crawled monolingual data.
- **A3108** (Yadav and Shrivastava, 2021) built a statistical machine translation (smt) system in both directions for English↔Marathi language pair. Its initial baseline experiments used various tokenization schemes to train models. By using optimal tokenization schemes, the team was able to create synthetic data and train an augmented dat aset to create more statistical models. Also, the team reordered English syntax to match Marathi syntax and further trained another set of baseline and data augmented models using various tokenization schemes.
- **CFILT-IITBombay** (Jain et al., 2021) buildt three different neural machine translation systems; a baseline English–Marathi system, a Baseline Marathi-English system, and a English–Marathi system that was based on back translation. The team explored the performance of the NMT systems between English and Marathi languages. Also, they explored the performance of back-translation using data obtained from NMT systems trained on a very small amount of data. From their experiments, the team observed that back-translation helped improve the MT quality over the baseline for English-Marathi.
- **UCF** (Chen and Fazio, 2021) used transfer learning, uni-gram and sub-word segmentation methods for English–Irish, Irish–English, English–Marathi and Marathi–English. The team conducted their experiment using an OpenNMT LSTM system. Efforts were constrained by using transfer learning and sub-word segmentation on small amounts of training data. Their models achieved the following BLEU scores when constraining on tracks of English–Irish, Irish–English, and Marathi–English: 13.5, 21.3, and 17.9, respectively.
- **adapt_dcu** (Lankford et al., 2021) used a transformer training approach carried out using OpenNMT-py and sub-word models for English–Irish. The team also explored domain adaptation techniques while using a Covid-adapted generic 55k corpus, fine-tuning, mixed fine-tuning and combined data set approaches were compared with models trained on an extended in-domain data set.

5 Results

As discussed, participants were allowed to use data sets other than those provided. The best three results for English-Irish, Irish-English, English-Marathi and Marathi-English language pairs are presented in Tables 4 and 5. The complete submitted systems results are available publicly[17]. Table 4 depicts how the UCF team were able to gain the highest and lowest results for Irish-English and English-Marathi with shared data. The highest scores were 21.3 BLEU, 0.45 CHRF and 0.711 TER, while the lowest scores were 5.1 BLEU, 0.22 CHRF and 0.872 TER. However, with the additional data and by using pre-trained models (see Table 5), adapt_dcu achieved the best results for English-Irish where scores were 36 BLEU, 0.6 CHRF and 0.531 TER. Contrastingly, UCF scored the lowest for English-Marathi. The lowest scores were 4.8 BLEU, 0.29 CHRF and 1.063 TER.

Team	System/task description	BLEU	CHRF	TER
adapt_dcu	en2ga-a	9.8	0.34	0.880
UCF	ga2en-TransferLearning-a	21.3	0.45	0.711
CFILT-IITBombay	en2mr-Backtranslation-a	12.2	0.38	0.979
CFILT-IITBombay	en2mr-Baseline_200-a	11	0.38	0.961
CFILT-IITBombay	en2mr-Baseline_1600-a	10.8	0.38	0.935
oneNLP-IIITH	en2mr-Method1-a	10.4	0.32	0.907
A3108	en2mr-Method29transliterate-a	11.8	0.45	0.95
A3108	en2mr-Method29unk-a	11.8	0.45	0.95
A3108	en2mr-Method10unk-a	11.4	0.43	0.934
UCF	en2mr-UnigramSegmentation-a	5.1	0.22	0.872
CFILT-IITBombay	mr2en-Baseline_1000-a	16.6	0.41	0.870
CFILT-IITBombay	mr2en-Baseline_1200-a	16.3	0.40	0.867
CFILT-IITBombay	mr2en-Baseline_1400-a	16.2	0.41	0.879
oneNLP-IIITH	mr2en-Method1-a	16.7	0.40	0.835
oneNLP-IIITH	mr2en-Method2-a	16.2	0.41	0.831
A3108	mr2en-Method7transliterate-a	14.6	0.47	0.945
A3108	mr2en-Method7unk-a	14.6	0.47	0.945
A3108	mr2en-Method20transliterate-a	14.5	0.42	0.866
UCF	mr2en-UnigramSegmentation-a	17.9	0.40	0.744

Table 4: Results of submitted systems at English↔Irish & English↔Marathi in the "-a" method

[17] https://github.com/loresmt/loresmt-2021

Team	System/task description	BLEU	CHRF	TER
adapt_dcu	en2ga-b	36.0	0.60	0.531
IIITT	en2ga-helsnikiopus-b	25.8	0.53	0.629
IIITT	ga2en-helsinkiopus-b	34.6	0.61	0.586
IIITT	en2mr-IndicTrans-b	24.2	0.59	0.597
oneNLP-IIITH	en2mr-Method2-c	22.2	0.56	0.746
oneNLP-IIITH	en2mr-Method3-c	22.0	0.56	0.753
oneNLP-IIITH	en2mr-Method1-c	21.5	0.56	0.746
UCF	en2mr-UnigramSegmentation-b	4.8	0.29	1.063
oneNLP-IIITH	mr2en-Method3-c	31.3	0.58	0.646
oneNLP-IIITH	mr2en-Method2-c	30.6	0.57	0.659
oneNLP-IIITH	mr2en-Method1-c	20.7	0.48	0.735
UCF	mr2en-UnigramSegmentation-b	7.7	0.24	0.833
IIITT	mr2en-IndicTrans-b	5.1	0.22	1.002

Table 5: Results of submitted systems at English↔Irish & English↔Marathi in the "-b" and "-c" method

6 Conclusion

We have reported the findings of the LoResMT 2021 Shared Task on COVID and sign language translation for low-resource languages as part of the fourth LoResMT workshop. All submissions used neural machine translation except for the one from oneNLP-IIITH. We conclude that in our shared tasks the use of transfer learning, domain adaptation, and back translation achieve optimal results when the data sets are domain specific as well as small-sized. Our findings show that uni-gram segmentation transfer learning methods provide comparatively low results for the following metrics: BLEU, CHRF and TER. The highest BLEU scores achieved are 36.0 for English-to-Irish, 34.6 for Irish-to-English, 24.2 for English-to-Marathi, and 31.3 for Marathi-to-English.

In future iterations of the LoResMT shared tasks, extended corpora of the three language pairs will be provided for training and evaluation. Human evaluation on system results will also be conducted. For sign language MT, the tasks will be fine-grained and evaluated separately.

7 Acknowledgements

This publication has emanated from research in part supported by Cardamom-Comparative Deep Models of Language for Minority and Historical Languages (funded by the Irish Research Council under the Consolidator Laureate Award scheme (grant number IRCLA/2017/129)) and we are grateful to them for providing English↔Irish parallel and monolingual COVID-related texts. We would like to thank Panlingua Language Processing LLP and Potamu Research Ltd for providing English↔Marathi parallel and monolingual COVID data and Taiwanese Sign Language↔Traditional Chinese linguistic data, respectively.

References

Anastasopoulos, A., Cattelan, A., Dou, Z.-Y., Federico, M., Federmann, C., Genzel, D., Guzmán, F., Hu, J., Hughes, M., Koehn, P., Lazar, R., Lewis, W., Neubig, G., Niu, M., Öktem, A., Paquin, E., Tang, G., and Tur, S. (2020). TICO-19: the translation initiative for COvid-19. In *Proceedings of the 1st Workshop on NLP for COVID-19 (Part 2) at EMNLP 2020*, Online. Association for Computational Linguistics.

Chen, W. and Fazio, B. (2021). The UCF Systems for the LoResMT 2021 Machine Translation Shared Task. In *Proceedings of the 4th Workshop on Technologies for MT of Low Resource Languages*.

Jain, A., Mhaskar, S., and Bhattacharyya, P. (2021). Evaluating the Performance of Back-translation for Low Resource English-Marathi Language Pair: CFILT-IITBombay @ LoResMT 2021. In *Proceedings of the 4th Workshop on Technologies for MT of Low Resource Languages*.

Karakanta, A., Ojha, A. K., Liu, C.-H., Abbott, J., Ortega, J., Washington, J., Oco, N., Lakew, S. M., Pirinen, T. A., Malykh, V., Logacheva, V., and Zhao, X., editors (2020). *Proceedings of the 3rd Workshop on Technologies for MT of Low Resource Languages*, Suzhou, China. Association for Computational Linguistics.

Karakanta, A., Ojha, A. K., Liu, C.-H., Washington, J., Oco, N., Lakew, S. M., Malykh, V., and Zhao, X. (2019). Proceedings of the 2nd workshop on technologies for mt of low resource languages. In *Proceedings of the 2nd Workshop on Technologies for MT of Low Resource Languages*.

Lankford, S., Afli, H., and Way, A. (2021). Machine Translation in the Covid domain: an English-Irish case study for LoResMT 2021. In *Proceedings of the 4th Workshop on Technologies for MT of Low Resource Languages*.

Liu, C.-H., editor (2018). *Proceedings of the AMTA 2018 Workshop on Technologies for MT of Low Resource Languages (LoResMT 2018)*, Boston, MA. Association for Machine Translation in the Americas.

Mujadia, V. and Sharma, D. M. (2021). English-Marathi Neural Machine Translation for LoResMT 2021. In *Proceedings of the 4th Workshop on Technologies for MT of Low Resource Languages*.

Ojha, A. K., Malykh, V., Karakanta, A., and Liu, C.-H. (2020). Findings of the LoResMT 2020 shared task on zero-shot for low-resource languages. In *Proceedings of the 3rd Workshop on Technologies for MT of Low Resource Languages*, pages 33–37, Suzhou, China. Association for Computational Linguistics.

Papineni, K., Roukos, S., Ward, T., and Zhu, W.-J. (2002). BLEU: a method for automatic evaluation of machine translation. In *Proceedings of the 40th annual meeting on association for computational linguistics*, pages 311–318. Association for Computational Linguistics.

Popović, M. (2015). chrF: character n-gram F-score for automatic MT evaluation. In *Proceedings of the Tenth Workshop on Statistical Machine Translation*, pages 392–395, Lisbon, Portugal. Association for Computational Linguistics.

Post, M. (2018). A call for clarity in reporting BLEU scores. In *Proceedings of the Third Conference on Machine Translation: Research Papers*, pages 186–191, Belgium, Brussels. Association for Computational Linguistics.

Puranik, K., Hande, A., Priyadharshini, R., D, T., Sampath, A., Thamburaj, K. P., and Chakravarthi, B. R. (2021). Attentive fine-tuning of Transformers for Translation of low-resourced languages @LoResMT 2021. In *Proceedings of the 4th Workshop on Technologies for MT of Low Resource Languages*.

Sennrich, R., Haddow, B., and Birch, A. (2016). Improving neural machine translation models with monolingual data. In *Proceedings of the 54th Annual Meeting of the Association for Computational Linguistics (Volume 1: Long Papers)*, pages 86–96, Berlin, Germany. Association for Computational Linguistics.

Yadav, S. and Shrivastava, M. (2021). A3-108 Machine Translation System for LoResMT Shared Task @MT Summit 2021 Conference. In *Proceedings of the 4th Workshop on Technologies for MT of Low Resource Languages*.

A3-108 Machine Translation System for LoResMT Shared Task @MT Summit 2021 Conference

Saumitra Yadav saumitra.yadav@research.iiit.ac.in
Manish Shrivastava m.shrivastava@iiit.ac.in
Machine Translation - Natural Language Processing Lab, Language Technologies Research Centre, Kohli Center on Intelligent Systems, International Institute of Information Technology - Hyderabad

Abstract

In this paper, we describe our submissions for LoResMT Shared Task @MT Summit 2021 Conference. We built statistical translation systems in each direction for English $\Longleftrightarrow$ Marathi language pair. This paper outlines initial baseline experiments with various tokenization schemes to train models. Using optimal tokenization scheme we create synthetic data and further train augmented dataset to create more statistical models. Also, we reorder English to match Marathi syntax to further train another set of baseline and data augmented models using various tokenization schemes. We report configuration of the submitted systems and results produced by them.

1 Introduction

Machine Translation systems are systems which translate from source language to target. There are multiple ways of creating such a system - rule based, data driven, hybrid etc. We are using data driven methods to create translation system. In data driven methods - statistical (Koehn et al., 2003) and neural methods (Bahdanau et al., 2014) have been employed to build decent MT systems in resource setting like English $\Longleftrightarrow$ French. In LoResMT shared task (Ojha et al., 2021) we are dealing with low resource setting for English, Marathi pair. According to Koehn and Knowles (2017), compared to statistical methods neural methods have a drawback when used in low resource setting. Hence, for this shared task we are using only phrase based statistical models to build translation models using Moses[1] (Koehn et al., 2007).

Marathi is morphologically richer, agglutinative language when compared to English. Also, former follows SOV as canonical syntactic structure while latter follows SVO. Level of difference in morphological richness and syntactic divergence between the two languages suggests to look for methods which can help to address them to certain extent in phrase based statistical models. Since we are in low resource setting, to address data sparsity problem, we use various tokenization schemes, e.g. BPE (Sennrich et al., 2016b), morfessor (Virpioja et al., 2013). Combinations of these tokenization schemes are used with SMT based method to create a baseline systems. After checking the optimal tokenization scheme, we use that scheme to augment training data with synthetic dataset using back translation (Sennrich et al., 2016a). As was the case in baseline systems, augmented dataset goes through prepossessing with various tokenization schemes and SMT method to build more systems. We elevate the amount of learning, the reordering model of SMT has to do, by making use of rule based reordering system

[1] `http://statmt.org/moses/`

Dataset	Baseline and Reordered Baseline		Augmented and Reordered Augmented	
Language	English	Marathi	English	Marathi
Monolingual	34891	40972	56789	57569
training	20651		59146	
dev	500		500	

Table 1: Data statistics, number of sentences for each set of experiments

(Patel et al., 2013), (Kunchukuttan et al., 2014) to reorder English to match Marathi syntax. With this we build another set of baseline systems for reordered English, Marathi pair. Like in baseline systems, mentioned above, here also we make use of various tokenization schemes. After comparing these schemes, we create synthetic dataset using back translation to augment reordered English, Marathi pair. Subsequent sections give more detailed overview of the systems developed.

2 SMT Systems

We use SMT model to make initial baseline systems using various tokenization schemes. We further make use of rule based reordering model to create another set of baseline systems using reordered English, Marathi pair. These two sets of systems are then used to create synthetic data set for data augmentation to train SMT models.

2.1 Data

For this shared task organisers provided parallel and monolingual corpus. We include Marathi training, dev dataset to already existing monolingual coprus to create Marathi monolingual corpus. For English monolingual corpus we joined English training and dev data from both (English $\Longleftrightarrow$ Marathi, English $\Longleftrightarrow$ Irish) language pair provided by organizers. As a first preprocessing step, we used the IndicNLP toolkit[2] to tokenize Marathi and Moses tokenizer[3] to tokenize English. Then we learned subwords using Byte pair encoding (Sennrich et al., 2016b) with 10000 merge operations on monolingual corpus and tokenized training and dev accordingly. We also used morfessor (Virpioja et al., 2013) as an alternative tokenization scheme. Morfessor model was also trained on full monolingual corpus. Table 1 provides statistics of datasets processed.

We made use of CFILT toolkit[4] to preorder English sentence in train, dev and monolingual text. Similar to previous sets of baseline systems, we use vairous tokenization schemes - moses tokenizer, BPE, Morfessor and train another set of baseline systems. Table 1 provides you with statistics of reordered English. We used all possible combination of tokenization schemes while training all models. These tokenization schemes are named as follow,

- BasicTok: Basic Tokenization using Indic NLP for Marathi and Moses tokenizer for English.
- BPE: text tokenized using BPE into subword.
- Morf: text tokenized using morfessor.

[2]https://anoopkunchukuttan.github.io/indic_nlp_library/

[3]https://github.com/moses-smt/mosesdecoder/blob/master/scripts/tokenizer/tokenizer.perl

[4]https://www.cfilt.iitb.ac.in/static/download.html

2.2 Translation Models

We made use of Moses toolkit (Koehn et al., 2007) to build statistical models trained with various tokenized bitext pairs. We also use GIZA++ (Och and Ney, 2003) to find alignments between parallel text and grow-diag-final-and method (Koehn et al., 2003) to extract aligned phrases. And utilize KenLM (Heafield, 2011) to train a trigram model with kneser ney smoothing on monolingual corpus of both languages. MERT (Och, 2003) is used for tuning the trained models. We also trained a reordering system for Reordered English to English so that we can have Reordered English as pseudo-pivot language.

2.2.1 Transliteration Module

Since we are building systems in low resource setting, its entirely possible to get unknown words while translating. To see if we can also counter unknown words in this resource constrained environments, we also made a small transliteration system. First a phrase based model was trained on English Marathi bitext using Moses(Koehn et al., 2007) with max phrase length[5] set to 1 to find tokens with very high alignment probability (we took average of 4 probabilities and took token pair with value > 0.79). We got 1557 pairs of tokens, we tokenized them character wise and used 1500 for training and 57 for tunning to build a transliteration system (by posing transliteration as translation problem). Since transliteration system is trained on very small corpus and hence prone to error, for each output from SMT translation system we give two outputs. One in which we made use of transliteration system for unknown words and another one in which we did not.

2.2.2 Performance on Dev sets

We used dev set to evaluate above mentioned models and all models which are described later on. Outputs were post processed according to the tokenization scheme of respective target language in each model, and then detokenized. After evaluating all systems using sacrebleu (Post, 2018), Table 2 lists the result on dev sets for baseline systems trained in English to Marathi Direction and Table 3 lists the result of systems trained on Marathi to English direction. If we

Tokenization Scheme	Baseline SMT		Augment SMT		Baseline Reordered SMT		Augment Reordered SMT	
	unk	transliterate	unk	transliterate	unk	transliterate	unk	transliterate
EnTok MrTok	58.2	58.1	57.6	57.5	59.2	59.1	62.7	62.7
EnBPE MrBPE	50.1	50.1	52.0	51.9	53.1	53.1	56.7	56.7
EnMorf MrMorf	41.3	41.3	43.6	43.6	45.7	45.6	51.3	51.3
EnTok MrBPE	49.3	49.1	50.7	50.6	51.5	51.4	54.7	54.7
EnTok MrMorf	47.4	47.3	47.3	47.2	49.8	49.7	54.7	54.7
EnBPE MrTok	54.3	54.3	54.4	54.4	56.7	56.7	58.9	58.9
EnBPE MrMorf	46.0	46.0	48.0	48.0	49.5	49.5	53.2	53.2
EnMorf MrTok	51.4	51.3	50.9	50.9	53.7	53.6	55.6	55.6
EnMorf MrBPE	44.3	44.2	45.9	45.8	47.8	47.8	52.3	52.3

Table 2: Results of systems for English To Marathi language direction. unk column contain output of systems where unknown were kept as they are, in transliterate column they were transliterated using small transliteration system

look at table 2, we can see that using reordering as preprocessing tool was helpful to system

[5] `http://www.statmt.org/moses/?n=FactoredTraining.TrainingParameters`

Tokenization Scheme	Baseline SMT		Augment SMT		Baseline Reordered SMT		Augment Reordered SMT	
	unk	transli-terate	unk	transli-terate	unk	transli-terate	unk	transli-terate
EnTok MrTok	70.4	70.4	72.4	72.4	55.6	55.7	61.3	61.3
EnBPE MrBPE	62.6	62.6	64.5	64.5	55.6	55.6	56.6	56.6
EnMorf MrMorf	56.0	56.0	57.5	57.5	51.1	51.1	53.4	53.4
EnTok MrBPE	62.0	62.0	64.8	64.8	54.4	54.4	56.0	56.0
EnTok MrMorf	62.9	62.9	63.6	63.6	55.5	55.5	57.5	57.5
EnBPE MrTok	67.9	68.0	69.6	69.6	55.6	55.5	58.1	58.1
EnBPE MrMorf	61.5	61.5	62.7	62.7	54.4	54.4	57.6	57.6
EnMorf MrTok	61.3	61.4	62.9	62.9	51.7	51.7	54.1	54.1
EnMorf MrBPE	54.9	54.9	59.1	59.1	51.3	51.3	52.3	52.3

Table 3: Results of systems for Marathi To English language direction. unk column contain output of systems where unknown were kept as they are, in transliterate column they were transliterated using small transliteration system

translating in English to Marathi direction. Whereas, training on Marathi to reordered English (Table 3) didnt get same positive result. Also surprising was dip in BLEU scores when using subwords. Using baseline systems with BasicTok as tokenization scheme for both scenarios (in both English and reordered English scenario) we created synthetic datasets using backtranslation(Sennrich et al., 2016a). Statistics for augmented datasets are given in Table 1. We used augmented data set with Moses to build SMT systems. Moses was used in same configuration as before. We employed all tokenization schemes combinations and result of same on dev sets are available in Table 2 and 3. Similar to trend seen in baseline systems on dev datasets, here also Augmented Reordered English to Marathi produce better score that Augmented English to Marathi. Marathi to English was better than Marathi to Reordered English to English. In most of the systems transliteration module was not helpful.

3 Result

For each language direction we submitted 72 output files. Table 4 shows the scores of top 3 systems for each direction. In case of English to Marathi translation direction, similar to trend seen on devsets, reordered English to Marathi systems fared better than canonical English to Marathi systems. Though tokenization scheme used was BPE for best system. While in case of Marathi to English translation direction, making a Marathi to reordered English did not preform better than Marathi to canonical English. Also we saw baseline system with BPE tokenized English and Marathi with morfessor as prepossessing step was better than all other system configurations, followed by Augmented Marathi with BPE to English with BPE . In terms of comparison to other teams, although our Marathi to English systems did not fare well, we were in top 3 for English to Marathi systems under constrained conditions.

References

Bahdanau, D., Cho, K., and Bengio, Y. (2014). Neural machine translation by jointly learning to align and translate. *arXiv preprint arXiv:1409.0473*.

Heafield, K. (2011). Kenlm: Faster and smaller language model queries. In *Proceedings of the sixth workshop on statistical machine translation*, pages 187–197.

Description of Translation System	Tokenization Scheme		Scores		
	Source	Target	BLEU	TER	CHRF
Augmented Reorder English to Marathi SMT system	BPE	BPE	11.8	0.45	0.95
Augmented Reorder English to Marathi SMT system	BPE	BPE	11.8	0.45	0.95
Baseline Reordered English to Marathi SMT system	basicTok	basicTok	11.4	0.43	0.934
Baseline Marathi to English SMT System	Morf	BPE	14.6	0.47	0.945
Baseline Marathi to English SMT System	Morf	BPE	14.6	0.47	0.945
Augmented Marathi to English SMT System	BPE	BPE	14.5	0.42	0.866

Table 4: Result of our top 3 systems on testsets in each translation direction

Koehn, P., Hoang, H., Birch, A., Callison-Burch, C., Federico, M., Bertoldi, N., Cowan, B., Shen, W., Moran, C., Zens, R., et al. (2007). Moses: Open source toolkit for statistical machine translation. In *Proceedings of the 45th annual meeting of the ACL on interactive poster and demonstration sessions*, pages 177–180. Association for Computational Linguistics.

Koehn, P. and Knowles, R. (2017). Six challenges for neural machine translation. *arXiv preprint arXiv:1706.03872*.

Koehn, P., Och, F. J., and Marcu, D. (2003). Statistical phrase-based translation. Technical report, UNIVERSITY OF SOUTHERN CALIFORNIA MARINA DEL REY INFORMATION SCIENCES INST.

Kunchukuttan, A., Mishra, A., Chatterjee, R., Shah, R., and Bhattacharyya, P. (2014). Sata-anuvadak: Tackling multiway translation of indian languages. *pan*, 841(54,570):4–135.

Och, F. J. (2003). Minimum error rate training in statistical machine translation. In *Proceedings of the 41st annual meeting of the Association for Computational Linguistics*, pages 160–167.

Och, F. J. and Ney, H. (2003). A systematic comparison of various statistical alignment models. *Computational linguistics*, 29(1):19–51.

Ojha, A. K., Liu, C.-H., Kann, K., Ortega, J., Satam, S., and Fransen, T. (2021). Findings of the LoResMT 2021 Shared Task on COVID and Sign Language for Low-Resource Languages. In *Proceedings of the 4th Workshop on Technologies for MT of Low Resource Languages*.

Patel, R. N., Gupta, R., Pimpale, P. B., and M, S. (2013). Reordering rules for English-Hindi SMT. In *Proceedings of the Second Workshop on Hybrid Approaches to Translation*, pages 34–41, Sofia, Bulgaria. Association for Computational Linguistics.

Post, M. (2018). A call for clarity in reporting BLEU scores. In *Proceedings of the Third Conference on Machine Translation: Research Papers*, pages 186–191, Belgium, Brussels. Association for Computational Linguistics.

Sennrich, R., Haddow, B., and Birch, A. (2016a). Improving neural machine translation models with monolingual data. In *Proceedings of the 54th Annual Meeting of the Association for Computational Linguistics (Volume 1: Long Papers)*, pages 86–96, Berlin, Germany. Association for Computational Linguistics.

Sennrich, R., Haddow, B., and Birch, A. (2016b). Neural machine translation of rare words with subword units. In *Proceedings of the 54th Annual Meeting of the Association for Computational Linguistics (Volume 1: Long Papers)*, pages 1715–1725, Berlin, Germany. Association for Computational Linguistics.

Virpioja, S., Smit, P., Grönroos, S.-A., Kurimo, M., et al. (2013). Morfessor 2.0: Python implementation and extensions for morfessor baseline.

The UCF Systems for the LoResMT 2021 Machine Translation Shared Task

William Chen wchen6255@knights.ucf.edu
Brett Fazio brettfazio@knights.ucf.edu
University of Central Florida

Abstract

We present the University of Central Florida systems for the LoResMT 2021 Shared Task, participating in the English-Irish and English-Marathi translation pairs. We focused our efforts on constrained track of the task, using transfer learning and subword segmentation to enhance our models given small amounts of training data. Our models achieved the highest BLEU scores on the fully constrained tracks of English-Irish, Irish-English, and Marathi-English with scores of 13.5, 21.3, and 17.9 respectively.

1 Introduction

In this paper, we describe the systems developed at the University of Central Florida for our participation in the Marathi and Irish tasks of the LoResMT 2021 Shared Task for low-resource supervised machine translation of COVID-19 related texts (Ojha et al., 2021). For these tasks, participants were asked to develop systems for the English to Irish, Irish to English, English to Marathi, or Marathi to English translation directions. Submissions are split into three tracks based on data constraints: a constrained track using only provided data, an unconstrained track allowing for publicly available corpora, and an unconstrained track allowing for both publicly available corpora and pre-trained models.

We utilize the Neural Machine Translation (NMT) approach, due to its prevalence in current research. While they are able to achieve state-of-the-art results in high-resource translation tasks, NMT systems tend to particularly struggle in low-resource scenarios. To alleviate this, our experiments focus primarily on data augmentation and transfer learning. We tried different techniques such as back-translation and subword segmentation, although they yielded little to no improvement in most cases. Our best performing systems during development for the Irish task utilized transfer learning from English-Marathi models. For the Marathi task, the best performances came from models trained on text pre-processed with subword segmentation via a unigram language model (Kudo, 2018). We submitted six systems for evaluation, one for each translation direction in the constrained track and two unconstrained Marathi models, which achieved the highest BLEU scores in the constrained tracks of English-Irish, Irish-English, and Marathi-English.

2 Data

We only utilize the data provided by the shared task organizers (Ojha et al., 2021) for our experiments. All text was pre-processed using Moses Tokenizer (Koehn et al., 2007) and lower-cased prior to training. We also experimented with a pre-trained SentencePiece (Kudo and

Richardson, 2018) tokenization model for Marathi from iNLTK (Arora, 2020). Final translation results were true-cased with Moses prior to submission.

We filtered out training sentences in the English-Marathi data that were also found in the development set from the training set to better evaluate our models during development. The parallel English-Marathi data was much larger than the English-Irish set, at 20,470 and 8,112 sentences respectively. A summary of the basic statistics of the final dataset used can be found in Table 1.

Data	Sentences	Vocabulary
EN Train (EN-GA)	8,112	15,761
GA Train (EN-GA)	8,112	17,026
EN Train (EN-MR)	20,470	27,717
MR Train (EN-MR)	20,470	42,116
EN Monolingual	8,826	20,037
MR Monolingual	21,902	39,942
EN Dev. (EN-GA)	502	2,128
GA Dev. (EN-GA)	502	2,455
EN Dev. (EN-MR)	500	3,740
MR Dev. (EN-MR)	500	4,767
EN Test (EN $\rightarrow$ GA)	500	1,912
GA Test (GA $\rightarrow$ EN)	250	1,056
EN Test (EN $\rightarrow$ MR)	500	2,344
MR Test (MR $\rightarrow$ EN)	500	2,528

Table 1: Statistics for the data used

3 System Description

We implement our models using OpenNMT-py (Klein et al., 2017). We initially tested both the Transformer (Vaswani et al., 2017) and LSTM (Hochreiter and Schmidhuber, 1997) architectures to obtain baseline results, but we found LSTMs to consistently yield better results despite attempts in optimizing Transformer parameters. As such, all of our experiments utilize LSTMs in a standard encoder-decoder setup.

We keep the majority of the parameters as their default values: we use 2 LSTM layers with 500 hidden units, an initial learning rate of 1, a dropout rate of 0.3, and stochastic gradient descent as the optimizer. We found the default step count of 100,000 to work well with the provided corpora with a batch size of 32.

3.1 Subword Segmentation

Subword segmentation is a common technique used for better dataset representation by reducing the amount of unique tokens and thus decreasing the chances of encountering unknown words. We explore Byte-Pair Encoding (BPE) (Sennrich et al., 2015) and Unigram (Kudo, 2018) segmentation, unsupervised algorithms commonly used in machine translation tasks. BPE is a greedy algorithm that initially represents a corpus at a character level, before conducting a certain number of merge operations to create subwords. Unigram initializes a large vocbulary from the corpus, before trimming down it down to meet a desired threshold.

3.2 Back-Translation

The addition of synthetic data via back-translation (Sennrich et al., 2016) has been shown to increase translation quality. To generate back-translated data, we train basic LSTM translation models on the provided parallel data. The models are then used to translate the provided monolingual data to create a parallel dataset. We also take advantage of the presence of English in both language pairs, translating the English portion of the English-Marathi training data to Irish and the English portion of the English-Irish training data to Marathi.

3.3 Transfer Learning

Transfer learning is a technique frequently used in low-resource translation, and is done by transferring the learned parameters of a high-resource parent model to low-resource child model (Zoph et al., 2016). We utilize transfer learning by training models on one language pair before fine-tuning them on the other (i.e. pre-training on English to Marathi and fine-tuning on English to Irish), leading to a total of four models trained with transfer learning: English-Marathi transferred to English-Irish, English-Irish transferred to English-Marathi, Marathi-English transferred to Irish-English, and Irish-English transferred to Marathi-English. We initialize these models with the weights of the trained LSTM baselines and fine-tune them for 100,000 steps on a new language pair. The optimizer is reset prior to fine-tuning to offset learning rate decay.

4 Experiments and Results

We first trained models using each technique to establish the effectiveness of a technique in each translation direction. Techniques that obtained a higher score than the baseline were then jointly used to develop additional models. We evaluated each model using the sacreBLEU (Post, 2018) implementation of BLEU (Papineni et al., 2002).

Model	EN→GA	GA→EN	EN→MR	MR→EN
1. LSTM	9.17	11.70	29.10	43.49
2. LSTM + BPE	8.04	10.47	27.70	39.94
3. LSTM + Unigram	8.87	9.30	28.39	43.79
4. LSTM + Back-Translation	8.75	11.32	22.26	40.29
5. LSTM + Transfer Learning	10.75	13.80	21.15	37.88
6. Model 1 + Pre-Trained Tokenizer			51.80	43.50
7. Model 2 + Pre-Trained Tokenizer			51.72	43.15
8. Model 3 + Pre-Trained Tokenizer			52.95	43.79
9. Model 4 + Pre-Trained Tokenizer			50.62	40.12
10. Model 5 + Pre-Trained Tokenizer			49.40	39.74

Table 2: BLEU scores on the validation set.

BLEU scores in the development stage are presented in Table 2. An unexpected outcome was the relative lack of benefit from subword segmentation and back-translation. We liken the former to the large vocabulary overlap between the training and validation set due to the COVID-19 specific context, as there would be fewer to no rare words that could be broken down into meaningful subwords by the segmentation algorithms.

Transfer learning from the higher resource English-Marathi models to the lower resource English-Irish models resulted in significant improvements in BLEU score (1.58 for English to Irish and 2.1 for Irish to English). However the reverse was not true, as English-Marathi models actually showed a large decrease in performance when knowledge was transferred from English-Irish.

The very high BLEU scores for the English-Marathi models can be explained by the domain overlap between data splits. We found the amount of common vocabulary between the training, development, and test sets of both language pairs to be rather large. For the Marathi texts, 94% of the development and 88% of the test vocabulary were found in the training portion.

The overlap was even more noticeable for English, with 93% of the vocabulary in development shared with training and 80% of vocabulary in testing shared with training.

Pair	Track	Model	BLEU	CHRF	TER
EN→GA	(A)	5	13.5	0.37	0.756
GA→EN	(A)	5	21.3	0.45	0.711
EN→MR	(A)	3	5.1	0.22	0.872
EN→MR	(B)	8	4.8	0.29	1.063
MR→EN	(A)	3	17.9	0.40	0.744
MR→EN	(B)	8	7.7	0.24	0.833

Table 3: Test scores via different metrics, provided by the organizers (Ojha et al., 2021)

For our final submissions, we participated in two tracks: the fully constrained track (A) and an unconstrained track (B). Track A was limited to using only data provided by the organizers. Track B allowed additional monolingual data and pre-trained models. We submitted translations generated from the systems with the highest BLEU scores in the development stage (Table 2) for each translation direction. We used LSTMs with transfer learning (Model 5) for the English to Irish and Irish to English directions, only submitting to track A. For track A of English to Marathi and Marathi to English, we used the LSTMs trained on text segmented with a unigram model (Model 3). For track B, we also used LSTMs trained on text segmented with a unigram model, but with the text pre-processed with a pre-trained language model tokenizer (Model 8). Table 3 shows the final scores of our systems on the test set, evaluated by BLEU (Papineni et al., 2002), CHRF (Popović, 2015), and TER (Snover et al., 2006).

5 Conclusion

We present systems for machine translation of Irish and Marathi to and from English. We improved over a developed baseline by incorporating transfer learning between language tasks and subword segmentation into our models. We also experimented with synthetic data generation via back-translation, which did not show any notable improvements during development. At test time, our models achieved the highest BLEU scores in the constrained tracks of English-Irish, Irish-English, and Marathi-English.

References

Arora, G. (2020). iNLTK: Natural language toolkit for indic languages. In *Proceedings of Second Workshop for NLP Open Source Software (NLP-OSS)*, pages 66–71, Online. Association for Computational Linguistics.

Hochreiter, S. and Schmidhuber, J. (1997). Long short-term memory. *Neural Computation*, 9(8):1735–1780.

Klein, G., Kim, Y., Deng, Y., Senellart, J., and Rush, A. (2017). OpenNMT: Open-source toolkit for neural machine translation. In *Proceedings of ACL 2017, System Demonstrations*, pages 67–72, Vancouver, Canada. Association for Computational Linguistics.

Koehn, P., Hoang, H., Birch, A., Callison-Burch, C., Federico, M., Bertoldi, N., Cowan, B., Shen, W., Moran, C., Zens, R., Dyer, C., Bojar, O., Constantin, A., and Herbst, E. (2007). Moses: Open source toolkit for statistical machine translation. In *Proceedings of the 45th Annual Meeting of the Association for Computational Linguistics Companion Volume Proceedings of the Demo and Poster Sessions*, pages 177–180, Prague, Czech Republic. Association for Computational Linguistics.

Kudo, T. (2018). Subword regularization: Improving neural network translation models with multiple subword candidates. In *Proceedings of the 56th Annual Meeting of the Association for Computational Linguistics (Volume 1: Long Papers)*, pages 66–75, Melbourne, Australia. Association for Computational Linguistics.

Kudo, T. and Richardson, J. (2018). SentencePiece: A simple and language independent subword tokenizer and detokenizer for neural text processing. In *Proceedings of the 2018 Conference on Empirical Methods in Natural Language Processing: System Demonstrations*, pages 66–71, Brussels, Belgium. Association for Computational Linguistics.

Ojha, A. K., Liu, C.-H., Kann, K., Ortega, J., Satam, S., and Fransen, T. (2021). Findings of the LoResMT 2021 Shared Task on COVID and Sign Language for Low-Resource Languages. In *Proceedings of the 4th Workshop on Technologies for MT of Low Resource Languages.*

Papineni, K., Roukos, S., Ward, T., and Zhu, W.-J. (2002). Bleu: a method for automatic evaluation of machine translation. In *Proceedings of the 40th Annual Meeting of the Association for Computational Linguistics*, pages 311–318, Philadelphia, Pennsylvania, USA. Association for Computational Linguistics.

Popović, M. (2015). chrF: character n-gram F-score for automatic MT evaluation. In *Proceedings of the Tenth Workshop on Statistical Machine Translation*, pages 392–395, Lisbon, Portugal. Association for Computational Linguistics.

Post, M. (2018). A call for clarity in reporting BLEU scores. In *Proceedings of the Third Conference on Machine Translation: Research Papers*, pages 186–191, Belgium, Brussels. Association for Computational Linguistics.

Sennrich, R., Haddow, B., and Birch, A. (2015). Neural machine translation of rare words with subword units. *CoRR*, abs/1508.07909.

Sennrich, R., Haddow, B., and Birch, A. (2016). Improving neural machine translation models with monolingual data.

Snover, M., Dorr, B., Schwartz, R., Micciulla, L., and Makhoul, J. (2006). A study of translation edit rate with targeted human annotation. In *Proceedings of the 7th Conference of the Association for Machine Translation in the Americas: Technical Papers*, pages 223–231, Cambridge, Massachusetts, USA. Association for Machine Translation in the Americas.

Vaswani, A., Shazeer, N., Parmar, N., Uszkoreit, J., Jones, L., Gomez, A. N., Kaiser, L., and Polosukhin, I. (2017). Attention is all you need. *arXiv:1706.03762. Version 5.*

Zoph, B., Yuret, D., May, J., and Knight, K. (2016). Transfer learning for low-resource neural machine translation. In *Proceedings of the 2016 Conference on Empirical Methods in Natural Language Processing*, pages 1568–1575, Austin, Texas. Association for Computational Linguistics.

Attentive fine-tuning of Transformers for Translation of low-resourced languages @LoResMT 2021

Karthik Puranik[1] **Adeep Hande**[1] **Ruba Priyadharshini**[2] **Thenmozi Durairaj**[3]
Anbukkarasi Sampath[4] **Kingston Pal Thamburaj**[5] **Bharathi Raja Chakravarthi**[6]
[1]Department of Computer Science, Indian Institute of Information Technology Tiruchirappalli
[2]ULTRA Arts and Science College, Madurai, Tamil Nadu, India
[3]Sri Sivasubramaniya Nadar College of Engineering, Tamil Nadu, India
[4]Kongu Engineering College, Erode, Tamil Nadu, India
[5]Sultan Idris Education University, Tanjong Malim, Perak, Malaysia
[6]Insight SFI Research Centre for Data Analytics, National University of Ireland Galway
{{karthikp, adeeph}18c@iiitt.ac.in, rubapriyadharshini.a@gmail.com, theni_d@ssn.edu.in,
anbu.1318@gmail.com, fkingston@gmail.com, bharathi.raja@insight-centre.org}

Abstract

This paper reports the Machine Translation (MT) systems submitted by the IIITT team for the English→Marathi and English⇔Irish language pairs LoResMT 2021 shared task. The task focuses on getting exceptional translations for rather low-resourced languages like Irish and Marathi. We fine-tune IndicTrans, a pretrained multilingual NMT model for English→Marathi, using external parallel corpus as input for additional training. We have used a pretrained Helsinki-NLP Opus MT English⇔Irish model for the latter language pair. Our approaches yield relatively promising results on the BLEU metrics. Under the team name IIITT, our systems ranked 1, 1, and 2 in English→Marathi, Irish→English, and English→Irish respectively. The codes for our systems are published[1].

1 Introduction

Today, a large number of text and written materials are present in English. However, with roughly around 6,500 languages in the world[2] (Chakravarthi, 2020; Hande et al., 2021a; Sarveswaran et al., 2021), every native monoglot should not be deprived of this knowledge and information. The manual translation is a tedious job involving much time and human resources, giving rise to Machine Translation (MT). Machine Translation involves the automated translation of text from one language to another by using various algorithms and resources to produce quality translation predictions (Pathak and Pakray, 2018; Krishnamurthy, 2015, 2019). Neural Machine Translation (NMT) brought about a great improvement in the field of MT by overcoming flaws of rule-based and statistical machine translation (SMT) (Revanuru et al., 2017; Achchuthan and Sarveswaran, 2015; Parameswari et al., 2012; Thenmozhi et al., 2018; Kumar et al., 2020b). NMT incorporates the training of neural networks on parallel corpora to predict the likeliness of a sequence of words. sequence-to-sequence neural models (seq2seq)

[1]https://github.com/karthikpuranik11/LoResMT
[2]https://blog.busuu.com/most-spoken-languages-in-the-world/

(Sutskever et al., 2014; Kalchbrenner and Blunsom, 2013) are the widely adopted as the standard approach by both industrial and research communities (Jadhav, 2020a; Bojar et al., 2016; Cheng et al., 2016).

Even though NMT performs exceptionally well for all the languages, it requires a tremendous amount of parallel corpus to produce meaningful and successful translations (Kumar et al., 2020a). With little research on low resourced languages, finding a quality parallel corpus to train the models can be arduous. The two low-resourced languages worked on in this paper are Marathi (mr) and Irish (ga). With about 120 million Marathi speakers in Maharashtra and other states of India, Marathi is recognized as one of the 22 scheduled languages of India[3]. The structural dissimilarity which occurs while translating from English (Subject-Verb-Object) to Marathi (Subject-Object-Verb) or vice versa adds up to issues faced while translation (Garje, 2014). The Irish language was recognized as the first official language of Ireland and also by the EU(Dowling et al., 2020a; Scannell, 2007). Belonging to the Goidelic language family and the Celtic family(Scannell, 2007; Lynn et al., 2015), Irish is also claimed as one of the low resourced languages due to its limited resources by the META-NET report (Dhonnchadha et al., 2012; Scannell, 2006).

Our paper represents the work conducted for the LoResMT @ MT Summit 2021[4] shared task to build MT systems for the low-resourced Marathi and Irish languages on COVID-19 related parallel corpus. We implement Transformer-based (Vaswani et al., 2017) NMT models to procure BLEU scores(Papineni et al., 2002) of 24.2, 25.8, and 34.6 in English→Marathi, Irish→English, and English→Irish respectively.

2 Related works

Neural Machine Translation has been exhaustively studied over the years (Kalchbrenner and Blunsom, 2013), with several intuitive approaches involving collective learning to align and translate (Bahdanau et al., 2016), and a language-independent attention bridge for multilingual translational systems (Vázquez et al., 2019). There have been several approaches to NMT, with zero-shot translational systems, between language pairs that have not seen the parallel training data during training (Johnson et al., 2017). The introduction of artificial tokens has reduced the architectural changes in the decoder (Ha et al., 2016). There have been some explorations towards neural machine translation in low resource languages, with the development of a multi-source translational system that targets the English string for any source language (Zoph and Knight, 2016).

There has been subsequent research undertaken by researchers for machine translation in low-resource Indian languages. Chakravarthi et al. surveyed orthographic information in machine translation, examining the orthography's influence on machine translation and extended it to under-resourced Dravidian languages (Chakravarthi et al., 2019a). Another approach of leveraging the information contained in rule-based machine translation systems to improve machine translation of low-resourced languages was employed (Torregrosa et al., 2019). Several approaches involving the improvement of WordNet for low-resourced languages have been explored (Chakravarthi et al., 2018, 2019b). Chakravarthi et al. constructed MMDravi, a multilingual multimodal machine translation dataset for low-resourced Dravidian languages, extending it from the Flickr30K dataset, and generating translations for the captions using phonetic transcriptions (U Hegde et al., 2021).

There have been relatively fewer approaches experimented with and benchmarked when it comes to translating from Marathi to English and vice versa. (Aharoni et al., 2019) tried to build multilingual NMT systems, comprising 103 distinct languages and 204 translational directions

[3]https://en.wikipedia.org/wiki/Marathi_language

[4]https://sites.google.com/view/loresmt/

simultaneously. (Jadhav, 2020b; Puranik et al., 2021) developed a machine translation system for Marathi to English using transformers on a parallel corpus. Other works on improving machine translation include (Adi Narayana Reddy et al., 2021) proposing an English-Marathi NMT using local attention. The same can be stated to Irish, as it is a poorly resourced language, as the quality of the MT outputs have struggled to achieve the same level as well-supported languages (Dowling et al., 2016; Rehm and Uszkoreit, 2012). In recent years, several researchers tried to overcome the resource barrier by creating artificial parallel data through back-translation (Poncelas et al., 2018), exploiting out-of-domain data (Imankulova et al., 2019), and leveraging other better-resourced languages as a pivot (Dowling et al., 2020b; Wu and Wang, 2007).

3 Dataset

We use the dataset provided by the organizers of LoResMT @ MT Summit 2021. The datasets can be found here[5]. It is a parallel corpus for English and the low resourced language, i.e., Irish and Marathi, mostly containing text related to COVID-19 (Ojha et al., 2021).

Language pair	English⇔Irish	English⇔Marathi
Train	8,112	20,933
Dev	502	500
Test	1,000	1,000
Total	9,614	22,433

Table 1: Number of sentences distribution

We have used bible-uedin[6] (Christodoulopoulos and Steedman, 2015) an external dataset for Marathi. It is a multilingual parallel corpus dataset containing translations of the Bible in 102 languages(Christodoulopoulos and Steedman, 2014) and shows the possibility of using the Bible for research and machine translation. English-Marathi corpus contains 60,495 sentences. CVIT PIB[7] (Philip et al., 2020) has also been used for the purpose of this research. It contains 1,14,220 parallel corpora for English-Marathi.

4 Methodology

4.1 IndicTrans

Fairseq PyTorch[8] (Ott et al., 2019) is an open-source machine learning library supported as a sequence modeling toolkit. Custom models can be trained for various tasks, including summarization, language, translation, and other generation tasks. Training on fairseq enables competent batching, mixed-precision training, multi-GPU and multi-machine training. IndicTrans (Ramesh et al., 2021), a Transformer-4x multilingual NMT model by AI4Bharat, is trained on the Samanantar dataset. The architecture of our approach is displayed in Fig.1. Samanantar[9] is the most extensive collection of parallel corpora for Indic languages available for public use. It includes 46.9 million sentence pairs between English and 11 Indian languages. IndicTrans is claimed to successfully outperform the existing best performing models on a wide variety of benchmarks. Even commercial translation systems and existing publicly available systems were surpassed for the majority of the languages. IndicTrans is based on fairseq, and it was

[5]https://github.com/loresmt/loresmt-2021
[6]https://opus.nlpl.eu/JRC-Acquis.php
[7]http://preon.iiit.ac.in/~jerin/bhasha/
[8]https://github.com/pytorch/fairseq
[9]https://indicnlp.ai4bharat.org/samanantar/

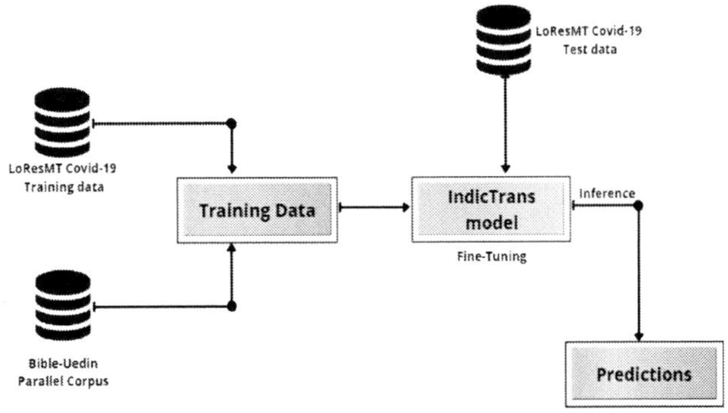

Figure 1: Our approach for the English→Marathi language pair.

fine-tuned on the Marathi training dataset provided by the organizers and the external datasets. The model was fine-tuned with the cross-entropy criterion to compute the loss function, Adam optimizer (Zhang, 2018), dropout of 0.2, fp16 (Micikevicius et al., 2017), maximum tokens of 256 for better learning, and a learning rate if 3e-5 in GPU. The process was conducted for a maximum of 3 epochs.

4.2 Helsinki-NLP Opus-MT

OPUS-MT (Tiedemann and Thottingal, 2020) supports both bilingual and multilingual models. It is a project that focuses on the development of free resources and tools for machine translation. The current status is a repository of over 1,000 pretrained neural MT models. We fine-tune a transformer-align model that was fine-tuned for the Tatoeba-Challenge[10]. ***Helsinki-NLP/opus-mt-en-ga*** model from the HuggingFace Transformers (Wolf et al., 2020) for English→ Irish and ***Helsinki-NLP/opus-mt-ga-en*** for Irish→ English were used.

Language pair	Method	BLEU
English→Marathi	IndicTrans baseline	14.0
English→Marathi	IndicTrans TRA	17.8
English→Marathi	IndicTrans CVIT-PIB	23.4
English→Marathi	IndicTrans bible-uedin	27.7
English→Irish	Opus MT	30.4
English→Irish	M2M100	25.6
Irish→English	Opus MT	37.2
Irish→English	M2M100	30.4

Table 2: BLEU scores obtained for the various models for the development set

5 Results and Analysis

For Marathi, it is distinctly visible that our system model, i.e., IndicTrans fine-tuned on the training data provided by the organizers or TRA and the bible-uedin dataset, gave the best BLEU

[10] `https://github.com/Helsinki-NLP/Tatoeba-Challenge`

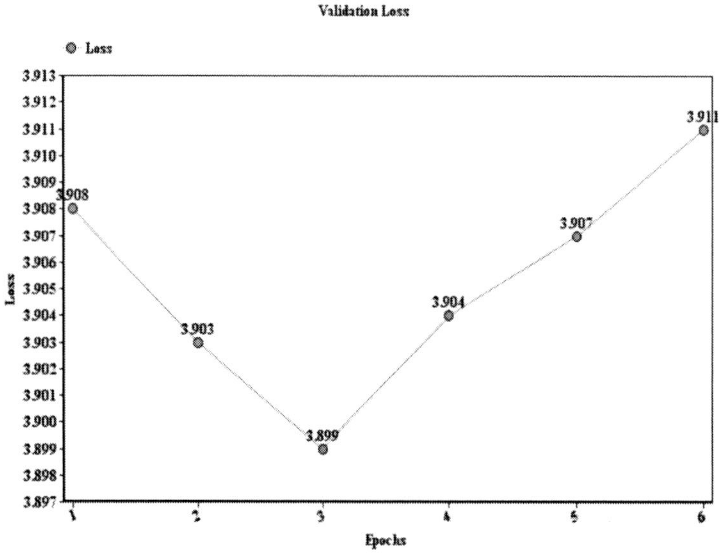

Figure 2: The graph depicting the increase in val lossafter the third epoch

scores. It was surprising how the model fine-tuned on a parallel corpus of 60,495 sentences of bible-uedin surpassed the model fine-tuned on 1,14,220 sentences from the CVIT PIB dataset. The possible explanation is the higher correlation between the sentences of the bible-uedin dataset with the test dataset than the CVIT PIB dataset. Another reason could be the presence of excessive noise in the CVIT PIB dataset. The other reason for this could be noise and a lower quality of translations in the CVIT PIB dataset compared to bible-uedin.

To infer the same, 1000 random pairs of sentences were picked from the datasets, and the average LaBSE or language-agnostic BERT Sentence Embedding (Feng et al., 2020) scores were found out. LaBSE gives a score between 0 and 1, depending on the quality of the translation. It was seen that the average was 0.768 for the bible-uedin dataset, while it was 0.58 for the CVIT PIB dataset. This might have been one of the reasons for the better BLEU scores. The model also showed constant overfitting after the second and third epoch, as the BLEU scores reduced considerably as they reached the 6th epoch. The BLEU scores decreased by a difference of 6.The validation loss starts increasing after the third epoch, thus, showing the overfitting occurring in training. So, the model was fine-tuned for three epochs while maintaining a low learning rate of around 3e-5 to get a BLEU score of 24.2.

Language pair	BLEU	CHRF	TER	Rank
English→Marathi	24.2	0.59	0.597	1
Irish→English	34.6	0.61	0.711	1
English→Irish	25.8	0.53	0.629	2

Table 3: Result and ranks obtained for the test dataset(Popović, 2015; Snover et al., 2006)

Training a model to predict for a low-resourced language was highly challenging due to the absence of prominent pretrained models (Kalyan et al., 2021; Yasaswini et al., 2021; Hande et al., 2021b). However, as an experiment, two models from HuggingFace Transformers[11], M2M100 (Fan et al., 2020) and Opus-MT from Helsinki NLP (Tiedemann, 2020) were compared. For the dev data, Opus MT produced a BLEU score of 30.4 while M2M100 gave 25.62 for translations from English to Irish and 37.2 and 30.37 respectively for Irish to English translations. Probably, the individual models pretrained on numerous datasets gave Opus MT an edge over M2M100. This led us to submit the Opus MT model for the LoResMT Shared task 2021. The model gave exceptional BLEU scores of 25.8 for English to Irish, which ranked second in the shared task, while 34.6 for Irish to English stood first.

6 Conclusion

It is arduous and unyielding to get accurate translations for low-resourced languages due to limited datasets and pretrained models. However, our paper puts forward a few methods to better the already existing accuracies. Ranked 1, 1, and 2 in English→Marathi, Irish→English, and English→Irish respectively in the LoResMT 2021 shared task, IndicTrans fine-tuned on the bible-uedin, and the dataset provided by the organizers manages to surpass the other models due to its high correlation with the test set and minimal noise for the Marathi language. The Irish language task was dominated by the Opus MT model by Helsinki-NLP, outperforming other Transformer models, M2M100.

References

Achchuthan, Y. and Sarveswaran, K. (2015). Language localisation of Tamil using statistical machine translation. In *2015 Fifteenth International Conference on Advances in ICT for Emerging Regions (ICTer)*, pages 125–129. IEEE.

Adi Narayana Reddy, K., Shyam Chandra Prasad, G., Rajashekar Reddy, A., Naveen Kumar, L., and Kannaiah (2021). English-marathi neural machine translation using local attention. In Garg, D., Wong, K., Sarangapani, J., and Gupta, S. K., editors, *Advanced Computing*, pages 280–287, Singapore. Springer Singapore.

Aharoni, R., Johnson, M., and Firat, O. (2019). Massively multilingual neural machine translation. In *Proceedings of the 2019 Conference of the North American Chapter of the Association for Computational Linguistics: Human Language Technologies, Volume 1 (Long and Short Papers)*, pages 3874–3884, Minneapolis, Minnesota. Association for Computational Linguistics.

Bahdanau, D., Cho, K., and Bengio, Y. (2016). Neural machine translation by jointly learning to align and translate.

Bojar, O., Chatterjee, R., Federmann, C., Graham, Y., Haddow, B., Huck, M., Jimeno Yepes, A., Koehn, P., Logacheva, V., Monz, C., Negri, M., Névéol, A., Neves, M., Popel, M., Post, M., Rubino, R., Scarton, C., Specia, L., Turchi, M., Verspoor, K., and Zampieri, M. (2016). Findings of the 2016 conference on machine translation. In *Proceedings of the First Conference on Machine Translation: Volume 2, Shared Task Papers*, pages 131–198, Berlin, Germany. Association for Computational Linguistics.

Chakravarthi, B. R. (2020). *Leveraging orthographic information to improve machine translation of under-resourced languages*. PhD thesis, NUI Galway.

Chakravarthi, B. R., Arcan, M., and McCrae, J. P. (2018). Improving wordnets for under-resourced languages using machine translation. In *Proceedings of the 9th Global Wordnet Conference*, pages 77–86.

[11] https://huggingface.co/transformers/

Chakravarthi, B. R., Arcan, M., and McCrae, J. P. (2019a). Comparison of different orthographies for machine translation of under-resourced dravidian languages. In *2nd Conference on Language, Data and Knowledge (LDK 2019)*. Schloss Dagstuhl-Leibniz-Zentrum fuer Informatik.

Chakravarthi, B. R., Arcan, M., and McCrae, J. P. (2019b). Wordnet gloss translation for under-resourced languages using multilingual neural machine translation. In *Proceedings of the Second Workshop on Multilingualism at the Intersection of Knowledge Bases and Machine Translation*, pages 1–7.

Chakravarthi, B. R., Priyadharshini, R., Stearns, B., Jayapal, A. K., Sridevy, S., Arcan, M., Zarrouk, M., and McCrae, J. P. (2019c). Multilingual multimodal machine translation for dravidian languages utilizing phonetic transcription. In *Proceedings of the 2nd Workshop on Technologies for MT of Low Resource Languages*, pages 56–63.

Chakravarthi, B. R., Rani, P., Arcan, M., and McCrae, J. P. (2021). A survey of orthographic information in machine translation. *SN Computer Science*, 2(4):1–19.

Cheng, Y., Xu, W., He, Z., He, W., Wu, H., Sun, M., and Liu, Y. (2016). Semi-supervised learning for neural machine translation. In *Proceedings of the 54th Annual Meeting of the Association for Computational Linguistics (Volume 1: Long Papers)*, pages 1965–1974, Berlin, Germany. Association for Computational Linguistics.

Christodoulopoulos, C. and Steedman, M. (2014). A massively parallel corpus: the bible in 100 languages. *Language Resources and Evaluation*, 49:1–21.

Christodoulopoulos, C. and Steedman, M. (2015). A massively parallel corpus: the bible in 100 languages. *Language Resources and Evaluation*, 49:375 – 395.

Dhonnchadha, E., Judge, J., Chasaide, A., Dhubhda, R., and Scannell, K. (2012). The irish language in the digital age: An ghaeilge sa ré dhigiteach.

Dowling, M., Castilho, S., Moorkens, J., Lynn, T., and Way, A. (2020a). A human evaluation of english-irish statistical and neural machine translation.

Dowling, M., Castilho, S., Moorkens, J., Lynn, T., and Way, A. (2020b). A human evaluation of English-Irish statistical and neural machine translation. In *Proceedings of the 22nd Annual Conference of the European Association for Machine Translation*, pages 431–440, Lisboa, Portugal. European Association for Machine Translation.

Dowling, M., Judge, J., Lynn, T., and Graham, Y. (2016). English to irish machine translation with automatic post-editing.

Fan, A., Bhosale, S., Schwenk, H., Ma, Z., El-Kishky, A., Goyal, S., Baines, M., Celebi, O., Wenzek, G., Chaudhary, V., Goyal, N., Birch, T., Liptchinsky, V., Edunov, S., Grave, E., Auli, M., and Joulin, A. (2020). Beyond english-centric multilingual machine translation.

Feng, F., Yang, Y., Cer, D., Arivazhagan, N., and Wang, W. (2020). Language-agnostic bert sentence embedding.

Garje, G. (2014). Marathi to english machine translation for simple sentences. *International Journal of Science and Research (IJSR)*, 3.

Ha, T.-L., Niehues, J., and Waibel, A. (2016). Toward multilingual neural machine translation with universal encoder and decoder. *ArXiv*, abs/1611.04798.

Hande, A., Puranik, K., Priyadharshini, R., and Chakravarthi, B. R. (2021a). Domain identification of scientific articles using transfer learning and ensembles. In *Trends and Applications in Knowledge Discovery and Data Mining: PAKDD 2021 Workshops, WSPA, MLMEIN, SDPRA, DARAI, and AI4EPT, Delhi, India, May 11, 2021 Proceedings 25*, pages 88–97. Springer International Publishing.

Hande, A., Puranik, K., Priyadharshini, R., Thavareesan, S., and Chakravarthi, B. R. (2021b). Evaluating pretrained transformer-based models for covid-19 fake news detection. In *2021 5th International Conference on Computing Methodologies and Communication (ICCMC)*, pages 766–772.

Imankulova, A., Dabre, R., Fujita, A., and Imamura, K. (2019). Exploiting out-of-domain parallel data through multilingual transfer learning for low-resource neural machine translation. In *Proceedings of Machine Translation Summit XVII Volume 1: Research Track*, pages 128–139, Dublin, Ireland. European Association for Machine Translation.

Jadhav, S. (2020a). Marathi to english neural machine translation with near perfect corpus and transformers. *ArXiv*, abs/2002.11643.

Jadhav, S. A. (2020b). Marathi to english neural machine translation with near perfect corpus and transformers.

Johnson, M., Schuster, M., Le, Q. V., Krikun, M., Wu, Y., Chen, Z., Thorat, N., Viégas, F., Wattenberg, M., Corrado, G., Hughes, M., and Dean, J. (2017). Google's multilingual neural machine translation system: Enabling zero-shot translation.

Kalchbrenner, N. and Blunsom, P. (2013). Recurrent continuous translation models. In *Proceedings of the 2013 Conference on Empirical Methods in Natural Language Processing*, pages 1700–1709, Seattle, Washington, USA. Association for Computational Linguistics.

Kalyan, P., Reddy, D., Hande, A., Priyadharshini, R., Sakuntharaj, R., and Chakravarthi, B. R. (2021). IIITT at CASE 2021 task 1: Leveraging pretrained language models for multilingual protest detection. In *Challenges and Applications of Automated Extraction of Socio-political Events from Text*, pages 98–104, Online. Association for Computational Linguistics.

Krishnamurthy, P. (2015). Development of Telugu-Tamil transfer-based machine translation system: With special reference to divergence index. In *Proceedings of the 1st Deep Machine Translation Workshop*, pages 48–54, Praha, Czechia. ÚFAL MFF UK.

Krishnamurthy, P. (2019). Development of Telugu-Tamil transfer-based machine translation system: An improvization using divergence index. *Journal of Intelligent Systems*, 28(3):493–504.

Kumar, A., Mundotiya, R. K., and Singh, A. K. (2020a). Unsupervised approach for zero-shot experiments: Bhojpuri–Hindi and Magahi–Hindi@LoResMT 2020. In *Proceedings of the 3rd Workshop on Technologies for MT of Low Resource Languages*, pages 43–46, Suzhou, China. Association for Computational Linguistics.

Kumar, B. S., Thenmozhi, D., and Kayalvizhi, S. (2020b). Tamil paraphrase detection using encoder-decoder neural networks. In *International Conference on Computational Intelligence in Data Science*, pages 30–42. Springer.

Lynn, T., Scannell, K., and Maguire, E. (2015). Minority language twitter: Part-of-speech tagging and analysis of irish tweets.

Micikevicius, P., Narang, S., Alben, J., Diamos, G., Elsen, E., Garcia, D., Ginsburg, B., Houston, M., Kuchaiev, O., Venkatesh, G., et al. (2017). Mixed precision training. *arXiv preprint arXiv:1710.03740*.

Ojha, A. K., Liu, C.-H., Kann, K., Ortega, J., Satam, S., and Fransen, T. (2021). Findings of the LoResMT 2021 Shared Task on COVID and Sign Language for Low-Resource Languages. In *Proceedings of the 4th Workshop on Technologies for MT of Low Resource Languages*.

Ott, M., Edunov, S., Baevski, A., Fan, A., Gross, S., Ng, N., Grangier, D., and Auli, M. (2019). fairseq: A fast, extensible toolkit for sequence modeling. In *Proceedings of NAACL-HLT 2019: Demonstrations*.

Papineni, K., Roukos, S., Ward, T., and Zhu, W. J. (2002). Bleu: a method for automatic evaluation of machine translation.

Parameswari, K., Sreenivasulu, N., Uma Maheshwar Rao, G., and Christopher, M. (2012). Development of Telugu-Tamil bidirectional machine translation system: A special focus on case divergence. In *proceedings of 11th International Tamil Internet conference*, pages 180–191.

Pathak, A. and Pakray, D. P. (2018). Neural machine translation for indian languages. *Journal of Intelligent Systems*, 28.

Philip, J., Siripragada, S., Namboodiri, V. P., and Jawahar, C. V. (2020). Revisiting low resource status of indian languages in machine translation. *8th ACM IKDD CODS and 26th COMAD*.

Poncelas, A., Shterionov, D., Way, A., Wenniger, G. M. D. B., and Passban, P. (2018). Investigating backtranslation in neural machine translation. *ArXiv*, abs/1804.06189.

Popović, M. (2015). chrF: character n-gram F-score for automatic MT evaluation. In *Proceedings of the Tenth Workshop on Statistical Machine Translation*, pages 392–395, Lisbon, Portugal. Association for Computational Linguistics.

Puranik, K., Hande, A., Priyadharshini, R., Thavareesan, S., and Chakravarthi, B. R. (2021). IIITT@LT-EDI-EACL2021-hope speech detection: There is always hope in transformers. In *Proceedings of the First Workshop on Language Technology for Equality, Diversity and Inclusion*, pages 98–106, Kyiv. Association for Computational Linguistics.

Ramesh, G., Doddapaneni, S., Bheemaraj, A., Jobanputra, M., AK, R., Sharma, A., Sahoo, S., Diddee, H., J, M., Kakwani, D., Kumar, N., Pradeep, A., Deepak, K., Raghavan, V., Kunchukuttan, A., Kumar, P., and Khapra, M. S. (2021). Samanantar: The largest publicly available parallel corpora collection for 11 indic languages.

Rehm, G. and Uszkoreit, H. (2012). The irish language in the digital age.

Revanuru, K., Turlapaty, K., and Rao, S. (2017). Neural machine translation of indian languages. In *Proceedings of the 10th Annual ACM India Compute Conference*, Compute '17, page 11–20, New York, NY, USA. Association for Computing Machinery.

Sarveswaran, K., Dias, G., and Butt, M. (2021). Thamizhimorph: A morphological parser for the Tamil language. *Machine Translation*, 35(1):37–70.

Scannell, K. P. (2006). Machine translation for closely related language pairs. In *Proceedings of the Workshop Strategies for developing machine translation for minority languages*, pages 103–109. Citeseer.

Scannell, K. P. (2007). The crúbadán project: Corpus building for under-resourced languages. In *Building and Exploring Web Corpora: Proceedings of the 3rd Web as Corpus Workshop*, volume 4, pages 5–15.

Snover, M., Dorr, B., Schwartz, R., Micciulla, L., and Makhoul, J. (2006). A study of translation edit rate with targeted human annotation.

Sutskever, I., Vinyals, O., and Le, Q. V. (2014). Sequence to sequence learning with neural networks.

Thenmozhi, D., Kumar, B. S., and Aravindan, C. (2018). Deep learning approach to English-Tamil and Hindi-Tamil verb phrase translations. In *FIRE (Working Notes)*, pages 323–331.

Tiedemann, J. (2020). The tatoeba translation challenge – realistic data sets for low resource and multilingual mt.

Tiedemann, J. and Thottingal, S. (2020). OPUS-MT – building open translation services for the world. In *Proceedings of the 22nd Annual Conference of the European Association for Machine Translation*, pages 479–480, Lisboa, Portugal. European Association for Machine Translation.

Torregrosa, D., Pasricha, N., Masoud, M., Chakravarthi, B. R., Alonso, J., Casas, N., and Arcan, M. (2019). Leveraging rule-based machine translation knowledge for under-resourced neural machine translation models. In *Proceedings of Machine Translation Summit XVII Volume 2: Translator, Project and User Tracks*, pages 125–133, Dublin, Ireland. European Association for Machine Translation.

U Hegde, S., Hande, A., Priyadharshini, R., Thavareesan, S., and Chakravarthi, B. R. (2021). UVCE-IIITT@DravidianLangTech-EACL2021: Tamil troll meme classification: You need to pay more attention. In *Proceedings of the First Workshop on Speech and Language Technologies for Dravidian Languages*, pages 180–186, Kyiv. Association for Computational Linguistics.

Vaswani, A., Shazeer, N., Parmar, N., Uszkoreit, J., Jones, L., Gomez, A. N., Kaiser, L., and Polosukhin, I. (2017). Attention is all you need.

Vázquez, R., Raganato, A., Tiedemann, J., and Creutz, M. (2019). Multilingual NMT with a language-independent attention bridge. In *Proceedings of the 4th Workshop on Representation Learning for NLP (RepL4NLP-2019)*, pages 33–39, Florence, Italy. Association for Computational Linguistics.

Wolf, T., Debut, L., Sanh, V., Chaumond, J., Delangue, C., Moi, A., Cistac, P., Rault, T., Louf, R., Funtowicz, M., Davison, J., Shleifer, S., von Platen, P., Ma, C., Jernite, Y., Plu, J., Xu, C., Le Scao, T., Gugger, S., Drame, M., Lhoest, Q., and Rush, A. (2020). Transformers: State-of-the-art natural language processing. In *Proceedings of the 2020 Conference on Empirical Methods in Natural Language Processing: System Demonstrations*, pages 38–45, Online. Association for Computational Linguistics.

Wu, H. and Wang, H. (2007). Pivot language approach for phrase-based statistical machine translation. In *Proceedings of the 45th Annual Meeting of the Association of Computational Linguistics*, pages 856–863, Prague, Czech Republic. Association for Computational Linguistics.

Yasaswini, K., Puranik, K., Hande, A., Priyadharshini, R., Thavareesan, S., and Chakravarthi, B. R. (2021). IIITT@DravidianLangTech-EACL2021: Transfer learning for offensive language detection in Dravidian languages. In *Proceedings of the First Workshop on Speech and Language Technologies for Dravidian Languages*, pages 187–194, Kyiv. Association for Computational Linguistics.

Zhang, Z. (2018). Improved adam optimizer for deep neural networks. In *2018 IEEE/ACM 26th International Symposium on Quality of Service (IWQoS)*, pages 1–2. IEEE.

Zoph, B. and Knight, K. (2016). Multi-source neural translation. In *Proceedings of the 2016 Conference of the North American Chapter of the Association for Computational Linguistics: Human Language Technologies*, pages 30–34, San Diego, California. Association for Computational Linguistics.

Machine Translation in the Covid domain: an English-Irish case study for LoResMT 2021

Séamus Lankford seamus.lankford@adaptcentre.ie
ADAPT Centre, School of Computing, Dublin City University, Dublin, Ireland.

Haithem Afli haithem.afli@adaptcentre.ie
ADAPT Centre, Department of Computer Science, Munster Technological University, Ireland.

Andy Way andy.way@adaptcentre.ie
ADAPT Centre, School of Computing, Dublin City University, Dublin, Ireland.

Abstract

Translation models for the specific domain of translating Covid data from English to Irish were developed for the LoResMT 2021 shared task. Domain adaptation techniques, using a Covid-adapted generic 55k corpus from the Directorate General of Translation, were applied. Fine-tuning, mixed fine-tuning and combined dataset approaches were compared with models trained on an extended in-domain dataset. As part of this study, an English-Irish dataset of Covid related data, from the Health and Education domains, was developed. The highest-performing model used a Transformer architecture trained with an extended in-domain Covid dataset. In the context of this study, we have demonstrated that extending an 8k in-domain baseline dataset by just 5k lines improved the BLEU score by 27 points.

1 Introduction

Neural Machine Translation (NMT) has routinely outperformed Statistical Machine Translation (SMT) when large parallel datasets are available (Crego et al., 2016; Wu et al., 2016). Furthermore, Transformer based approaches have demonstrated impressive results in moderate low-resource scenarios (Lankford et al., 2021). NMT involving Transformer model development will improve the performance in specific domains of low-resource languages (Araabi and Monz, 2020). However, the benefits of NMT are less clear when using very low-resource Machine Translation (MT) on in-domain datasets of less than 10k lines.

The Irish language is a primary example of a low-resource language that will benefit from such research. This paper reports the results for the MT system developed for the English–Irish shared task at LoResMT 2021 (Ojha et al., 2021). Relevant work is presented in the background section followed by an overview of the proposed approach. The empirical findings are outlined in the results section. Finally, the key findings are presented and discussed.

2 Background

2.1 Transformer

A novel architecture called Transformer was introduced in the paper 'Attention Is All You Need' (Vaswani et al., 2017). Transformer is an architecture for transforming one sequence into another with the help of an Encoder and Decoder without relying on Recurrent Neural Networks.

Transformer models use attention to focus on previously generated tokens. This approach allows models to develop a long memory which is particularly useful in the domain of language translation.

2.2 Domain adaptation

Domain adaptation is a proven approach in addressing the paucity of data in low-resource settings. Fine-tuning an out-of-domain model by further training with in-domain data is effective in improving the performance of translation models (Freitag and Al-Onaizan, 2016; Sennrich et al., 2016). With this approach an NMT model is initially trained using a large out-of-domain corpus. Once fully converged, the out-of-domain model is further trained by fine-tuning its parameters with a low resource in-domain corpus.

A modification to this approach is known as mixed fine-tuning (Chu et al., 2017). With this technique, an NMT model is trained on out-of-domain data until fully converged. This serves as a base model which is further trained using the combined in-domain and out-of-domain datasets.

3 Proposed Approach

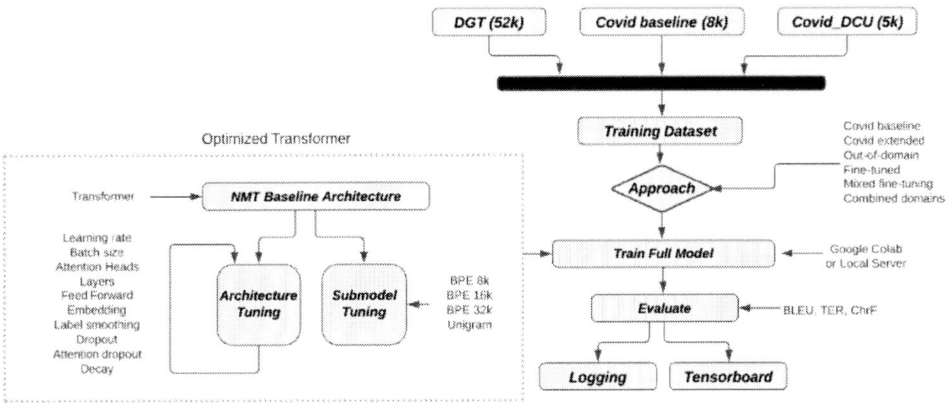

Figure 1: Proposed Approach. Optimal hyperparameters are applied to Transformer models which are trained using one of several possible approaches. The training dataset composition is determined by the chosen approach. Models are subsequently evaluated using a suite of metrics.

Hyperparameter optimization of Recurrent Neural Network (RNN) models in low-resource settings has previously demonstrated considerable performance improvements (Sennrich and Zhang, 2019). The extent to which such optimization techniques may be applied to Transformer models in similar low-resource scenarios was evaluated in a previous study (Lankford et al., 2021). Evaluations included modifying the number of attention heads, the number of layers and experimenting with regularization techniques such as dropout and label smoothing. Most importantly, the choice of subword model type and the vocabulary size were evaluated.

In order to test the effectiveness of our approach, models were trained using three English-Irish parallel datasets: a general corpus of 52k lines from the Directorate General for Translation (DGT) and two in-domain corpora of Covid data (8k and 5k lines). All experiments involved concatenating source and target corpora to create a shared vocabulary and a shared SentencePiece (Kudo and Richardson, 2018) subword model. The impact of using separate source and target subword models was not explored.

Approach	**Source**	**Lines**
Covid baseline	Baseline	8k
Covid extended	Baseline + Covid_DCU	13k
Out-of-domain	DGT	52k
Fine-tuned	Baseline + Covid_DCU + DGT	65k
Mixed fine-tuned	Baseline + Covid_DCU + DGT	65k
Combined domains	Baseline + Covid_DCU + DGT	65k

Table 1: Datasets used in proposed approach

Hyperparameter	**Values**
Learning rate	0.1, 0.01, 0.001, **2**
Batch size	1024, **2048**, 4096, 8192
Attention heads	**2**, 4, **8**
Number of layers	5, **6**
Feed-forward dimension	**2048**
Embedding dimension	128, **256**, 512
Label smoothing	**0.1**, 0.3
Dropout	0.1, **0.3**
Attention dropout	**0.1**
Average Decay	0, **0.0001**

Table 2: Hyperparameter optimization for Transformer models. Optimal parameters are highlighted in bold (Lankford et al., 2021).

The approach adopted is illustrated in Figure 1 and the datasets used in evaluating this approach are outlined in Table 1. All models were developed using a Transformer architecture.

3.1 Architecture Tuning

Long training times associated with NMT make it costly to tune systems using conventional Grid Search approaches. A previous study identified the hyperparameters required for optimal performance (Lankford et al., 2021). Reducing the number of hidden layer neurons and increasing dropout led to significantly better performance. Furthermore, within the context of low-resource English to Irish translation, using a 16k BPE submodel resulted in the highest performing models. The Transformer hyperparameters, chosen in line with these findings, are outlined in Table 2.

4 Empirical Evaluation

4.1 Experimental Setup

4.1.1 Datasets

The performance of the Transformer approach is evaluated on English to Irish parallel datasets in the Covid domain. Three datasets were used in the evaluation of our models. These consisted of a baseline Covid dataset (8k) provided by MT Summit 2021 (Ojha et al., 2021), an in-domain Covid dataset (5k) developed at DCU and a publicly available out-of-domain dataset (52k) provided by DGT (Steinberger et al., 2013).

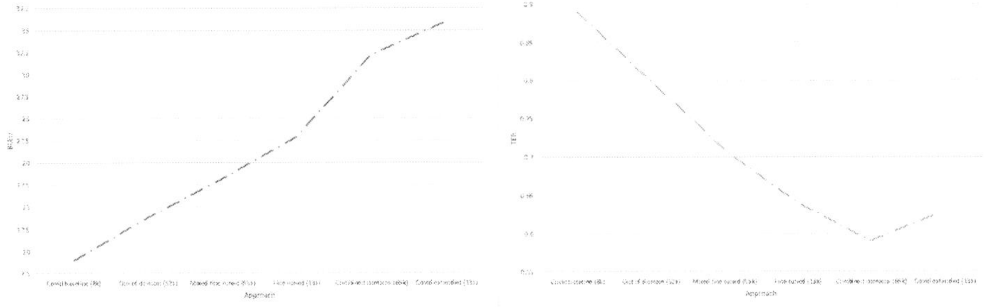

(a) BLEU (b) TER

Figure 2: Translation performance of all approaches using Transformers with 2 heads

4.1.2 Infrastructure

Models were developed using a lab of machines each of which has an AMD Ryzen 7 2700X processor, 16 GB memory, a 256 SSD and an NVIDIA GeForce GTX 1080 Ti. Rapid prototype development was enabled through a Google Colab Pro subscription using NVIDIA Tesla P100 PCIe 16 GB graphic cards and up to 27GB of memory when available (Bisong, 2019).

Our MT models were trained using the Pytorch implementation of OpenNMT 2.0, an open-source toolkit for NMT (Klein et al., 2017).

4.1.3 Metrics

Automated metrics were used to determine the translation quality. All models were trained and evaluated using the BLEU (Papineni et al., 2002), TER (Snover et al., 2006) and ChrF (Popović, 2015) evaluation metrics. Case-insensitive BLEU scores, at the corpus level, are reported. Model training was stopped once an early stopping criteria of no improvement in validation accuracy for 4 consecutive iterations was recorded.

4.2 Results

Experimental results achieved using a Transformer architecture, with either 2 or 8 attention heads, are summarized in Table 3 and in Table 4. Clearly in the context of our low-resource experiments, it can be seen there is little performance difference using Transformer architectures with a differing number of attention heads. The largest difference occurs when using a fine-tuned approach (2.1 BLEU points). However the difference between a 2 head and an 8 head approach is less than 1 BLEU point for all other models. The highest performing approach uses the extended Covid dataset (13k) which is a combination of the MT summit Covid baseline and a custom DCU Covid dataset. This Transformer model, with 2 heads, performs well across all key translation metrics (BLEU: 36.0, TER: 0.63 and ChrF3: 0.32).

The worst performing model uses the Covid baseline which is not surprising given that only 8k lines are available. The performance of the higher resourced models (out-of-domain, fine-tuned, mixed fine-tuned and combined domains) all lag that of the Covid extended model. In particular, the out-of-domain model, using the DGT dataset, performs very poorly with a BLEU score of just 13.9 on a Transformer model with 2 heads.

The BLEU and TER scores for all approaches are illustrated in Figure 2a and Figure 2b. As expected, there is a high level of inverse correlation between BLEU and TER. Well-performing models, with high BLEU scores, also required little post editing effort as indicated by their lower TER scores.

System	Heads	Lines	Steps	BLEU ↑	TER ↓	ChrF3 ↑
Covid baseline	2	8k	35k	9.0	0.89	0.32
Covid extended	2	13k	35k	36.0	0.63	0.54
Out-of-domain	2	52k	200k	13.9	0.80	0.41
Fine-tuned	2	65k	35k	22.9	0.64	0.42
Mixed fine-tuned	2	65k	35k	18.2	0.71	0.42
Combined domains	2	65k	35k	32.2	0.59	0.55

Table 3: Comparison of optimized Transformer performance with 2 attention heads

System	Heads	Lines	Steps	BLEU ↑	TER ↓	ChrF3 ↑
Covid baseline	8	8k	35k	9.6	0.91	0.33
Covid extended	8	13k	35k	35.7	0.61	0.55
Out-of-domain	8	52k	200k	13.0	0.80	0.40
Fine-tuned	8	65k	35k	25.0	0.63	0.43
Mixed fine-tuned	8	65k	35k	18.0	0.71	0.42
Combined domains	8	65k	35k	32.8	0.59	0.57

Table 4: Comparison of optimized Transformer performance with 8 attention heads

5 Discussion

Standard Transformer parameters identified in a previous study were observed to perform well (Lankford et al., 2021). Reducing hidden neurons to 256 and increasing regularization dropout to 0.3 improved translation performance and these hyperparameters were chosen when building all Transformer models. Furthermore a batch size of 2048 and using 6 layers for the encoder / decoder were chosen throughout.

The results demonstrate that translation performance for specific domains is driven by the amount of data which is available for that specific domain. It is noteworthy that an in-domain dataset of 13k lines (Covid extended), trained for just 35k steps outperformed by 22.1 BLEU points the corresponding out-of-domain 52k dataset (DGT) which was trained for 200k steps.

6 Conclusion and Future Work

In the official evaluation for LoResMT 2021, our English–Irish system was ranked first according to the BLEU, TER and ChrF scores. We demonstrate that a high performing in-domain translation model can be built with a dataset of 13k lines. Developing a small in-domain dataset, of just 5k lines, improved the BLEU score by 27 points when models were trained with the combined Covid baseline and custom Covid dataset.

Following on from our previous work, careful selection of Transformer hyperparameters, and using a 16k BPE SentencePiece submodel, enabled rapid development of high performing translation models in a low-resource setting.

Within the context of our research in low-resource English to Irish translation, we have shown that augmenting in-domain data, by a small amount, performed better than approaches which incorporate fine-tuning, mixed fine-tuning or the combination of domains.

As part of our future work, we plan to develop English-Irish MT models trained on a dataset derived from the health domain. Domain adaptation, through fine-tuning such models with the Covid extended dataset may further improve Covid MT performance.

Acknowledgements

This work was supported by ADAPT, which is funded under the SFI Research Centres Programme (Grant 13/RC/2016) and is co-funded by the European Regional Development Fund. This research was also funded by the Munster Technological University.

References

Araabi, A. and Monz, C. (2020). Optimizing transformer for low-resource neural machine translation. *arXiv preprint arXiv:2011.02266.*

Bisong, E. (2019). Google colaboratory. In *Building Machine Learning and Deep Learning Models on Google Cloud Platform*, pages 59–64. Springer.

Chu, C., Dabre, R., and Kurohashi, S. (2017). An empirical comparison of domain adaptation methods for neural machine translation. In *Proceedings of the 55th Annual Meeting of the Association for Computational Linguistics (Volume 2: Short Papers)*, pages 385–391.

Crego, J., Kim, J., Klein, G., Rebollo, A., Yang, K., Senellart, J., Akhanov, E., Brunelle, P., Coquard, A., Deng, Y., et al. (2016). Systran's pure neural machine translation systems. *arXiv preprint arXiv:1610.05540.*

Klein, G., Kim, Y., Deng, Y., Senellart, J., and Rush, A. M. (2017). Opennmt: Open-source toolkit for neural machine translation. *arXiv preprint arXiv:1701.02810.*

Kudo, T. and Richardson, J. (2018). Sentencepiece: A simple and language independent subword tokenizer and detokenizer for neural text processing. *arXiv preprint arXiv:1808.06226.*

Lankford, S., Alfi, H., and Way, A. (2021). Transformers for low resource languages: Is feidir linn. In *Proceedings of the 18th Conference of the Association for Machine Translation in the Americas (Volume 1: Research Papers).*

Ojha, A. K., Liu, C.-H., Kann, K., Ortega, J., Satam, S., and Fransen, T. (2021). Findings of the LoResMT 2021 Shared Task on COVID and Sign Language for Low-Resource Languages. In *Proceedings of the 4th Workshop on Technologies for MT of Low Resource Languages.*

Papineni, K., Roukos, S., Ward, T., and Zhu, W.-J. (2002). Bleu: a method for automatic evaluation of machine translation. In *Proceedings of the 40th annual meeting of the Association for Computational Linguistics*, pages 311–318.

Popović, M. (2015). chrf: character n-gram f-score for automatic mt evaluation. In *Proceedings of the Tenth Workshop on Statistical Machine Translation*, pages 392–395.

Sennrich, R. and Zhang, B. (2019). Revisiting low-resource neural machine translation: A case study. *arXiv preprint arXiv:1905.11901.*

Snover, M., Dorr, B., Schwartz, R., Micciulla, L., and Makhoul, J. (2006). A study of translation edit rate with targeted human annotation. In *Proceedings of association for machine translation in the Americas*, volume 200. Citeseer.

Steinberger, R., Eisele, A., Klocek, S., Pilos, S., and Schlüter, P. (2013). Dgt-tm: A freely available translation memory in 22 languages. *arXiv preprint arXiv:1309.5226.*

Vaswani, A., Shazeer, N., Parmar, N., Uszkoreit, J., Jones, L., Gomez, A. N., Kaiser, L., and Polosukhin, I. (2017). Attention is all you need. *arXiv preprint arXiv:1706.03762.*

Wu, Y., Schuster, M., Chen, Z., Le, Q. V., Norouzi, M., Macherey, W., Krikun, M., Cao, Y., Gao, Q., Macherey, K., et al. (2016). Google's neural machine translation system: Bridging the gap between human and machine translation. *arXiv preprint arXiv:1609.08144*.

English-Marathi Neural Machine Translation for LoResMT 2021

Vandan Mujadia vandan.mu@research.iiit.ac.in
Dipti Misra Sharma dipti@iiit.ac.in
Machine Translation - Natural Language Processing Lab
Language Technologies Research Centre
Kohli Center on Intelligent Systems
International Institute of Information Technology
Hyderabad

Abstract

In this paper, we (team - oneNLP-IIITH) describe our Neural Machine Translation approaches for English-Marathi (both direction) for LoResMT-2021[1]. We experimented with transformer based Neural Machine Translation and explored the use of different linguistic features like POS and Morph on subword unit for both English-Marathi and Marathi-English. In addition, we have also explored forward and backward translation using web-crawled monolingual data. We obtained 22.2 (overall 2nd) and 31.3 (overall 1st) BLEU scores for English-Marathi and Marathi-English on respectively.

1 Introduction

Machine Translation (MT) is a field of Natural Language Processing which aims to translate a text from one natural language (i.e English) to another (i.e Marathi). The meaning of the source text must be fully preserved in the resulting translated text in the target language. Recent years have seen significant quality advancements in machine translation with the advent of Neural Machine Translation. For the translation task, different types of machine translation systems have been developed and they are mainly categorized into Rule based Machine Translation (RBMT)(Forcada et al., 2011), Statistical Machine Translation (SMT) (Koehn, 2009) and Neural Machine Translation (NMT) (Bahdanau et al., 2014).

Rule based Machine Translation (RBMT) translates on the basis of grammatical rules. It involves a grammatical analysis of the source language and the target language. Based on the analysis, it generates the translated sentence (Dwivedi and Sukhadeve, 2010). Statistical Machine Translation (SMT) is based on statistical models, which analyse large parallel and monolingual text and tries to determine the correspondence between a source language word and a target language word. NMT (Bahdanau et al., 2014) is an end to end approach for automatic machine translation without heavy hand crafted feature engineering. Due to recent advances, NMT has been receiving heavy attention and achieved state of the art performance in the task of language translation. With this work, we intend to check how NMT systems could be developed for low resource machine translation.

[1]https://sites.google.com/view/loresmt/

This paper describes our experiments for LoResMT-2021[2](Ojha et al., 2021). The third edition of LoResMT-2021 aims at building MT systems for low-resource language pairs on COVID-related texts. For our work, we focused only on English-Marathi language pair (both directions) and participated for categories where in first, we only used given parallel training data (constrained) and in second, we utilized available parallel corpora from different sources for English-Marathi and English-Hindi (unconstrained).

In this work, we experimented only with Transformer (Vaswani et al., 2017) based Neural Machine Translation throughout. Along with it, we also explored the morph (Virpioja et al., 2013) induced sub-word segmentation with byte pair encoding (BPE)(Sennrich et al., 2016b) to enable open vocabulary translation. We used POS tags as linguistic feature for English-Marathi direction along with forward and back translation to leverage synthetic data for machine translation. We also explored the use of English-Hindi parallel data for English-Marathi as origin of these two languages are the same and they are Indo-aryan languages (wikipedia, 2021). Hindi is said to have evolved from Sauraseni Prakrit (wikipedia Hindi, 2021) whereas Marathi is said to have evolved from Maharashtri Prakrit (wikipedia Marathi, 2021) and they both use the same writing script - Devanagari[3]. In LoResMT-2021, we participated as team "oneNLP-IIITH".

2 Data

Data (Language)	#Sentences	#Token	#Type
Train - English (Parallel)	20,933	0.3M	28K
Train - Marathi (Parallel)	20,933	0.29M	42K
Validation - English (Parallel)	500	12K	3.7K
Validation - Marathi (Parallel)	500	10K	4.7K
English (Monolingual)	8K	0.1M	200K
Marathi (Monolingual)	21K	0.2M	39K

Table 1: English-Marathi LoResMT-2021 Training data (for Constrained)

Data (Language)	#Sentences	#Token	#Type
Train - English (Parallel)	7M	13M	0.5M
Train - Hindi (Parallel)	7M	5.6M	0.9K
Train - English (Parallel)	1.8M	2.5M	0.1K
Train - Marathi (Parallel)	1.8M	2.2M	0.6K
English (Monolingual)	0.1M	-	-
Marathi (Monolingual)	0.1M	-	-

Table 2: Other Utilised data (for Unconstrained)

We utilized provided parallel and monolingual corpora for the Machine Translation task on English<->Marathi language pairs. Table-1 describes the training (parallel and monolingual) and validation data (parallel) after cleaning (i.e removed parallel data from training which are also in validation). We carried out constrained experiments on this data. For unconstrained experiments we use additional parallel dataset from samanantar (Ramesh et al., 2021). For back

[2]https://sites.google.com/view/loresmt/
[3]https://en.wikipedia.org/wiki/Devanagari

and forward translation, we web-crawled monolingual data for both English and Marathi to aid relatively new NLP domain Covid. Table-2 describes this additional dataset in terms of number of sentences, token and type.

3 Data Pre-Processing

For data pre-precessing, we used IndicNLP Tool[4] with in-house tokenizer to tokenize and clean both English and Marathi corpora (train, test, valid and monolingual) as a first step. Following subsections explain other pre-processing steps for our MT experiments.

3.1 Morph + BPE Segmentation

Based on token/type ratio, Marathi is morphologically richer compared to English from Table-1. Translating from morphologically-rich agglutinative languages is more difficult due to their complex morphology and large vocabulary. We address this issue with a segmentation method which is based on morphology and BPE segmentation (Sennrich et al., 2016b) as a pre-processing step as prescribed in (Mujadia and Sharma, 2020). We utilized unsupervised

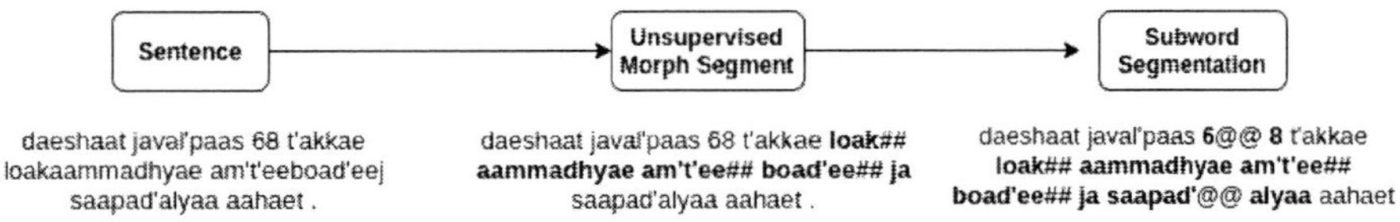

Figure 1: Morph and Subword based pre-processing for a Marathi sentence. Here ## denotes UMorph based segmentation and @@ denotes subword based segmentation

Morfessor (Virpioja et al., 2013) by training it on monolingual data for Marathi. We then applied this trained Morfessor model on our corpora (train, test, validation) to get meaningful stem, morpheme, suffix segmented sub-tokens for each word in a sentence. Subsequently, we applied the subword algorithm on top of the morph segmentation as shown in Figure-1. For English, we only applied subword segmentation throughout the experiments.

3.2 Features

We carried out experiments using Part of Speech (POS) tag as a word and subword level feature (Sennrich and Haddow, 2016) only for English. We used Spacy (Honnibal et al., 2020) toolkit to get POS tags for English and used them by concatenating their embedding with word embedding for NMT training as shown in Figure-2.

3.3 Hindi centric parallel data

For unconstrained experiments, we experimented and studied the use of available parallel data. Along with the English-Marathi parallel data, we utilized a small chunk of English-Hindi parallel data from Samanantar corpus (Ramesh et al., 2021) as Hindi is a close and related language to Marathi. We appended the English-Hindi parallel data to the existing English-Marathi data and maintained 1:1 ratio of them for overall training.

3.4 Forward and Back Translation

Back translation is a widely used data augmentation method for low resource neural machine translation (Sennrich et al., 2016a). Here, we utilized the provided and web crawled monolin-

[4]http://anoopkunchukuttan.github.io/indic nlp library/

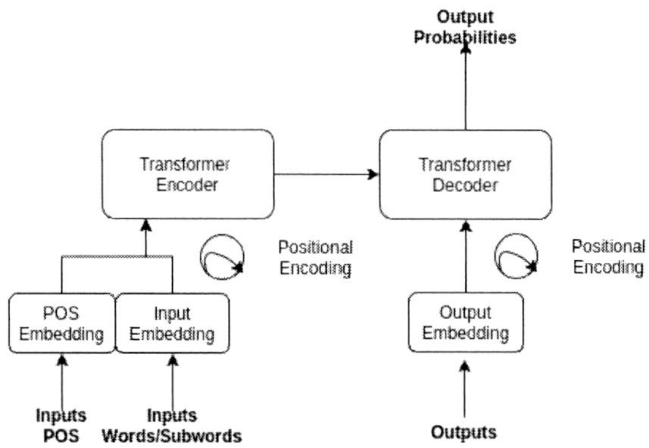

Figure 2: Modeling POS tags as feature along with word embedding for English in Transformer Network

gual data (for Marathi and English). We used around 0.1M forward and back translated pairs for both translation directions.

4 Training Configuration

Throughout all experiments, we used Transformer sequence to sequence architecture with the following configuration for constrained and unconstrained experiments.

- **Constrained**
  Morph + BPE based subword segmentation, POS tags as feature, Embedding size : 512 Transformer for encoder and decoder, rnn_size 512 feature_Embedding 100 (only for POS), heads 4 encoder - decoder layers : 2, label smoothing : 1.0, dropout : 0.30, Optimizer : Adam, Beam size : 4 (train) and 10 (test), training steps : 20K

- **Unconstrained**
  Morph + BPE based subword segmentation, Embedding size : 512 Transformer for encoder and decoder, RNN_size 512, heads 8 encoder - decoder layers : 6, label smoothing : 1.0, dropout : 0.30, Optimizer : Adam, Beam size : 4 (train) and 10 (test), training steps : 20K

For these experiments, we used shared vocab across trainings. We used Opennmt-py (Klein et al., 2020) toolkit with above configuration for our experiments.

Using the above described configuration, we performed experiments based on different parameter (feature) configurations. We trained and tested our models on word level, BPE level and morph + BPE level for input and output. We also used POS tagger and experimented with shared vocabulary across the translation task. The results are discussed in following Result section.

5 Result

Table-3 and Table-4 show performance of our systems with different configurations in terms of BLEU score (Papineni et al., 2002) for English-Marathi and Marathi-English respectively on the validation and Test data. We achieved highest 17.9 development and 22.2 test BLEU scores for English-Marathi and highest 32.88 development and 31.6 test BLEU scores for

Type	Feature	BPE	Valid	Test
C	Word	-	13.03	-
C	BPE	7.5K	13.25	-
C	Morph + BPE + POS	-	14.17	10.4
C	Morph + BPE + POS	7.5K	14.03	-
C	Morph + BPE + POS	15K	14.54	11.5
C	Morph+BPE+POS + BT(1L sent)	15K	14.89	**14.0**
UC	BPE + (Eng-Mar ExtData)	10K	11.73	-
UC	BPE+(Eng-Mar&Eng-Hin ExtData ExtData)	10K	13.73	21.5
UC	BPE+(Eng-Mar&Eng-Hin ExtData)+F-BT	10K	**16.25**	**22**
UC	Morph+BPE+(Eng-Mar&Eng-Hin ExtData)+F-BT	10K	**17.90**	**22.2**

Table 3: BLEU scores for English-Marathi. Here C stands Constrained and UC for Unconstrained, BPE stands for byte pair encoding (subword), Morph for Morphological segment and POS for Part of Speech and F-BT for forward and backward translation

Type	Feature	BPE	Valid Data	Test Data
C	BPE	10K	19.11	16.2
C	BPE	7.5K	19.47	16.4
C	Morph+BPE	7.5K	19.67	**16.7**
UC	BPE + (Eng-Mar ExtData)	7.5K	20.10	20.7
UC	BPE+(Eng-Mar&Eng-Hin ExtData)	10K	**29.80**	**30.6**
UC	BPE+(Eng-Mar&Eng-Hin ExtData)+F-BT	10K	**32.88**	**31.6**

Table 4: BLEU scores for Marathi-English. Here C stands Constrained and UC for Unconstrained, BPE stands for byte pair encoding (subword), Morph for Morphological segment and F-BT for forward and backward translation

Marathi-English systems respectively.

The results show that for low resource settings, transformer network based MT models can be improved with linguistic information like morph and POS features. The results also indicate that morph based segmentation along with byte pair encoding improves BLEU score and can be used for morph rich languages. The results also suggest that performance drastically improves when model is exposed to more parallel data (for unconstrained setting). Our experiments suggest that use of English-Hindi parallel data gives performance boost by 3.0+ BLEU points for English-Marathi and almost 10.0+ BLEU points for Marathi-English. Also, forward and back translated synthetic data obtained from same Covid domain improves quality of NMT models marginally, as they could be helping models to do better generalization. From the Test results (Table-3 and Table-4), we stand at overall 2nd and 1st for English-Marathi and Marathi-English respectively.

6 Conclusion

From our experiments, we conclude that linguistic feature driven NMT for low resource languages is a promising approach and use of similar language training data gives a significant boost in performance to the low resource language.

References

Bahdanau, D., Cho, K., and Bengio, Y. (2014). Neural machine translation by jointly learning to align and translate. *arXiv preprint arXiv:1409.0473*.

Dwivedi, S. K. and Sukhadeve, P. P. (2010). Machine translation system in indian perspectives. *Journal of computer science*, 6(10):1111.

Forcada, M. L., Ginestí-Rosell, M., Nordfalk, J., O'Regan, J., Ortiz-Rojas, S., Pérez-Ortiz, J. A., Sánchez-Martínez, F., Ramírez-Sánchez, G., and Tyers, F. M. (2011). Apertium: a free/open-source platform for rule-based machine translation. *Machine translation*, 25(2):127–144.

Honnibal, M., Montani, I., Van Landeghem, S., and Boyd, A. (2020). spaCy: Industrial-strength Natural Language Processing in Python.

Klein, G., Hernandez, F., Nguyen, V., and Senellart, J. (2020). The opennmt neural machine translation toolkit: 2020 edition. In *Proceedings of the 14th Conference of the Association for Machine Translation in the Americas (AMTA 2020)*, pages 102–109.

Koehn, P. (2009). *Statistical machine translation*. Cambridge University Press.

Mujadia, V. and Sharma, D. M. (2020). Nmt based similar language translation for hindi-marathi. In *Proceedings of the Fifth Conference on Machine Translation*, pages 414–417.

Ojha, A. K., Liu, C.-H., Kann, K., Ortega, J., Satam, S., and Fransen, T. (2021). Findings of the LoResMT 2021 Shared Task on COVID and Sign Language for Low-Resource Languages. In *Proceedings of the 4th Workshop on Technologies for MT of Low Resource Languages*.

Papineni, K., Roukos, S., Ward, T., and Zhu, W.-J. (2002). Bleu: a method for automatic evaluation of machine translation. In *Proceedings of the 40th annual meeting of the Association for Computational Linguistics*, pages 311–318.

Ramesh, G., Doddapaneni, S., Bheemaraj, A., Jobanputra, M., AK, R., Sharma, A., Sahoo, S., Diddee, H., J, M., Kakwani, D., Kumar, N., Pradeep, A., Deepak, K., Raghavan, V., Kunchukuttan, A., Kumar, P., and Khapra, M. S. (2021). Samanantar: The largest publicly available parallel corpora collection for 11 indic languages.

Sennrich, R. and Haddow, B. (2016). Linguistic input features improve neural machine translation. In *Proceedings of the First Conference on Machine Translation: Volume 1, Research Papers*, pages 83–91.

Sennrich, R., Haddow, B., and Birch, A. (2016a). Improving neural machine translation models with monolingual data. In *Proceedings of the 54th Annual Meeting of the Association for Computational Linguistics (Volume 1: Long Papers)*, pages 86–96.

Sennrich, R., Haddow, B., and Birch, A. (2016b). Neural machine translation of rare words with subword units. In *Proceedings of the 54th Annual Meeting of the Association for Computational Linguistics (Volume 1: Long Papers)*, pages 1715–1725.

Vaswani, A., Shazeer, N., Parmar, N., Uszkoreit, J., Jones, L., Gomez, A. N., Kaiser, Ł., and Polosukhin, I. (2017). Attention is all you need. In *Advances in neural information processing systems*, pages 5998–6008.

Virpioja, S., Smit, P., Grönroos, S.-A., Kurimo, M., et al. (2013). Morfessor 2.0: Python implementation and extensions for morfessor baseline.

wikipedia (2021). Indo-aryan languages - wikipedia. https://en.wikipedia.org/wiki/Indo-Aryan_languages.

wikipedia Hindi (2021). Shauraseni prakrit - wikipedia. https://en.wikipedia.org/wiki/Shauraseni_Prakrit.

wikipedia Marathi (2021). Maharashtri prakrit - wikipedia. https://en.wikipedia.org/wiki/Maharashtri_Prakrit.

Evaluating the Performance of Back-translation for Low Resource English-Marathi Language Pair: CFILT-IITBombay @ LoResMT 2021

Aditya Jain adityajainiitb@cse.iitb.ac.in
Shivam Mhaskar shivammhaskar@cse.iitb.ac.in
Pushpak Bhattacharyya pb@cse.iitb.ac.in
Department of Computer Science and Engineering, IIT Bombay, India.

Abstract

In this paper, we discuss the details of the various Machine Translation (MT) systems that we have submitted for the English-Marathi LoResMT task. As a part of this task, we have submitted three different Neural Machine Translation (NMT) systems; a Baseline English-Marathi system, a Baseline Marathi-English system, and an English-Marathi system that is based on the back-translation technique. We explore the performance of these NMT systems between English and Marathi languages, which forms a low resource language pair due to unavailability of sufficient parallel data. We also explore the performance of the back-translation technique when the back-translated data is obtained from NMT systems that are trained on a very less amount of data. From our experiments, we observe that the back-translation technique can help improve the MT quality over the baseline for the English-Marathi language pair.

1 Introduction

In this work, we explore various ways to perform Machine Translation (MT) in low resource settings, that is, when very less amount of parallel data is available to train the model. We also explore the performance of the back-translation technique, which is one of the data augmentation techniques to overcome the problem of low resource in neural machine translation. In our work, we focus on the Neural Machine Translation (NMT) systems, which requires a large amount of parallel training data to produce good quality translations. This is the major reason behind NMT systems to be considered as *data hungry*. The language pair for which less amount of parallel data is available is considered a low resource language pair.

As compared to parallel data, monolingual data is easier to obtain and is available in relatively large quantity. This monolingual data can also be used to improve the performance of the NMT system. We explore the back-translation technique to make use of the available monolingual data to create an augmented pseudo-parallel data which can then be used to train the NMT system. In back-translation, the monolingual data is first translated using a machine translation system. In case of low resource languages, this machine translation system is trained on very less amount of data and hence, the translation of the monolingual data produced may not be of very high quality. If the model is trained using this low quality back-translated parallel data, it can degrade the performance of the system. We explore the performance of the NMT system when it is trained using back-translation technique in which the back-translated data is generated from a NMT system which is trained on a less amount of data. From the experiments that we have performed as part of the LoResMT 2021 (Ojha et al., 2021) task, we observe that the back-translation technique gives a BLEU score improvement of up to 1.2 points over the baseline model for the English-Marathi MT task.

2 Related Work

Neural Machine Translation systems were initially based on Recurrent Neural Network (RNN) based approaches (Cho et al., 2014; Sutskever et al., 2014). But Recurrent Neural Network based architectures were not able to capture long term dependencies in long sentences. In order to overcome this problem, Attention (Bahdanau et al., 2014) mechanism was introduced. The Attention-based RNN architecture still suffered from problems like longer training time because of their sequential nature. Later Transformer architecture (Vaswani et al., 2017) was introduced which improved the performance of the NMT systems and also lead to faster training due to its non-sequential nature.

Sennrich et al. (2016) introduced the technique of back-translation in which monolingual data is used to create augmented pseudo-parallel data. Sen et al. (2018) used Statistical Machine Translation (SMT) system by extracting phrases generated during SMT training and using them along with the training data for NMT systems. Zoph et al. (2016) introduced a transfer learning techniques in which a parent NMT model is initially trained on a high resource language pair and then the parameters of this parent model are used to initialize a child model, which is then trained on a low resource language pair. Kim et al. (2019) introduced a transfer learning technique based on a pivot language in which a pivot language is used to pre-train the encoder and decoder of a NMT model, which are then used to initialize the encoder and decoder of the final NMT model which is then fine-tuned on the low resource language pair. Multi-lingual NMT models (Zoph and Knight, 2016; Firat et al., 2016; Johnson et al., 2017) that can translate to or from multiple languages have shown performance improvements in the case of low resource language pairs when the system also includes high resource language pairs.

3 Approaches

In this section, we discuss the various techniques that we have used to implement our English-Marathi and Marathi-English MT systems.

3.1 Baseline Model

In our Baseline English-Marathi and Marathi-English MT models, we train a NMT system using the given English-Marathi parallel corpus for 1600 epochs and we save the model for every 200 epochs starting from 200, to test the performance.

3.2 Back-Translation

Back-translation technique makes use of monolingual data of source or target language to generate source-target parallel sentences using a trained NMT system. From the provided English-Marathi parallel data and Marathi monolingual data, we first train a Marathi-English NMT system using the English-Marathi parallel data. We then use this Marathi-English model to translate the Marathi monolingual data to get the corresponding English output. Finally we combine the given English-Marathi parallel data and this back-translated English-Marathi pseudo-parallel data to train our English-Marathi back-translation NMT system.

4 Experiments

In this section, we discuss the various experiments that we have performed as a part of this work.

4.1 Dataset

Type of Data	Number of sentences
Parallel	20,933
Monolingual	21,902

Table 1: Dataset

We used the English-Marathi parallel corpus provided by the LoResMT 2021 organizers, which consisted of 20,933 English-Marathi parallel sentences. Further, for our back-translation experiment we used the Marathi monolingual corpus provided by the LoResMT 2021 organizers which consisted of 21,902 Marathi sentences.

4.2 Training Setup

For all of the NMT systems discussed in this paper, we have used the transformer-based architecture which we have implemented using the fairseq Ott et al. (2019) library. This transformer-based architecture consisted of 6 encoder layers and 6 decoder layers. The number of encoder and decoder attention heads used were 4 each. We used encoder and decoder embedding dimension of 512 each. For training the system, the optimizer used was Adam optimizer with betas (0.9, 0.98). The inverse square root learning rate scheduler was used with initial learning rate of 5e-4 and 4,000 warm-up updates. The criterion used was label smoothed cross entropy with label smoothing of 0.1. The dropout probability value of 0.3 was used.

5 Results and Analysis

Model	English-Marathi	Marathi-English
Baseline-200	11	16.8
Baseline-400	10.4	17.1
Baseline-600	—	17.2
Baseline-800	10.6	17.2
Baseline-1000	10.5	16.6
Baseline-1200	10.7	16.3
Baseline-1400	10.5	16.2
Baseline-1600	10.8	—
Back-translation	12.2	—

Table 2: BLEU scores of English-Marathi language pair where for a model named Baseline-X, X represents the number of epochs for which the model was trained.

Table 2 shows the results of the different techniques used to implement the MT systems for the English-Marathi language pair. We used BLEU (Papineni et al., 2002) metric to measure the performance of the MT systems. The baseline English-Marathi system produced a BLEU score of 11 and the baseline Marathi-English System produced a BLEU score of 17.2. We observe that the English-Marathi and Marathi-English NMT were trained using the same English-Marathi parallel data, the Marathi-English system produced higher BLEU scores than that produced by the English-Marathi system. We also observe that the English-Marathi system gives the best BLEU score after 400 epochs and after that the scores decrease and fluctuate between a small range. The Marathi-English model gives the best score after 600 epochs and after that the scores starts decreasing. We have used this Marathi-English NMT system to translate the Marathi monolingual data to English. Then we trained the English-Marathi back-translation system using the given English-Marathi parallel data and the English-Marathi back-translated pseudo-parallel data. This back-translation system produced a BLEU score of 12.2. We observe that even though the Marathi-English back-translated data was produced using a machine translation system which was trained on very low amount of data, there is still an increase in BLEU score of around 1.2 points over the baseline model.

6 Conclusion

In this work, we implement various English-Marathi and Marathi-English baseline NMT systems and use the given monolingual Marathi data to implement the back-translation technique for data augmentation. From our experiments, we observe that the technique of back-translation can help improve the MT quality over the baseline for the English-Marathi MT task for which less amount of parallel data is available.

References

Bahdanau, D., Cho, K., and Bengio, Y. (2014). Neural machine translation by jointly learning to align and translate. *arXiv preprint arXiv:1409.0473.*

Cho, K., van Merrienboer, B., Bahdanau, D., and Bengio, Y. (2014). On the properties of neural machine translation: Encoder-decoder approaches. *CoRR*, abs/1409.1259.

Firat, O., Cho, K., and Bengio, Y. (2016). Multi-way, multilingual neural machine translation with a shared attention mechanism. In *Proceedings of the 2016 Conference of the North American Chapter of the Association for Computational Linguistics: Human Language Technologies*, pages 866–875, San Diego, California. Association for Computational Linguistics.

Johnson, M., Schuster, M., Le, Q. V., Krikun, M., Wu, Y., Chen, Z., Thorat, N., Viégas, F., Wattenberg, M., Corrado, G., Hughes, M., and Dean, J. (2017). Google's multilingual neural machine translation system: Enabling zero-shot translation. *Transactions of the Association for Computational Linguistics*, 5:339–351.

Kim, Y., Petrov, P., Petrushkov, P., Khadivi, S., and Ney, H. (2019). Pivot-based transfer learning for neural machine translation between non-English languages. In *Proceedings of the 2019 Conference on Empirical Methods in Natural Language Processing and the 9th International Joint Conference on Natural Language Processing (EMNLP-IJCNLP)*, pages 866–876, Hong Kong, China. Association for Computational Linguistics.

Ojha, A. K., Liu, C.-H., Kann, K., Ortega, J., Satam, S., and Fransen, T. (2021). Findings of the LoResMT 2021 Shared Task on COVID and Sign Language for Low-Resource Languages. In *Proceedings of the 4th Workshop on Technologies for MT of Low Resource Languages.*

Ott, M., Edunov, S., Baevski, A., Fan, A., Gross, S., Ng, N., Grangier, D., and Auli, M. (2019). fairseq: A fast, extensible toolkit for sequence modeling. *arXiv preprint arXiv:1904.01038.*

Papineni, K., Roukos, S., Ward, T., and Zhu, W.-J. (2002). Bleu: a method for automatic evaluation of machine translation. In *Proceedings of the 40th annual meeting of the Association for Computational Linguistics*, pages 311–318.

Sen, S., Hasanuzzaman, M., Ekbal, A., Bhattacharyya, P., and Way, A. (2018). Neural machine translation of low-resource languages using smt phrase pair injection. *Natural Language Engineering*, pages 1–22.

Sennrich, R., Haddow, B., and Birch, A. (2016). Improving neural machine translation models with monolingual data. In *Proceedings of the 54th Annual Meeting of the Association for Computational Linguistics (Volume 1: Long Papers)*, pages 86–96, Berlin, Germany. Association for Computational Linguistics.

Sutskever, I., Vinyals, O., and Le, Q. V. (2014). Sequence to sequence learning with neural networks. *CoRR*, abs/1409.3215.

Vaswani, A., Shazeer, N., Parmar, N., Uszkoreit, J., Jones, L., Gomez, A. N., Kaiser, L., and Polosukhin, I. (2017). Attention is all you need. *CoRR*, abs/1706.03762.

Zoph, B. and Knight, K. (2016). Multi-source neural translation. In *Proceedings of the 2016 Conference of the North American Chapter of the Association for Computational Linguistics: Human Language Technologies*, pages 30–34, San Diego, California. Association for Computational Linguistics.

Zoph, B., Yuret, D., May, J., and Knight, K. (2016). Transfer learning for low-resource neural machine translation. In *Proceedings of the 2016 Conference on Empirical Methods in Natural Language Processing*, pages 1568–1575, Austin, Texas. Association for Computational Linguistics.

Association for Computational Linguistics
209 N. Eighth Street
Stroudsburg, Pennsylvania 18360

ISBN 978-1-7138-3922-4

CURRAN ASSOCIATES INC. proceedings.com